CREDIBILITY AND THE INTERNATIONAL MONETARY REGIME

The present global monetary regime is based on change to floating exchange rates among the major advanced countries. A key underlying factor behind the present regime is credibility to maintain stable monetary policies. The origin of credibility in monetary regimes goes back to the pre-1914 classical gold standard. In that regime, adherence by central banks to the rule of convertibility of national currencies in terms of a fixed weight of gold provided a nominal anchor to the price level. Between 1914 and the present, several monetary regimes gradually moved away from gold, with varying success in maintaining price stability and credibility. In this book, the editors present ten studies combining historical narrative with econometrics that analyze the role of credibility in four monetary regimes, from the gold standard to the present managed float.

Michael D. Bordo is professor of economics and director of the Center for Monetary and Financial History at Rutgers University, New Brunswick, New Jersey. He is a research associate of the National Bureau of Economic Research, Cambridge, Massachusetts. He holds a BA from McGill University, an MSc(Econ) from the London School of Economics, and a PhD from the University of Chicago. He has published many articles in leading journals in monetary economics and economic history. Recent publications include *A Retrospective on the Bretton Woods International Monetary System* (1993, with Barry Eichengreen), *The Defining Moment: The Great Depression and the American Economy in the Twentieth Century* (1998, with Claudia Goldin and Eugene White), *Essays on the Gold Standard and Related Regimes* (Cambridge University Press 1999, paperback 2005), and *Globalization in Historical Perspective* (2003, with Alan Taylor and Jeffrey Williamson).

Ronald MacDonald is currently the Adam Smith Professor of Political Economy at the University of Glasgow. He is also a Fellow of the Royal Society of Edinburgh, Research Fellow of the CESifo Research Network Munich, and an International Fellow of the Kiel Institute of Economics. He holds a BA in economics from Heriot Watt University, Edinburgh, and an MA and PhD from the University of Manchester. He has published widely in the areas of macroeconomics, monetary economics, and international finance in journals such as the *Journal of Monetary Economics*; *Journal of Money, Credit and Banking*; *Economic Journal*; and *European Economic Review*. His recent books include *Exchange Rate Economics: Theories and Evidence* (2007), *The Political Economy of Financing Scottish Government* (2009, with C. Paul Hallwood), and *Currency Union and Exchange Rate Issues* (2010, with Abdulrazak Al Faris).

Studies in Macroeconomic History

Series Editor:
Michael D. Bordo, *Rutgers University*

Editors:
Marc Flandreau, *Institut d'Etudes Politiques de Paris*
Chris Meissner, *University of California, Davis*
François Velde, *Federal Reserve Bank of Chicago*
David C. Wheelock, *Federal Reserve Bank of St. Louis*

The titles in this series investigate themes of interest to economists and economic historians in the rapidly developing field of macroeconomic history. The four areas covered include the application of monetary and finance theory, international economics, and quantitative methods to historical problems; the historical application of growth and development theory and theories of business fluctuations; the history of domestic and international monetary, financial, and other macroeconomic institutions; and the history of international monetary and financial systems. The series amalgamates the former Cambridge University Press series *Studies in Monetary and Financial History* and *Studies in Quantitative Economic History*.

Other Books in the Series:

(Continued after index)

Credibility and the International Monetary Regime

A Historical Perspective

Edited by

MICHAEL D. BORDO

Rutgers University

RONALD MACDONALD

University of Glasgow

CAMBRIDGE UNIVERSITY PRESS

Figures

Tables

Contributors

Myrvin Anthony, International Monetary Fund

Michael D. Bordo, Rutgers University

Hali Edison, International Monetary Fund

C. Paul Hallwood, University of Connecticut

Ronald MacDonald, University of Glasgow

Ian W. Marsh, Cass Business School

Michael J. Oliver, ESC Rennes School of Business

PART ONE

INTRODUCTION

ONE

Credibility in Fixed Exchange Rate Regimes

Theoretical and Historical Perspectives

Michael D. Bordo and Ronald MacDonald

At present, the global monetary regime is based on floating exchange rates among the major advanced countries: the United States, Japan, the United Kingdom, Canada, Australia, and the Eurozone. The Eurozone is a monetary union. The rest of the world has a gamut of regimes, ranging from floating to hard pegs. A key underlying factor behind the current regime is credibility to maintain stable monetary policies.

The origins of credibility in monetary regimes go back to the classical gold standard, 1880–1914. In that regime, in the advanced countries, adherence by the monetary authorities to the rule of convertibility of national currencies in terms of gold provided a credible nominal anchor. Today gold is no longer the nominal anchor; instead this anchor is based on the credibility of independent central banks dedicated to keeping inflation low. Between 1914 and the present, the world exhibited several regimes that gradually did away with gold as the nominal anchor and that had varying success in maintaining credibility. In this book, we present nine studies of how credibility functioned in four monetary regimes, from the gold standard to the present regime of managed floating.

The issue of the appropriate exchange rate regime for a country has been a central theme in the international finance literature. Numerous currency crises in the last three decades of the twentieth century have given fixed but adjustable exchange rate regimes something of a bad name. The perceived wisdom is that such regimes are likely to be blown off track if the underlying macroeconomic fundamentals are at variance with the peg, or even if they are not, sunspot effects and pure contagion effects can produce the same unsatisfactory outcome. These apparent problems with fixed but adjustable rates led to the emergence of the so-called corners hypothesis as the perceived wisdom: To avoid the frenzy of speculative attacks and the consequent implications for the real economy and, more generally, the international monetary system, countries should irrevocably lock their currencies to other currencies in some way (a monetary union or currency board), or they should allow their currencies to float freely, with little or no foreign exchange market intervention.

At the heart of the issue of how sustainable a fixed rate is likely to be is the credibility of the peg: A credible peg is much less likely to suffer the ignominy of a speculative attack than one that is not. Furthermore, the existence of a credible exchange rate can allow a central bank some flexibility in its ability to change monetary policy, despite the fact that the exchange rate is pegged. In this book, we focus on the issue of credibility. In particular, we bring together a group of papers that examine the credibility of a number of key regimes of the international monetary system, from the classical and interwar gold standards to the exchange rate mechanism (ERM) experience with fixed but adjustable exchange rates.

One key outcome of our work is that it would seem that credibility is a function of the particular international monetary regime in existence. For example, the classical and interwar gold standard systems seem to have a superior performance in terms of credibility compared to other regimes, such as the ERM experience with fixed exchange rates and sterling's experience under Bretton Woods. Therefore, in designing architecture for the International Monetary System (IMS), and indeed designing a reform of the IMS per se, a key question that arises from our work is: Do we need gold, or some other commodity, as the anchor, to impart credibility, or are there other mechanisms, institutions, and regulations that can replace a commodity-based system?

A further aspect of the work reported in this volume is that although the two main gold standard regimes did exhibit considerable credibility, there were key periods when they were non-credible. However, we show that there is usually an intuitive explanation for such non-credibility in terms of either economic or political fundamentals, and that such lack of credibility was short-lived. Another theme we seek to address in this book is what extent the existence of credibility in fixed-rate regimes lends to monetary authorities the ability to engage in independent monetary policies.

OVERVIEW

The book is divided into four sections after this introduction representing four exchange rate regimes: Part II, Classical Gold Standard; Part III, The Interwar Period; Part IV, Bretton Woods; and Part V, The European Monetary System Period.

Classical Gold Standard

In Chapter 2, C. Paul Hallwood, Ronald MacDonald, and Ian W. Marsh focus specifically on the issue of credibility in the classical and interwar gold standard periods. They adopt a target zone interpretation of the gold standard period and implement two categories of tests: tests of the mean-reverting properties of certain key exchange rates and the calculation of credibility confidence intervals for these currencies. Although the credibility test of Svensson is often seen as the simplest test of credibility, a test of the mean-reverting properties of exchange rate behavior in a target zone is in fact even simpler because it relies only on the time series properties of the exchange rate. To test mean reversion, the authors use variance ratio statistics and Dickey-Fuller type tests; for the classical gold standard period, evidence of very fast and significant mean reversion is reported: Within four months, half of a deviation is extinguished. For the interwar period, the authors also report evidence of mean reversion for key currencies, although this is not as clear-cut (as fast or as significant) as in the classical period.

In Chapter 3, Michael D. Bordo and Ronald MacDonald offer a framework to test the degree of monetary independence conferred on a central bank in a credible target zone arrangement. In the context of the classical gold standard regime, they show how to test the "stylized fact" of a failure of central banks to play by the rules of the game – sterilize gold flows and follow domestic policies independent of concern for convertibility – combined with an apparently credible IMS. Using an uncovered interest rate parity condition and a term structure relationship, the authors derive three testing systems. System one involves estimating Uncovered Interest Parity (UIP) as a long-run co-integrating relationship and then calculating the mean reversion speed to this equilibrium. The speed of mean reversion provides information on the degree of monetary independence.

The second system combines the UIP relationship with a term structure relationship. The latter is included to gauge how much long-term and short-term interest rates diverge as a result of a monetary impulse. If the target zone/central bank independence story is correct, long rates should be relatively insensitive to shocks (because any monetary independence can only be short-lived in this model), and this is demonstrated to hold in the data – long rates change by very little in response to impulses, and adjustment of long rates is relatively rapid.

The third system consists of the second system plus a vector of "short-run" fundamentals: the change in gold reserves, the change in industrial production, the change in prices, and the volatility of short-term interest rates. This system is designed to capture the interest rate responses to temporary shocks in "fundamentals." The authors demonstrate, as expected, that the amount of policy independence is transitory, lasting about a year. Furthermore, the results show that interest rate adjustments do not need to be very large to accommodate 1 percent shocks in the fundamentals, and the magnitude of short rate adjustment proves to be much larger than that for long rates.

In Chapter 4, C. Paul Hallwood, Ronald MacDonald, and Ian W. Marsh examine in some detail a key feature of the results reported in Chapter 2, namely that the expected rate of re-alignment for the U.S. dollar was persistently non-zero for the period between 1879 and 1896. What explains this apparent lack of credibility? Because Friedman and Schwartz (1963) have argued that political factors rather than economic factors explain this behavior, the authors of the chapter use a modeling framework that seeks to disentangle the effect of economic fundamentals, expectational failures, time-varying risk premia, and political factors. The model used to assess this relies on splitting the interest differential into four components: a risk premium; the probability of re-alignment, which is a function of both economic and political factors; a peso effect, the expected rate of devaluation scaled by the probability of re-alignment; and the expected change in the exchange rate.

In sum, Hallwood, MacDonald, and Marsh find that the non-zero expected rate of re-alignment is predominately driven by a peso effect, and their explanation of this phenomenon is that financial markets were predicting a regime change – specifically the monetization of silver alongside gold – that would have increased both the U.S. money supply and the rate of inflation relative to the gold standard's "core" country, Britain. The specific events that gave rise to the belief in a regime change were the Bland-Allison Act of 1878, the prolonged agitation for the free coinage of silver – which lasted at least from 1879 until its weakening in late 1896 – the Sherman Silver Purchase Act of 1890, the draining of U.S. gold reserves during the 1890s, and the support given to the free-silver movement by influential elements in the Democratic Party. The authors argue that their finding of a significant dollar-peso problem quantifies the keen insights of Friedman and Schwartz (1963) and adds to the quantitative findings of some other investigators.

The Interwar Period

In Chapter 5, Michael D. Bordo and Ronald MacDonald apply the methods used in Chapter 3 to test for monetary independence in the interwar gold exchange standard period, a period that Hallwood, MacDonald, and Marsh in Chapter 2 found to be credible. Interestingly, and in terms of its credibility, Bordo and MacDonald find that the system behaves much as in the classical gold standard period.

In Chapter 6, C. Paul Hallwood, Ronald MacDonald, and Ian W. Marsh push the analyses of Chapter 2 one step further and attempt to assess the importance of economic fundamentals in forcing both the United Kingdom and the United States off the gold standard in 1931 and 1933, respectively. For the United Kingdom they assume that the expected rate of re-alignment is a function of standard macroeconomic fundamentals, such as relative money supplies, current accounts, and relative income, whereas for the U.S. dollar they test Brown's (1940) hypothesis that the expected rate of re-alignment is driven by gold reserves and banking crises. Such simple models are shown to work for the interwar period, in the sense that they have good in-sample explanatory power and coefficients are in general correctly signed and statistically significant. The authors show that for the United Kingdom, simply graphing the fitted expected devaluation along with the actual value shows the former leads the turning point and also the direction of the final change correctly. For the United States, a Vector Autoregression (VAR) analysis shows that both bank failures and gold flows are significant determinants of expected devaluation, and gold (out)flows cause bank failures. The authors interpret this result as reflecting that the Fed's commitment to the gold standard constrained its internal monetary policy.

In Chapter 7, C. Paul Hallwood, Ronald MacDonald, and Ian W. Marsh consider whether the impending war in Europe helped destroy the Gold Bloc in 1936. Specifically, they investigate how the Gold Bloc operated between France, the Netherlands, Switzerland, and Belgium, especially from the time the United States left the gold standard in March 1933 to its end in September 1936. They distinguish two different causes of the abandonment of gold by the Gold Bloc members (France, Netherlands, and Switzerland) in September 1936 – the external and internal inconsistency hypotheses. The external inconsistency hypothesis, extant in the literature, takes the form of an argument that economic causes – high price levels in the Gold Bloc relative to non–Gold Bloc countries (such as the United States and the United Kingdom) – exerted deflationary pressures in the Gold Bloc, which eventually became intolerable. The internal inconsistency hypothesis is that the Gold Bloc became unworkable because of asymmetric military-political shocks emanating from Germany and Italy, which adversely affected confidence in the French franc to a greater extent than either the Swiss franc or the Dutch gilder. The tests employed are based on the kind of credibility tests considered elsewhere in the book, specifically those relying on interest yield differentials. Although Hallwood, MacDonald, and Marsh find some support for the internal inconsistency hypothesis, the available data does not allow a researcher to claim that either the internal or external inconsistency hypothesis dominates.

Bretton Woods

In Chapter 8, Michael D. Bordo, Ronald MacDonald, and Michael J. Oliver examine the experience of UK sterling in the crisis period between 1964 and 1967. Evidence from credibility tests as conducted in earlier chapters shows that the sterling peg was often not credible and that the speculative attacks that occurred were justified. New archival daily data on sterling reserves shows that UK reserves were lower than official estimates at the time and were in worse shape than policy makers admitted to the public and their own creditors. The authors find that reserve movements driven by monetary and fiscal indiscipline were a key driver of the expected rate of re-alignment. They also show that the Bank of England was sensitive to movements of the exchange rate with respect to the exchange rate band.

The European Monetary System Period

The mean-reverting properties of the ERM experience with fixed exchange rates is tested by Myrvin Anthony and Ronald MacDonald in Chapter 9 for the narrow-band period of the ERM (1979–1992). For this period, the authors show, in contrast to the gold standard periods, a considerable lack of credibility, although they do note that when the other member central banks followed policies consistent with that of the Bundesbank, they were able to buy into its credibility, the Netherlands being a case in point. Proponents of wide-band target zones argue that they can be more stabilizing than narrow bands because, by reducing the likelihood of a relatively safe one-way bet on a re-alignment, they limit speculation against a currency. The likelihood of a safe one-way bet is regarded as more likely in a narrow-band target zone (see Kenen, 1995). In other words, by making it more costly (less safe) for speculators who may attempt to gain from a one-way bet on a re-alignment of the currency, a wide-band target zone tends to be more stabilizing than a narrow zone.

Finally, in Chapter 10, Hali Edison and Ronald MacDonald apply the first system's methods of Chapter 2 to the ERM period and find that this system behaves very much like the classical gold standard in the sense that countries whose currencies exhibit credibility, such as the Netherlands and Belgium, had some monetary independence, but that this was transitory and only lasted for about a year (a metric similar to what Bordo and MacDonald found in Chapter 3 for the classical period).

MEASURING CREDIBILITY AND MEAN REVERSION IN TARGET ZONE REGIMES

One key issue in a number of chapters in this volume relates to the measurement of credibility in a target zone regime. In this section, we sketch a few methods for testing credibility, which have been widely used in the literature and are used in a number of the chapters in this book. We also briefly summarize the so-called variance *ratio* tests, which are also used in a number of chapters in this book.

Perhaps the simplest test of credibility involves plotting the forward exchange rate against the upper and lower bands of the target zone (Svensson, 1993). The idea here is that in a credible target zone, the forward exchange rate will be the market's expected exchange rate and should be bounded by the upper and lower bands of the target zone:

$$s^l \leq f_t \leq s^u, \tag{1.1}$$

where s^l is the lower band of the target zone and s^u is the upper band. If the forward rate were to lie outside the band, this would be prima facie evidence that the target zone was non-credible.

More precise measures of credibility rely on measuring re-alignment expectations, and in this we follow the methodology of Svensson (1991, 1993) and Bertola and Svensson (1993). In natural logarithms, define the current exchange rate, s_t, as:

$$s_t \equiv x_t + c_t, \tag{1.2}$$

where c_t represents the central parity and x_t represents the deviation of the exchange rate from central parity ($x_t \equiv s_t - c_t$). Using this expression and taking time derivatives, the expected change in the exchange rate may, in turn, be defined as:

$$E[ds_t]/dt \equiv E_t[dx_t]/dt + E_t[dc_t]/dt, \tag{1.3}$$

where $E_t[dx_t]/dt$ is the expected rate of currency depreciation within the band and $E_t[dc_t]/dt$ is the expected rate of re-alignment. So the rationally expected rate of change of the exchange rate is divided into the expected movement "within the band," ($E_t[dx_t]/dt$), plus the expected rate of depreciation of the central parity, ($E_t[dc_t]/dt$).

Let x_t^u and x_t^l denote the upper and lower limits of an exchange rate's deviation from the central parity. The maximum possible changes in the exchange rate within the band are then given by the following weak inequality:

$$\left(x_t^l - x_t\right)/d_t \leq E_t[dx_t]/dt \leq \left(x_t^u - x_t\right)/d_t. \qquad (1.4)$$

Assuming that the interest differential measures the total expected change in the exchange rate, the following weak inequality expresses Svensson's "100 percent" confidence interval:

$$\left(i_t - i_t^*\right) - \left(x_t^u - x_t\right)/d_t \leq E_t[dc_t]/dt \leq \left(i_t - i_t^*\right) - \left(x_t^l - x_t\right)/d_t. \qquad (1.5)$$

This re-alignment expectation can be calculated if we know the expected change in the exchange rate, $E_t[ds]/dt$, which is easily calculated from the interest differential on the basis that uncovered interest parity is assumed to hold (i.e., in discrete time: $E\Delta s_{t+k} = i_t - i_t^*$). To calculate the expected movement of the exchange rate within the band, $E_t[dx]/dt$, the maximum possible changes in the exchange rate within the band for a particular fixed exchange rate regime must be determined, which requires using the values of the upper and lower limits of the band. For the gold standard periods, these are defined by the gold points; for other regimes considered in this book, these are defined by the allowed movement of the exchange rate above and below the central parity (which for Bretton Woods, for example, was plus or minus 1 percent).[1] It is only when both the left and right sides of the inequality signs are of the same sign that we reject the null hypothesis of no re-alignment expectation.[2]

---

[1] A numerical illustration may be helpful. Suppose that the expected change in the exchange rate as measured by the interest differential is 5% and that the exchange rate is currently at the center of the zone (i.e., $x_t = 0$ and, therefore, $x_t^u - x_t = 0.5\%$, or approximately half the width of the historical gold points). It follows that $4.5\% \leq E_t[dc]/dt \leq 5.5\%$, and we are confident that depreciation of the central parity is expected. The idea that we are "100%" confident derives from the fact that we are assuming the edges of the target zone, x^l and x^u, are known for certain. But supposing that the exchange rate is again at the center of its zone but that the expected depreciation is only 0.25%, we now calculate $-0.25\% \leq E_t[dc]/dt \leq 0.75\%$. In this case, the range of expectations spans both a possible appreciation of the central parity and a depreciation. As this range spans zero, we do not reject the null hypothesis that no re-alignment is expected.

[2] The expected rate of re-alignment can be interpreted as the expected devaluation size multiplied by the frequency of re-alignment. Suppose that, conditional on there being a devaluation, the devaluation will be 5%. An expected rate of re-alignment of 2.5% (roughly the average for the sterling-dollar rate through the less credible early part of the classical gold standard for the United States between 1879 and 1896 [see Hallwood,

Svensson (1993) has argued that a more precise measure of re-alignment expectations can be obtained from the so-called 95 percent confidence interval. This relies on a basic theoretical proposition by Krugman (1991) and to Miller and Weller (1991), and is discussed in more detail in succeeding chapters, that within a target zone the exchange rate should be a mean-reverting – or stationary – time series. Based on this, Svensson (1993) calculates the expected movement of the exchange rate within the band as a linear function of the current deviation, x_t, of the exchange rate from the central parity. Imposing rational expectations, the expected movement of the exchange rate within the band over the subsequent m months is the fitted value from the regression:

$$x_{t+m} - x_t = \alpha_0 + \alpha_1 x_t + u_t. \tag{1.6}$$

The availability of the fitted value then facilitates calculation of the discrete time 95 percent confidence interval as:

$$\left(i_t - i_t^*\right) - \left(x_t^{+5} - x_t\right) \le E_t \Delta c_t \le \left(i_t - i_t^*\right) - \left(x_t^{-5} - x_t\right), \tag{1.7}$$

where x_t^{+5} and x_t^{-5} represent the plus and minus 5 percent values of x_t.

As we have noted, and as we shall see in more detail later, a relatively straightforward way of testing for mean reversion would be to use a standard unit root test, such as the Dickey-Fuller type test. However, it is now widely accepted that such tests are not very powerful in detecting whether a series is stationary or not, particularly when the series contains a root that lies close to the unit circle. An alternative way of testing for unit roots is provided by the variance ratio test, recently popularized in the economics literature by Cochrane (1988). The variance ratio test is, we believe, especially useful for the kind of exchange rate behavior analyzed in this volume because it can indicate three types of potential behavior in a time series: whether a series contains a unit root and is therefore non-stationary; whether the series is non-stationary and, additionally, exhibits what we refer to as super-persistence (that is, it has a root greater than unity); or whether the series is mean-reverting and therefore stationary. For the last two outcomes, the variance ratio test can be regarded as particularly useful

MacDonald, and Marsh, 1995]) implies that the expected frequency of re-alignment is 0.5 per annum. That is, the market expects a 5% devaluation within the year to happen with a 50% probability. Equivalently, the expected time to a 5% devaluation of the dollar is two years. Thus, although the average expected rate of re-alignment may appear to be small, it can be consistent with quite substantial devaluation expectations. Of course, when the confidence interval spans zero, we cannot reject the hypothesis that the expected probability of a devaluation of any magnitude is zero.

because it gives a very straightforward interpretation of how rapidly a series reverts back to, or diverges from, its mean value.

The variance ratio test is potentially a powerful way of testing for the univariate mean-reverting properties of a series because it can capture potential long auto-correlations that are unlikely to be captured in standard Dickey-Fuller type tests, and that can be important in producing mean reversion. Under the null hypothesis that a variable, such as the exchange rate, follows a random walk, the variance of the kth difference should equal k times the first difference. That is,

$$Var(q_t - q_{t-k}) = kVar(q_t - q_{t-1}). \tag{1.8}$$

On re-arranging this expression, we have:

$$V_k = (1/k).[(Var(q_t - q_{t-k})).(Var(q_t - q_{t-1}))^{-1}] = 1, \tag{1.9}$$

where V_k denotes the variance ratio based on lag k. So a finding that an estimated value of V_k equals unity would imply that the exchange rate follows a random walk. However, if V_k turns out to be less than unity, this would imply that the exchange rate was stationary and mean-reverting. The intuition for this is straightforward – if the underlying process driving the real exchange rate is mean- reverting, the variance of the series would decrease as k becomes larger. Alternatively, if V_k turns out to be greater than 1, the exchange rate may be regarded as exhibiting super-persistence. Lo and MacKinlay (1988) define the test statistic:

$$M(k) = \hat{V}_k - 1$$

and show that the normalized statistic,

$$z(k) = M(k)\left(\frac{2(2k-1)(k-1)}{3Tk}\right), \tag{1.10}$$

is asymptotically distributed as standard normal. Lo and MacKinlay also derive a version that is robust to heteroscedasticity. We refer to the former statistic as $z_1(k)$ and the latter as $z_2(k)$.

CONCLUSIONS

A number of conclusions can be drawn from the collection of works in this volume. First, a number of chapters make clear that both the classical and interwar gold standard systems represented highly credible international monetary systems. Moreover, it is possible to understand and explain this credibility in terms of economic fundamentals.

Second, the evident non-credibility of the U.S. dollar in the classical gold standard period, discussed in Chapter 2, can be best understood in terms of political factors, specifically the free-silver movement, rather than inappropriate economic fundamentals.

Third, the existence of credible target zone systems in both gold standard systems seems to have given central banks some limited monetary independence of up to a year, which, Bordo and MacDonald (Chapter 3) show, could have been used for interest-rate-smoothing objectives or to absorb shocks to economic variables. The findings of Chapter 3 confirm, therefore, the predictions of Lars Svensson's theoretical model (see Svensson, 1994) that even with a fixed exchange rate, a central bank has some monetary independence as long as the fixed rate is regarded by market participants as a credible rate.

Fourth, Chapter 8 provides the first econometric study of foreign exchange market intervention for the United Kingdom during the sterling crises from 1964 to 1967 and clearly highlights the perils faced by a non-credible exchange rate arrangement. The use of daily data in this study allows a more precise description of the loss of credibility during four currency crises and shows that reserve losses are consistent with exchange rate crises.

Fifth, the chapter on the Gold Bloc, which develops concepts of internal (to the Gold Bloc) and external (or relative international price level) inconsistency and tests these hypotheses, finds that both economic fundamentals and military-political factors can have an important role to play in undermining the credibility of a fixed exchange rate system. We have demonstrated in this volume how non-economic factors can be measured and modeled.

Sixth, the two chapters on the ERM experience clearly indicate that a country can buy credibility for its monetary policy if it is prepared to lock its currency with the currency of a central bank that is credible, and the width of the target zone band appears not to affect this result. However, countries unprepared to have disciplined monetary policies will face a continual lack of credibility and repeated currency crises when such non-credibility becomes too large.

The lessons learned on the importance of credibility in the success or failure of the different experiences we covered across the four historical pegged exchange rate regimes have resonance for today's environment. Today, many of the advanced countries as well as a few emerging countries have floating exchange rates, independent central banks, and a commitment to low inflation. The successful operation of this non-regime depends on the central banks having both credibility and the ability to conduct their monetary policy actions independent of the government's fiscal needs. The historical experience of the twentieth century in the episodes we examine when credibility was lacking may have served as a learning experience for central banks in the past twenty years and helped create the Great Moderation. Once the dust settles on the recent financial crisis and recession, it will be interesting to see if the monetary authorities get back to the practices based on credibility learned from the earlier record in the era of pegged exchange rates.

PART TWO

THE CLASSICAL GOLD STANDARD

TWO

Credibility and Fundamentals

Were the Classical and Inter-War Gold Standards Well-Behaved Target Zones?

C. Paul Hallwood, Ronald MacDonald, and Ian W. Marsh

INTRODUCTION

This chapter investigates the question of whether the international gold standard constituted a credible target zone. The question is not a narrow one, for the answer has a bearing on whether adherence to the gold standard was sufficient to render monetary policy time-consistent. In other words, the question is: Did the markets believe that the authorities were truly committed to the international standard, or were the policies adopted seen as threatening the link with gold? Given that the Classical gold standard lasted from about 1873 to 1914 and, according to economic historians, operated more or less according to the rules of the game, it would not be so surprising to find that during this long period, the authorities did create a credible reputation for responsible monetary and interest rate policies. It may be somewhat more surprising if it were discovered that the troubled and short-lived reconstituted inter-war gold standard of 1925 to the early 1930s was similarly credible. This is one of the key issues which we investigate in this chapter.

The literature on the theory of freely floating exchange rates – which typically uses the asset approach to the exchange rate – is normally formulated using a linear relationship between an exchange rate and its fundamental determinants, say, the quantity of money and its velocity of circulation (see, for example, the well-known works of Dornbusch 1976, Frenkel 1976, Mussa 1976). These models are usually based on the assumption that purchasing power parity holds, at least in the long run. However, by contrast, a feature of "fixed" exchange rate systems is that an exchange rate is usually allowed to float between upper- and lower-intervention points, but is not allowed to move outside of this narrow intervention range, or what a recent burgeoning literature calls a target zone. Two examples of this type of target zone are the European Monetary System (1979–1990), and the Bretton Woods System (c. 1959–1971), where members of either system committed themselves actively to intervene in the foreign exchange market if the market exchange rate threatened to deviate outside the target zone. The gold standard is an interesting member of the class of target zone exchange rate systems. However, a significant difference between the managed exchange rate systems mentioned earlier and either version of the gold standard is that whereas in the former, the width of the target zone was defined by international convention, under the gold standard, the limits of the target zone were defined in the market – in fact, being governed by the cost of international gold arbitrage. In fact, if empirical research on the European Monetary System as a target zone is compared with our empirical findings set out later in the chapter, it seems that both the classical and inter-war gold standards were the more credible target zones – as judged by exchange rate behaviour. Bordo and Kydland (1992) raise a related point, specifically, that the classical gold standard was time-consistent. That is, in practice, adherence by the monetary authorities to the "rules of the game" effectively constrained monetary policy and constituted a credible commitment not to inflate prices. Relatedly, the implications (if not the theory) of time inconsistency of Britain not returning to the gold standard were well understood at the time by Sir Otto Niemeyer, a Treasury advisor, who wrote in 1924 that if it was seen that the United Kingdom had lost its nerve over a return to the gold standard, "the immediate consequence would be considerable withdrawal of balances and investment (both foreign and British) from London; a heavy drop in Exchange; and to counteract that tendency, a substantial increase in Bank rate" (quoted in Moggridge, 1969, p. 47).

As we have indicated, the key issue we intend investigating in this chapter is the credibility of the classical and inter-war versions of the international gold standards. In general terms, we intend to illuminate this issue by examining the behaviour of market exchange rates in these two periods, both in a time series context and in relation to their fundamental determinants within the target zone. We proceed as follows. The next section outlines the operation of the gold standard within the framework of the target zone literature. The third section presents the theory of target zones, and the two subsequent sections present the results of our empirical work. We close with a brief summary of our conclusions.

THE GOLD STANDARD AS A TARGET ZONE

The U.S. mint price of gold was set by the Mint Act of 1873 at $18.8047 per ounce of gold 9/10 fine and the mint price of gold in Britain had been set ever since 1717 at £3 17s 10.5d per ounce of gold 11/12 fine. Officer (1986) adjusts these prices for the quality differences and calculates the mint parity exchange rate as $4.8665 dollars per pound. If the underlying mint prices were fixed and arbitragers' transactions costs were zero, the market exchange rate would also be this rate. Naturally, however, transaction costs were positive and resulted in the determination of gold export and import points (see Spiller and Wood, 1988). Contemporaneous estimates of gold import and export points, made by the *Economist*, put the U.S. gold export and import points at, respectively, $4.890 and $4.827. A later estimate by Morgenstern (1959) is not very different from this. Nor are the still later estimates made by Clark (1984), Officer (1986) and Spiller and Wood (1988). In these three latter cases, the gold points are taken to vary with transaction costs – in the approximate range, according to Officer (1986), of 0.47 to 0.78 per cent or mint par prices. Transaction costs were a function of a number of variables including interest cost (which fluctuated with short-term money rates), the time taken to cross the Atlantic and, sometimes, in waiting to be paid by the authorities while they melted foreign gold, freight and insurance costs, abrasion of coin (which reduced coin weight below face value), any premium that the authorities might set above the mint price, normal profit and arbitragers' risk premiums.

In Officer's (1986) study and that of Spiller and Wood (1988), both the relatively high level and variability of transaction costs are used to explain apparent frequent gold point violations "discovered" by Morgenstern (1959) and Clark (1984). This is an important matter, because frequent violations of the gold points would question the efficiency of the gold standard as a target zone. As it is, this most recent research on gold point violations supports the views of contemporaries and economic historians that arbitrage was in fact effective in constraining exchange rates between the gold points. Thus Spiller and Wood (1988) conclude that "the gold standard seems to have been a relatively efficient system to provide bounds to exchange rate movements" (p. 89).

The finding that dollar-sterling gold points were rarely breached during the period of the classical gold standard is complemented by Officer's (1993) first meticulous study of dollar-sterling gold point arbitrage during the inter-war period. He explains how gold arbitrage by New York and London banks acted to keep the dollar-sterling exchange rate within the gold points. He also introduces the concept of "speculation points" which define the range of exchange rate movements given efficient uncovered arbitrage. Further, he shows that the dollar-sterling exchange rate remained within the gold points over the entire period that the United Kingdom was on the gold standard, May 1925 to August 1931. This, and the fact that forward rates also remained within the range, can be used to buttress the notion that the gold points defined credible bounds for exchange rate movements.[1] Officer's (1993) discussion of speculation points utilises the assumption that speculators' expected exchange rate was at the middle of the gold point range.[2] Although this may be somewhat arbitrary, as we shall see, it is not very different from the results obtained from Krugman's (1991) target zone model which exploits the idea that the expected exchange rate will revert towards the centre of the target zone. In addition to Officer's finding that the gold points set credible bounds to exchange rate movements, he also shows that rates fluctuated sufficiently within the centre of the zone as to be usually consistent with his calculated speculation points. The implication of this is that the credible target zone induces stabilising uncovered interest arbitrage which further boosts the stability of exchange rates. Had the target zone, as defined by gold points, not been credible then, as expected exchange rates moved outside the zone, speculators would have acted to push actual exchange rates outside the zone – but this did not happen.

TARGET ZONES: SOME THEORY

The literature on target zones concerns the relationship between an exchange rate and its fundamental determinants. Krugman (1991) models an exchange rate which is restricted to a narrow band, such as between the gold points, as a "target zone."[3] A target zone is credible, in the sense that the market believes that the exchange rate will be contained within it, if it is believed that the monetary authorities are committed to managing fundamentals, such as its discount rate and the monetary base, to that end. Thus, at the edges of the target zone, monetary policy must be geared exclusively to the exchange rate and not towards influencing, say, domestic business conditions. The seminal contribution was made by Krugman (1991) and extended by Miller and Weller (1991). Their theory is briefly outlined in this section.

---

[1] Officer (1996) introduces the concept of regime efficiency and applies it to the inter-war sterling-dollar gold link.

[2] Officer justifies this bold assumption by arguing that speculators had no reason to favour one point estimate over another whilst the exchange rate was within the gold points. This implies that their probability distributions of expected exchange rates were rectangular, with mean in the centre of the range.

[3] Empirical investigation of gold standard as a target zone is undertaken by Hallwood, MacDonald, and Marsh (1995), Giovannini (1993) and Flood, Rose and Mathieson (1991).

The argument assumes that the market believes that the target zone is credible. Credibility requires that the authorities purposely or automatically adapt monetary policy to defend the zone. As a simplification, it is further assumed that the target zone is defended only when the exchange rate reaches the upper or lower edges of the zone (so-called intra-marginal intervention is ruled out). The exchange rate is determined as

$$s_t = m_t + v_t + \alpha E_t[ds_t]/dt \tag{2.1}$$

where, in natural logarithms, s_t is the domestic currency price of foreign exchange, m_t is the money supply (which is an exogenous policy variable), α is the semi-elasticity of the demand for money, and v_t is a general-purpose term which includes anything else impacting on the demand or supply for money (e.g. changes in real income). Most simply, v_t is taken to be the "cumulative value of velocity" (Miller and Weller, 1991). Shocks to velocity are random with mean zero, and normally distributed such that the cumulative value of v_t follows a continuous-time random walk. The sum of m_t and v_t is usually referred to as the composite fundamental term, f_t. The final term is the instantaneous rationally expected rate of change of the exchange rate. Absolute purchasing power parity ($s_t = p_t - p_t^*$) and uncovered interest rate parity ($i_t = i_t^* + E_t[ds_t]/dt$) are assumed to hold continuously. Moreover, as the country is small, i_t^* and p_t^* are assumed to be parametrically given.

Figure 2.1 shows how the exchange rate is expected to behave in response to shocks to v_t. If the exchange rate was permitted to float freely, then from Equation 2.1 we see that it would be expected to move along the dashed 45 ray line (because the exchange rate is homogeneous of degree one with respect to both the fundamentals entering f_t). However, there is a target zone, with s_0 and s_1 as the maximum permitted depreciation and appreciation (under a gold standard, respectively, the gold export and import points). According to the theory of target zones, the S-shaped curve defines the relationship between the exchange rate and its fundamental determinants.

To see how the exchange rate behaves inside the band, suppose that there is a positive random shock to v_t. In this case, f_t increases and, to balance the domestic money market, i_t falls. However, given uncovered interest parity (UIP), a fall in i_t is only possible if $E_t[ds_t]/dt$ is negative – the exchange rate is expected to appreciate. From Equation 2.1 we see that a negative value of $E_t[ds_t]/dt$ will attenuate the movement of s_t; that is, s_t moves by less than it would have done had $E_t[ds_t]/dt$ not become negative. This is called the honeymoon effect, which represents a free benefit from the announcement of a credible target zone and indicates that there should be a negative association

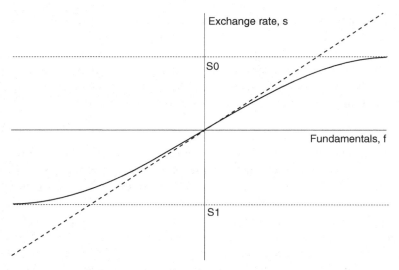

Figure 2.1. Exchange rate in a target zone.

between the expected change in the exchange rate and the actual exchange rate in a credible target zone system. The generation of the expected appreciation of s_t may be illustrated by considering the situation whereby s_t has already reached the upper edge of the band. A further random increase in v_t will be offset by a gold-outflow-induced reduction in m_t. Therefore, s_t cannot rise because f_t has an upper limit; but it might fall because the next random shock to v_t could be negative, in which case f_t and s_t fall. Thus on balance, s_t must be expected to fall. It is this expected appreciation, given that UIP holds at all times, that allows i_t to fall below i_t^*. Moreover, the argument holds for any value of s between its upper and central limit.

The target zone model discussed earlier may be regarded as the baseline model. A rather more sophisticated version, introduced by Bertola and Svensson (1993), pushes the model further. In particular, Bertola and Svensson note that Krugman's basic formulation ignores potential realignments of the fixed parity; such realignments have been fairly frequent in the exchange rate mechanism (ERM) experience with quasi-fixed rates, and although they did not occur during the gold standard, this does not preclude the possibility that agents held expectations of non-zero realignments. If market participants, at least in part, anticipate such realignments, the target zone cannot be perfectly credible, as is assumed in the basic target zone model. The Bertola and Svensson's variant notes first of all that the exchange rate is by definition equal to the sum of the central parity rate, and the deviation from the central parity, as given by Equation 1.2. Using the expression for the expected change in the exchange rate as given by Equation 1.3 in Equation 2.1, and on subtracting c_t from the resulting expression, we obtain an equation describing the exchange rate within the band as:

$$x_t = h_t + \alpha E_t [dx_t]/dt \qquad (2.2)$$

where h_t is the new composite fundamental and is equal to $f_t - c_t + \alpha E_t [dc_t]/dt$. Equation 2.2 has two immediate implications for any empirical test of the target zone model. First, even if UIP holds continuously, this extended target zone model suggests that one cannot say a priori what the relationship between the exchange rate and the interest rate differential will be like. This is because UIP holds for the total expected change in the exchange rate which from Equation 1.3 is equal to two elements. As in our discussion of the Krugman model, one would expect there to be a negative association between the expected rate of currency depreciation within the band and the exchange rate, but one cannot say anything about the relationship between the expected rate of realignment and the exchange rate. Because the latter component of Equation 1.3 is time-varying, it could easily swamp the former component, resulting in a positive or negative relationship between the exchange rate and the interest differential. A second implication of Equation 2.2 for an empirical test is that one should include the expected rate of realignment in ones' measure of the composite fundamentals term. An implication of Equation 1.3 is that the expected rate of realignment can be backed out of the total expected change in the exchange rate given by the interest rate differential:

$$E[dc_t]/dt \equiv E_t [ds_t]/dt - E_t [dx_t]/dt. \qquad (2.3)$$

All that is needed is a measure of the expected change in the exchange rate within the band, which, as we noted in the previous chapter, can be estimated via a simple linear regression.

IMPLICATIONS OF THE TARGET ZONE MODEL AND EMPIRICAL EVIDENCE

The first prediction of the theory of target zones is that, in terms of the basic model, there should be a negative relationship between the expected total change in the exchange rate (given by the interest differential) and the level of the exchange rate. If, however, the target zone is not perfectly credible, one cannot make any a priori prediction about the relationship. However, the existence of a positive relationship would be prima facie evidence of the existence of less-than-full credibility. Second, there should be a non-linear relationship between the exchange rate and fundamentals, where following our discussion of potential realignments, care must be taken in the definition of the fundamentals.

For the gold standard period, the tests of these two predictions have been conducted by Flood, Rose and Mathieson (1991). With respect to the interest differential/exchange rate relationship, using scatterplot analysis, they find some evidence of a negative association for the classical gold standard period, whereas for the inter-war gold standard, they report six out of the nine currencies having a negative relationship (the three with a positive relationship are Germany, Italy and the Netherlands). Furthermore, for both the classical gold standard and inter-war periods, the relationship between the exchange rate and fundamentals "seems to be decidedly more non-linear than for the EMS." Indeed, for the classical gold standard period, the scatterplots seem to suggest an S-shaped relationship. Given that our databases are very similar to those used by Flood, Rose and Mathieson, we do not intend repeating them here.

The other testable implications of the target zone model relate to the assumptions underpinning the model. By far the most important assumption is that the zone is indeed credible. Svensson (1992) summarises the results of testing this assumption by arguing that they clearly indicate that perfect credibility is rejected for most modern exchange rate target zones and sample periods. Given that a detailed examination of this assumption has not been conducted, we make it the focal point for both gold standard experiences in this chapter. We discuss our methods and apply them to the classical gold standard in the following sub-section. We then contrast the findings with those pertaining to the inter-war experience.

Credibility of the Classical Gold Standard

Unfortunately, data limitations restrict the number of currencies which can be analysed in the target zone framework, and for the classical gold standard we are forced to focus on the pound-dollar and pound-French franc exchange rates. Two data sets are available: one monthly and the other annual. The annual data include a limited range of fundamental variables (which will be used later) and are available for the full classical gold standard period from the 1870s to the start of World War I (exact dates depend upon the countries examined). The shorter monthly series on exchange and interest rates span January 1889 through December 1907. Further details and sources are given in the Data Appendix.

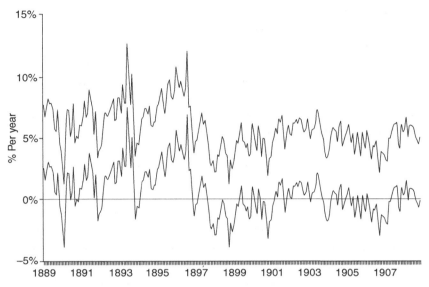

Figure 2.2. Expected realignment rate, 100% confidence interval.

One Hundred Per Cent Confidence Interval Test

In this section we provide estimates of the "100 per cent" confidence interval, introduced in the previous chapter (see Equation 1.5), for the expected devaluation of the classical gold standard exchange rates noted earlier. We have placed quotes around the 100 per cent because the gold points are themselves only estimates. Several authors, both contemporary and modern, have tried to estimate the gold points, each arriving at different values. Most have been forced to provide an average estimate of the gold points for a sub-period of the classical gold standard, albeit acknowledging that the component costs of arbitrage were certainly not constant through time (an exception is Spiller and Wood, 1988). Here we use the *Economist*'s relatively wide estimates of the gold points to obtain our 100 per cent confidence interval for the expected rate of realignment, plotted in Figure 2.2. As can be seen, for most of the 1890s, this interval lay above zero, indicating an expected devaluation of the dollar. After 1897, the confidence interval appears to shift down and spans zero more often than not. Narrower estimates of the gold points would of course provide more examples of expected devaluation over the whole sample period.[4]

---

[4] Calomiris (1992), using a different methodology, has calculated realignment expectations for the short period between 1893 and 1896. Giovannini (1993) uses a methodology similar to ours, applying it to the years between 1889 and 1909.

Stationarity of the Exchange Rate within the Band

The simple credibility test assumes no knowledge of the time series behaviour of the exchange rate within the band. However, according to the target zone theory, the expected change in the exchange rate within the band should be mean-reverting – when the exchange rate is near the top of the band, it should be expected to fall back towards the middle. It should be noted that the gold standard target zones were not symmetric about the gold parity rates due to the asymmetries in the costs of gold arbitrage (typically foreign interest rates were above London rates). The exchange rate would therefore be expected to revert towards the middle of the band rather than the parity rate.

To test the mean reversion of our two currencies, we estimate the variance ratio tests, introduced in the previous chapter, and our estimates of V_k, $z_1(k)$ and $z_2(k)$ are presented in Table 2.1. The tables should be read in the following way. The figures not in parentheses give the estimated variance ratios. The first figure in parentheses immediately below this number is $z_1(k)$, and the second figure is the estimated value of $z_2(k)$. The statistics are calculated for a range of values between two and twelve months. Note that both currencies are strongly mean-reverting. Thus, at the 1 per cent significance level, the estimated value of $z_2(k)$ for the United Kingdom is significantly below unity from lag two onwards, whereas it is significantly below unity from lag three onwards for France.

Bertola and Svensson's Test of Credibility

Having established that exchange rates are stationary, the question remains, however, of how to estimate the mean reversion expected by market participants. Usefully, Bertola and Svensson (1993) suggest that the expected future change in the exchange rate within the band may be approximated by the current exchange rate; both Svensson (1993) and Rose and Svensson (1991) demonstrate empirical support for this proposition using data for currencies participating in the ERM. Conditional on no realignment, the m-period change in the exchange rate within the band may be estimated from Equation 1.6 which indicates that the single determinant of the expected change within the band is the current deviation of the exchange rate from the centre of the band.[5] In principle, the relationship should be non-linear, but Bertola and Svensson argue that a linear relationship ought

---

[5] In their empirical implementation of Equation 1.6, for ERM currencies, Rose and Svensson (1991) include levels of other ERM exchange rates, because the latter may be relevant in a multilateral exchange rate target zone model. Given the wide range of country-specific sample periods, and also the fact that the gold standard experiences do not seem to

Table 2.1. *Variance ratio tests of classical gold standard exchange rates*

	US/UK	FR/UK
2	0.813	0.858
	$(2.81)^1$	$(2.14)^2$
	$(2.42)^1$	$(1.70)^3$
3	0.633	0.719
	$(3.71)^1$	$(2.84)^2$
	$(4.72)^1$	$(3.38)^1$
4	0.545	0.635
	$(3.67)^1$	$(2.94)^1$
	$(4.85)^1$	$(3.65)^1$
6	0.447	0.441
	$(3.36)^1$	$(3.40)^1$
	$(5.34)^1$	$(5.13)^1$
8	0.338	0.379
	$(3.78)^1$	$(3.17)^1$
	$(6.05)^1$	$(5.41)^1$
12	0.195	0.258
	$(3.22)^1$	$(2.97)^1$
	$(6.87)^1$	$(6.08)^1$

Notes: The first figure in each cell gives the ratio of variances. The first figure in parentheses directly below this gives the estimated value of the $z_1(k)$ statistic, and the second gives the estimated value of $z_2(k)$. A 1, 2 and 3 denote, respectively, significance at the 1, 5 and 10 per cent levels.

to be acceptable for typical parameter values. In fact, many studies of modern target zones use the linear approximation and find that it produces more sensible estimates than other, more complicated methods (see Lindberg et al., 1993, and Rose and Svensson, 1991).[6]

As we have noted, the gold points were not necessarily symmetric about the gold parity level. The centre of the band therefore changes with the costs of arbitrage and, if the gold points are unknown, is itself unknown. To remove the possible problems with the gold point estimates, we measure the deviation in the exchange rate from the gold parity level. Because

resemble a multilateral target zone system as much as a group of bilateral relationships, we do not include other gold standard currencies in our estimated relationships.

[6] Because the dependent variable consists of overlapping observations Newey and West (1987) generalised method of moments (GMM), standard errors are reported. These allow for both serial correlation and heteroscedasticity.

Table 2.2. *Expected change in exchange rate
within the band – classical period*

	US/UK	FR/UK
Constant	−0.000611	−0.000673
	(2.29)	(3.35)
X	−0.616857	−0.632450
	(7.90)	(9.30)
R^2	0.313	0.325
'DF test'	4.905	8.301

Notes: Figures in parentheses are t-statistics computed with GMM standard errors. The "DF tests" are t-tests of the hypothesis that $\alpha_1 = 1$.

a constant is included in the regression, this does not constrain the parity level to be the point to which exchange rates revert, but it does force this point to be constant. As the majority of reliable estimates of the gold points are themselves constant, we do not feel that any other approach would be profitable.

Our estimates of Equation 1.6, the mean-reversion equation, for the classical gold standard are presented in Table 2.2. Notice that all of the t-ratios on the α_1 coefficients are, in absolute terms, above the critical values of Dickey and Fuller, again confirming that the exchange rate series are stationary. Bertola and Svensson then show that the 95 per cent confidence interval for the resulting estimates of expected mean reversion can be subtracted from the interest differential to provide a 95 per cent confidence interval for the expected realignment rate. This will be independent of any estimated gold points and should therefore allow an independent check on the credibility of the gold standard. Furthermore, because we are also able to apply this technique to the franc-pound rate, this gives us a wider perspective on the operation of the gold standard system during its Classical incarnation.[7]

These are plotted using our monthly and annual data sets in Figures 2.3–2.6.[8] The first point to note is that the sterling-dollar intervals are little different to the 100 per cent versions presented earlier. If anything, the 95

[7] We could not find any reliable estimates of the gold points for the French franc exchange rate and so we were unable to produce "100 per cent" confidence intervals. This also applies to the inter-war period examined later.

[8] To obtain the confidence intervals based on annual data, the mean reversion parameters estimated with the monthly data are combined with the annual exchange and interest rate data.

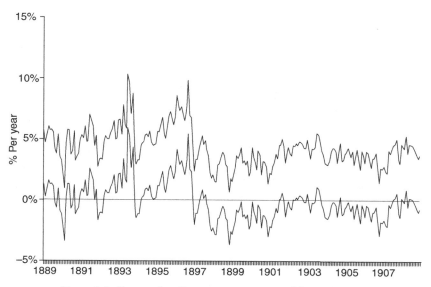

Figure 2.3. Expected realignment rate, 95% confidence interval.

Figure 2.4. Expected realignment rate, 95% confidence interval.

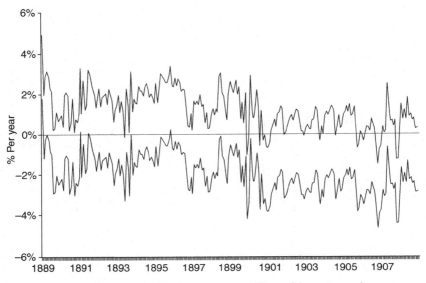

Figure 2.5. Expected realignment rate, 95% confidence interval.

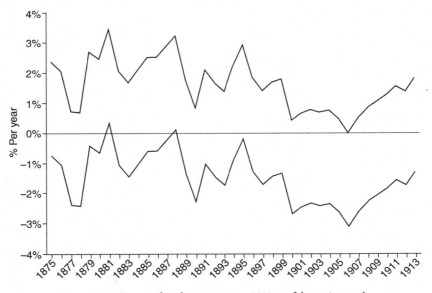

Figure 2.6. Expected realignment rate, 95% confidence interval.

percent interval is slightly wider, with fewer instances of the range lying above zero. This would seem to indicate that even the widest gold point estimates are too narrow. Nevertheless, instances of positive devaluation expectations of the dollar are still common, and it would appear that one of the key rates of the classical gold standard was less than perfectly credible.

The expected rate of realignment can be interpreted as the expected devaluation size multiplied by the frequency of realignment. Suppose that, conditional on there being a devaluation, the devaluation will be 5 per cent. An expected rate of realignment of 2.5 per cent (roughly the average level for the sterling-dollar rate through the less-credible early part of the classical gold standard) implies that the expected frequency of realignment is 0.5 per annum. That is, the market expects a 5 per cent devaluation within the year to happen with a 50 per cent probability. Equivalently, the expected time to a 5 per cent devaluation of the pound is two years. Thus, although the average expected rate of realignment is small, it is consistent with substantial devaluation expectations. Of course, for those later periods where the confidence interval spans zero we cannot reject the hypothesis that the expected probability of a 5 per cent devaluation is zero.

It is reassuring to note that the occurrences of large devaluation expectations coincide with notable periods of tension. Officer (1989) highlights the "eight-year period from 1890 to 1897 [where] there was an acute lack of confidence in the ability of the United States to remain on the gold standard" (p. 24). The cause of this tension was almost certainly the pro-bimetallist 1890 Sherman Silver Purchase Act. Over the thirty-five months following the passing of the Act, beginning December 1890 and ending with the repeal of the silver clause in November 1893, there were twenty-nine months with significant dollar realignment expectations. The dramatic rise in the confidence of the sterling-dollar link following the repeal proved very temporary, however, mainly because silver still rode high on the political agenda. The persistent devaluation expectations were finally ended by the November 1896 defeat of the pro-silver presidential candidate, William Jennings Bryan. Figure 2.3 shows that dollar realignment expectations disappeared almost immediately after the election.[9]

---

[9]   The significant devaluation expectations of the late 1880s are less easily attributed to a single cause. The Bland-Allison Act of 1878 reinstated silver as legal tender and may have led the markets to question the America's commitment to the monometalic gold standard. However, it has also been suggested that the rise of the Populist Movement may have been sufficiently threatening to the banking community to affect the currency's credibility.

We note that our results are also compatible with those of Giovannini (1993) who, using a similar database, found periods of expected dollar devaluation in the 1890s.

By contrast, the sterling-franc exchange rate band appears to have been very credible. Using the annual data, in only one instance was the expected rate of realignment significantly different from zero (and then only very marginally). Using the monthly data, a few more periods of less than perfect credibility are revealed, but they were not persistent and were small in magnitude.

Credibility of the Inter-war Gold Standard

For the inter-war period, a greater availability of reliable data should, in principle, allow us to cover a wider range of currencies. The major data constraint we face is related to the assumption that uncovered interest parity holds. Interest data of comparable maturity and quality are not readily available for many countries for these years. Fortunately, Einzig (1937a) lists weekly spot exchange rates and three-month forward premia against sterling for the dollar, French franc, German mark, Dutch florin and Swiss and Belgian francs. Using triangular arbitrage, these were all converted to dollar bilateral exchange rates.[10] Note that our base country has changed as we move from classical to inter-war standards. In the former, the United Kingdom plays the central role, whereas the United States assumes this position after World War I. Assuming covered interest parity, we take the forward premium as our measure of the interest differential. Given that monthly series on several fundamental variables are available for this period, we sample the data using the observation relating to the last Saturday of each month to produce a monthly database.[11] Because the pound-dollar exchange rate was still dominant in the inter-war period, we constrain our analysis to the interval May 1925 to August 1931 during which the sterling-dollar gold link was maintained.

Mean Reversion of the Exchange Rate

Using the same methods as for the classical period, the degree of mean reversion of the exchange rate can be assessed for the inter-war experiment. The Bertola and Svensson's simple regression technique reveals very significant mean reversion of a similar magnitude to that experienced during the classical gold standard. The results for a range of exchange rates are given

---

[10] We should point out that our choice of currencies, dictated by data availability, is likely to be favourable to the gold standard. Belgium, France, the Netherlands and Switzerland all became members of the Gold Bloc after 1931.

[11] The foreign exchange market was typically open on Saturdays during this period. For days when the market was closed, the nearest business day is used instead.

Table 2.3. *Expected change in exchange rate within the band – inter-war period*

	UK/US	FR/US	GE/US	NE/US	SW/US	BE/US
Const. ($\times 10^{-3}$)	0.854	−0.550	0.478	0.430	−0.380	−1.612
	(1.86)	(1.05)	(0.10)	(0.94)	(0.64)	(2.71)
X	−0.622	−0.669	−0.518	−0.737	−0.605	−0.701
	(3.53)	(3.74)	(3.63)	(4.76)	(3.72)	(4.99)
R^2	0.310	0.335	0.248	0.362	0.253	0.352
Std. Error ($\times 10^{-2}$)	0.197	0.257	0.252	0.281	0.335	0.230

Notes: Figures in parentheses are t-statistics computed with GMM standard errors.

in Table 2.3. The potentially more powerful variance ratio tests give similar results, although the statistical significance is somewhat weaker than for the classical period. In particular, the ratios for the sterling-dollar rate fall below unity after lag 4, but never significantly so. The ratios for the French franc exchange rate are practically always less than 1 but only marginally significant at long lags. However, we ascribe these problems to the short data span rather than any lack of mean reversion in the exchange rate because, as we shall see in the following section, the key sterling-dollar spot rate never left the confines of the Officer (1993) gold points. The evidence of mean reversion is much more clear-cut for Belgium, the Netherlands and Switzerland. The full set of variance ratio results are reported in Table 2.4.[12]

Devaluation Expectations

Although widely interpreted as less credible than the classical incarnation, there was never a violation of the gold points by the key sterling-dollar exchange rate during the inter-war gold standard. Figure 2.7 shows the spot exchange rate fluctuating widely but always within the Officer (1993) gold points. Notice how the latter also fluctuated, typically narrowing as time passed. We stress, however, that this is not a sufficient condition for there to have been no expectations of realignment.

Based on the Officer (1993) gold points, a 100 per cent confidence interval for the expected rate of realignment of the pound-dollar exchange rate can be estimated. This is plotted in Figure 2.8. Most of the time we are unable to reject the hypothesis that there were no expectations of realignment, as the interval spans zero. At the end of the period, however,

---

[12] One interesting extension of our mean reversion tests would be to implement them using recursive methods. In theory, this could shed light on potential variations in mean reversion in the two gold standard periods. Data considerations, however, mean that only the classical period would be a suitable candidate for such work.

Table 2.4. *Variance ratio tests of inter-war gold standard rates*

	UK/US	FR/US	GE/US	NE/US	SW/US	BE/US
2	1.062	1.005	0.896	1.263	0.994	0.920
	(0.54)	(0.03)	(0.85)	(2.26)	(0.05)	(0.61)
	(0.63)	(0.03)	(0.80)	(2.66)	(0.06)	(0.84)
3	1.059	0.918	0.793	1.160	0.918	0.822
	(0.34)	(0.40)	(1.13)	(0.92)	(0.45)	(0.91)
	(0.60)	(0.58)	(1.58)	(1.62)	(0.72)	(1.88)
4	1.037	0.875	0.733	0.907	0.833	0.684
	(0.17)	(0.48)	(1.17)	(0.43)	(0.73)	(1.26)
	(0.31)	(0.71)	$(1.74)^3$	(0.78)	(1.13)	$(2.52)^2$
5	0.966	0.812	0.739	0.676	0.706	0.588
	(0.13)	(0.63)	(0.94)	(1.26)	(1.06)	(1.43)
	(0.28)	(1.08)	$(1.70)^3$	$(2.73)^1$	$(1.99)^2$	$(3.29)^1$
6	0.908	0.756	0.791	0.585	0.591	0.529
	(0.32)	(0.73)	(0.66)	(1.44)	(1.29)	(1.41)
	(0.67)	(1.26)	(1.26)	(3.09)	$(2.44)^2$	$(3.16)^1$
7	0.866	0.733	0.767	0.586	0.472	0.504
	(0.42)	(0.71)	(0.70)	(1.24)	(1.58)	(1.31)
	(0.97)	(1.38)	(1.41)	(3.08)	$(3.16)^1$	$(3.33)^1$
8	0.816	0.738	0.807	0.633	0.418	0.537
	(0.52)	(0.64)	(0.51)	(1.04)	(1.54)	(1.14)
	(1.24)	(1.25)	(1.11)	$(2.54)^1$	$(3.24)^1$	$(2.84)^1$
9	0.787	0.718	0.833	0.653	0.391	0.547
	(0.56)	(0.63)	(0.41)	(0.92)	(1.49)	(1.01)
	(1.43)	(1.35)	(0.96)	$(2.40)^1$	$(3.39)^1$	$(2.78)^1$
10	0.765	0.678	0.815	0.619	0.365	0.556
	(0.58)	(0.64)	(0.41)	(0.93)	(1.42)	(0.99)
	(1.51)	(1.47)	(1.02)	$(2.51)^1$	$(3.37)^1$	$(2.57)^1$
11	0.762	0.619	0.773	0.559	0.337	0.553
	(0.53)	(0.76)	(0.51)	(0.99)	(1.48)	(0.89)
	(1.53)	$(1.74)^3$	(1.24)	$(2.91)^1$	$(3.52)^1$	$(2.59)^1$
12	0.728	0.570	0.698	0.528	0.288	0.479
	(0.61)	(0.75)	(0.60)	(1.06)	(1.42)	(1.04)
	(1.68)	$(1.89)^2$	(1.60)	$(2.99)^1$	$(3.63)^1$	$(2.88)^1$

Notes: See Table 2.1 for definitions.

there was a substantial deterioration in confidence in the currency link, and devaluation expectations rose significantly above zero in the final two months.

Similarly, a 95 per cent confidence interval can be constructed using the results from the mean reversion equation (reported as Figure 2.9). Once more a similar picture is revealed, and although the 95 per cent confidence

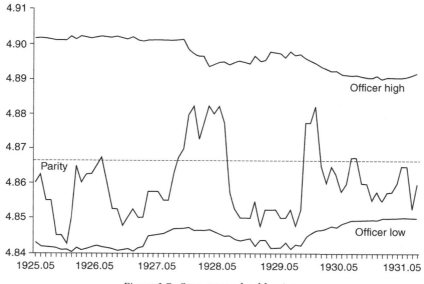

Figure 2.7. Spot rate and gold points.

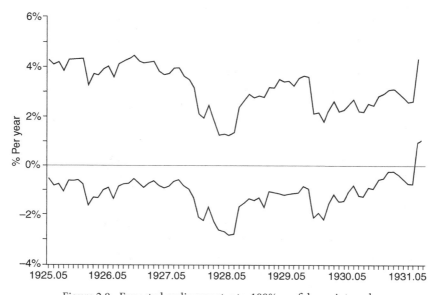

Figure 2.8. Expected realignment rate, 100% confidence interval.

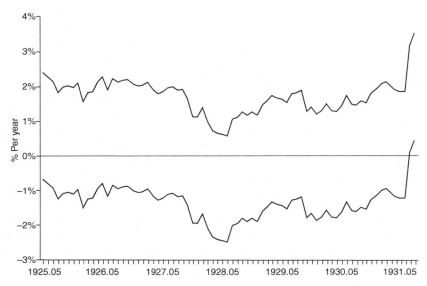

Figure 2.9. Expected realignment rate, 95% confidence interval.

interval band is narrower than that derived from the simple method, the
more relevant lower bound is practically identical. The sterling-dollar
exchange rate was almost fully credible during the inter-war gold standard, but the expected rate of realignment became significantly positive in
the last few months of the regime, indicating correctly that the pound was
expected to devalue. Nevertheless, the expected devaluation indicated by
both methods is small when compared to estimates made of ERM devaluation expectations. Svensson (1993) plots similar 95 per cent confidence
intervals for the ERM exchange rates against the German mark and shows
that in the run-up to realignments, devaluation expectations usually
exceed 10 per cent pa and often exceed 20 per cent pa. This compares with
a maximum of around 4 per cent for the pound-dollar during the inter-
war period.

The 95 per cent confidence interval for the expected rate of realignment
of the French franc-dollar rate is plotted in Figure 2.10.[13] As in the classical period, the franc link with the central currency (this time the U.S.
dollar) appears to have been robust. Realignment expectations were

[13] We have been unable to locate any gold point estimates for exchange other than for
sterling-dollar. This precludes the reporting of confidence intervals.

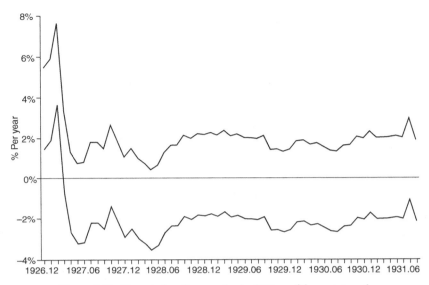

Figure 2.10. Expected realignment rate, 95% confidence interval.

non-zero for the first three months of the regime, but once the markets had settled down, confidence in the link rose. Reflecting the perceived under-valuation of the franc, the mean realignment expectation was negative, indicating that an upward revaluation of the franc was deemed most likely by investors.

Confidence in the mark-dollar link was more volatile (Figure 2.11). There were four periods when the confidence interval did not span zero, each instance reflecting expectations of a mark devaluation. A sustained crisis of confidence in mid-1926 (five consecutive months of devaluation expectations) was overcome, but the mean predicted rate of realignment was positive throughout the period. Although realignment expectations were marginally significant, warning bells were not exactly sounding at the end of the regime, reflecting the sudden onset of the banking crisis that eventually forced the German currency to break with gold and precipitated the end of the inter-war gold standard. Figure 2.12 plots realignment expectations for the Dutch, Swiss and Belgian currencies. Without exception, expectations were insignificantly different from zero for all currencies, and indeed these three currencies plus the French franc maintained their gold links for many more years. The graph clearly shows common trends in confidence for these closely related currencies.

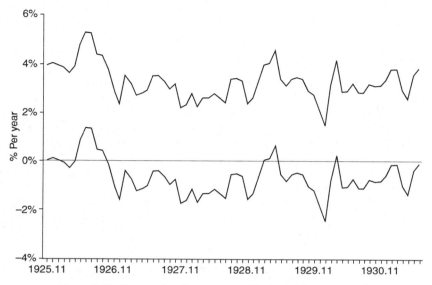

Figure 2.11. Expected realignment rate, 95% confidence interval.

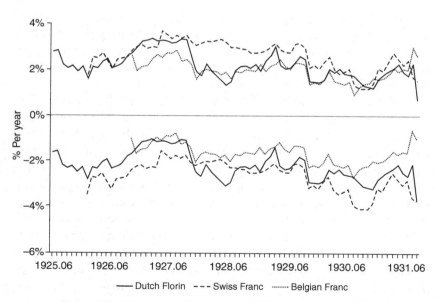

Figure 2.12. Expected realignment rate, 95% confidence interval.

FUNDAMENTAL DETERMINANTS OF CREDIBILITY

Once time series of realignment expectations have been estimated, the next logical step is to relate these measures of credibility to other parameters which influence exchange rates. Several researchers have examined the determinants of the credibility of modern target zones (see Caramazza, 1993, and Chen and Giovannini, 1994). However, determinants of devaluation expectations during the gold standards have not, until now, been examined. Data limitations for the classical gold standard period mean that we can only consider a few possible determinants of realignment expectations, namely money supplies, income levels and inflation rates. Nevertheless, these are key variables in most modern theories of the exchange rate and should shed some light on whether the state of the economy and the policies of governments influenced the credibility of the system. We regress the realignment expectations series on a constant and the lagged (log) differences in each variable between the home country and the United Kingdom. The results are reported in Table 2.5.

Although the equations have reasonably good explanatory power, especially when judged by the criterion for a satisfactory exchange rate equation given by Mussa (1979), only one of the variables is significantly different from zero (the difference between income levels in the UK-France relationship). Furthermore, F-tests indicate that the three fundamental terms are jointly insignificant in both equations. This indicates that the paths of these key fundamental variables were not sufficiently out of line with each other to suggest to market participants that the gold link was under threat. We can therefore find no evidence to contradict the hypothesis that governments played according to the rules of the game under the classical gold standard. The fact, of course, remains that credibility was not perfect for the dollar-sterling link for the early part of the period. Further investigation of the importance of the dramatic changes in U.S. reserve gold holdings which occurred in the early 1890s would appear to be of particular relevance.[14]

For the inter-war period where data are more readily available, we can include several variables which may be important in explaining the credibility of the regime. In particular, we estimate regressions of the following form

$$
\begin{aligned}
E_t[dc_t]/dt = \beta_0 + \beta_1 \Big[r - r^* \Big]_{t-1} + \beta_2 \Big[\pi - \pi^* \Big]_{t-1} + \beta_3 \Big[m - m^* \Big]_{t-1} \\
+ \beta_4 \Big[bp - bp^* \Big]_{t-1} + \beta_5 \Big[y - y^* \Big]_{t-1} \\
+ \beta_6 [q]_{t-1} + \beta_7 E_{t-1}[dc_{t-1}] dc + \varepsilon_t
\end{aligned}
\tag{2.4}
$$

---

[14] See Officer (1993) for a discussion of events in this period.

Table 2.5. *Fundamental determinants of realignment*
expectations – classical

	US/UK	FR/UK
m–m*(−1)	0.000053	−0.001034
	(0.01)	(0.11)
y–y*(−1)	−0.009735	0.039011
	(0.36)	(1.92)
π–π*(-1)	−0.018076	−0.069565
	(0.28)	(1.33)
$E[dc]/dt(−1)$	0.445554	0.458618
	(2.55)	(2.98)
R^2	0.293	0.487
Std. Error	0.0089	0.0066
F-test	0.344 (0.79)	2.065 (0.12)
No. observations	34	38

Notes: The figures in parentheses under the coefficient estimates
are t-statistics. m denotes the money supply, y denotes income and
π denotes inflation. All independent variables are lagged by one
period, and a * denotes a foreign (UK) variable. F-tests are tests that
the fundamental determinants excluding the lagged dependent variable are insignificant. The figures in parentheses after the F-test statistics are the marginal significance level.

where r denotes reserves, π the inflation rate, m the money supply, b
the balance of payments ratio (exports/imports), y income (proxied by
industrial production), and q the real exchange rate. All variables are in
logarithms, and an asterisk denotes a foreign (U.S.) variable. Our results are
reported in Table 2.6 for the three currencies for which non-zero devaluation expectations were found.

The regressions of Equation 2.4 exhibit a good explanatory power for
all exchange rates. Additionally, all of the equations contain a high pro-
portion of significant explanatory variables; however, are they correctly
signed? In the United Kingdom, notice that the change in reserves is significantly negative, suggesting, as theory would predict, that an increase in
domestic foreign exchange reserves results in a decrease in the expected
rate of realignment. The money supply term, which is usually interpreted as
a government financing term, is also strongly significant, with the expected
positive sign. The significantly negative effect of relative UK industrial production indicates that an increase in UK industrial production relative to
that in the United States reduces the expected rate of devaluation because
it increases the demand for money relative to the supply. Notice that of the

Table 2.6. *Fundamental determinants of realignment expectations – inter-war*

	UK/US	FR/US	GE/US
r–r*(−1)	−0.009374	0.004114	0.006242
	(2.11)	(1.13)	(0.97)
π–π*(-1)	−0.075969	−0.156256	−0.061398
	(0.43)	(3.22)	(0.27)
m–m*(−1)	0.043533	0.008630	−0.01777
	(2.63)	(0.70)	(1.40)
bp–bp*(−1)	0.004023	−0.002192	0.003465
	(2.59)	(0.43)	(1.11)
y–y*(−1)	−0.004411	−0.010759]	−0.016547
	(2.74)	(1.70)	(1.85)
q(−1)	0.069823	0.698732	0.021525
	(0.46)	(2.44)	(0.06)
E[dc]/dt(−1)	0.694615	0.411907	0.411707
	(7.75)	(5.05)	(3.69)
R^2	0.800	0.614	0.556
Std. Error	0.0024	0.0040	0.0052
X^2-test	11.569 (0.07)	33.836 (0.00)	15.865 (0.01)
No. observations	74	53	64

Notes: Figures in parentheses under the coefficient estimates are t-statistics computed with GMM standard errors. r denotes reserves, π denotes inflation, m denotes money supply (M1 for the United Kingdom, M2 for France, Money base for Germany and matching series for the United States), bp denotes the balance of payments (exports/imports), y denotes income, and q denotes the real exchange rate. All independent variables are lagged by one period, and a * denotes a foreign (U.S.) variable. X^2-tests are tests that the fundamental determinants excluding the lagged dependent variable are insignificant. The figures in parentheses after the test statistics are the marginal significance level. Seasonal dummies are included in the estimated equations.

other non-monetary variables, one enters with an incorrect sign (the balance of payments) and one with the correct sign (the real exchange rate) and that both are strongly significant.

The sign pattern of the variables is more mixed in the French and German equation. For example, although the French inflation term is very significant, it is wrongly signed, suggesting that an increase in French inflation led to a decrease in the expected rate of devaluation. Of the other marginally significant variables, the French industrial production and real exchange rate terms appear with the correct sign. Significance levels are low in the German equation, with only the industrial production spread being correctly signed and significant.

However, perhaps the sign differences in the inter-war period should not be overemphasised. It is important to remember that the equation under consideration here is a reduced form, and the different sign patterns across countries could simply reflect different policy reaction functions. What is important and worth emphasising, however, is the (joint and individual) significance of the explanatory variables for the inter-war equations. This contrasts quite sharply with the picture for the classical period and indicates that governments may have been pursuing goals in addition to the maintenance of gold parity. Thus the evolution of the fundamental variables was felt by the markets to have an impact on the credibility of the governments' links to gold. These findings may be thought to confirm those of Eichengreen, Watson and Grossman (1985), who argue that the Bank of England's policy towards Bank Rate, a critical monetary variable, was driven by other than simply following the rules of the game which simply state-linked changes in interest rates to changes in international reserves. For example, they show that Bank Rate policy also reacted to domestic business conditions, with the Bank of England being reluctant to raise Bank Rate when business conditions were weak.

Nevertheless, realignment expectations were only very rarely significant for all exchange rates and, with the exception of the last few months of the dollar-sterling link and the immediate aftermath of the entry of the French franc, were of small magnitude. However, this is not necessarily a contradiction. The entirety of our results indicates that even though the Bank of England (and other central banks) may have deviated somewhat from the strict rules of the game, it did not do so enough so as to threaten the credibility of its commitment to the gold standard, at least until the final few months.

SUMMARY

We now summarise our conclusions regarding the credibility of the two gold standard experiences. For the classical gold standard period we found that the key dollar sterling rate was not fully credible, particularly at the start of the period and in the 1890s. In contrast, however, the franc-sterling rate appears to be reasonably credible throughout. Interestingly, we could find no significant association between fundamentals and the expected rate of realignment. Rather, political influences, particularly the Populist Movement of the late 1880s and the Free Silver Movement of the 1890s, appear to have been the source of the dollar's weakness.

Although a priori we would have expected the inter-war experience to be much less credible than the classical period, our results suggest a remarkable degree of stability for this period. For example, the sterling-dollar standard lasted around six years within a band of approximately plus/minus 0.6 per cent. This compares very favourably with the much more liberal plus/minus 2.25 per cent ERM, in which the longest period between realignments for the central franc-mark rate was for the period from January 1987 to June 1993. Our tests suggest that fundamentals were an important determinant of credibility in the inter-war period. We interpret this as suggesting that governments were more willing to take account of economic conditions besides the exchange rate in conducting policy during this period, but that this was not sufficient to completely undermine the credibility of the system. One interesting result from our inter-war database was the finding that for both Germany and the United Kingdom, devaluation expectations rose sharply towards the end of these countries' time on the gold standard. The fact that there was little warning of devaluation from these countries' interest rates (a finding which parallels Rose and Swenson's [1994] study of sterling's ERM crisis) suggests the possibility of a speculative attack (in Germany's case because of the banking crisis) rather than problems with fundamentals.

We also think that our finding of no substantial differences between the credibility of the inter-war and (latter part of the) classical gold standards should be of interest to economic historians. Indeed, it will come as a surprise to some specialists in this area who have pointed to certain supposed fundamental weaknesses associated with the latter period: for example, that Britain re-entered the gold standard in 1925 with an overvalued exchange rate and that as both France and, to a lesser extent, the United States acted as "sinks" for monetary gold, world monetary gold became grossly maldistributed. However, this is not to say that we think that the inter-war gold standard was necessarily as efficient an international monetary mechanism as was the classical standard, primarily because the inter-war gold standard had to be supported from time to time by international co-operation. That is, Britain's key role during the inter-war period was shored up through the United States and France making loans to the Bank of England and, in the early years at least, the Federal Reserve trimming its discount rate to accommodate the Bank of England. However, our findings can be used to support the propositions that for several years international actions such as these probably did help to underpin the credibility of the system. Future research could usefully develop explanations of why the inter-war gold standard was so credible despite the apparent flaws in the international financial regime.

Acknowledgements

The authors are grateful to Tam Bayoumi, Michael Bordo, Barry Eichengreen, and an anonymous referee for their helpful comments on an earlier draft of this chapter. MacDonald and Marsh are grateful to the ESRC's Global Economic Institutions Programme for research support (Grant No. L120251014).

APPENDIX: DATA DESCRIPTION AND SOURCES

Classical Gold StandardAnnual Data: All series are annual averages. Exact calculation methods are given in cited source.

Exchange Rates:
Sterling-dollar rates from Friedman and Schwartz (1982).
Sterling-franc rates from Mitchell (1993).

Bill Rates:
United States: Prime sixty-to-ninety-day commercial paper from Homer (1963).
United Kingdom: Open market rate of discount from Homer (1977).
France: Open market rate of discount from Homer (1977).

Money Supplies:
United States: Money stock from Friedman and Schwartz (1982).
United Kingdom: Money stock from Friedman and Schwartz (1982).
France: Bank notes in circulation from Mitchell (1993).

Income Levels:
United States: Real national income from Friedman and Schwartz (1982).
United Kingdom: Real income from Friedman and Schwartz (1982).
France: Real GDP from Mitchell (1993).

Price Series:
United States: Implicit price deflator from Friedman and Schwartz (1982).
United Kingdom: Implicit price deflator from Friedman and Schwartz (1982).
France: Implicit price deflator from Mitchell (1993).

Monthly Data:
Exchange Rates: National Monetary Commission (1910).
Bill Rates: National Monetary Commission (1910).

Inter-War Gold StandardExchange Rates:
All countries: Spot and three-month forward data from Einzig (1937a), appendix 1.

Reserves:

All countries: Gold reserves from various issues of the League of Nations Monthly Bulletin of Statistics.

Money Supplies:

United States: Money base, M1 and M2 from Friedman and Schwartz (1970).

United Kingdom: Money base and M1 from Capie and Webber (1985).

France: M2 from Patat and Luffalla (1990).

Germany: Money base (liabilities of Reichsbank) from Federal Reserve Board (1943).

Industrial Production Indices:

United States: Industrial production from Federal Reserve Board (1943).

All other countries: Industrial production from various League or Nations Monthly Bulletin of Statistics. UK data is interpolated from quarterly data.

Balance of Payments:

All countries: Imports and Exports series from various issues of the League of Nations Monthly Bulletin of Statistics.

Price Series:

All countries: Price levels from Federal Reserve Board (1943).

THREE

Interest Rate Interactions in the Classical Gold Standard, 1880–1914

Was There Any Monetary Independence?

Michael D. Bordo and Ronald MacDonald

INTRODUCTION

This chapter examines the operation of monetary policy within the context of the recent literature on target zones (Krugman, 1991). We argue that under the classical gold standard, gold parity was bounded by a two-sided target zone set by the gold points. Within the zone, stabilizing expectations allowed monetary authorities to use their policy tools to set short-term interest rates independently of those in the rest of the world. Our approach builds upon a recent paper by Svensson (1994). He argues that the conventional view on fixed exchange rate systems in a world of perfect capital mobility – that central banks have no power to conduct an independent monetary policy – does not hold in a system with exchange rate bands, such as the Bretton Woods regime or the classical gold standard. In a fixed exchange rate system with bands, monetary authorities have the latitude for independent action because of stabilizing rational expectations.

For example, in the case where a central bank lowers short-term rates, instead of an immediate capital outflow as in the textbook case, the exchange rate (domestic currency price of foreign currency) rises above the central parity rate until the expected rate of appreciation relative to central parity has become so large as to match the initial decline in the short-term rate. When the short-term interest rate is raised, the exchange rate declines (appreciates) relative to central parity such that the expected rate of depreciation relative to central parity matches the initial rise in the exchange rate. Thus, when central banks gear monetary policy to domestic goals, they are simply exploiting mean reversion of the exchange rate relative to central parity towards the long-run mean (Svensson, 1994, p. 162).

The classical gold standard is an example of a fixed exchange rate system with bands and with a high degree of capital mobility (see, for example,

46

Bordo, Eichengreen, and Kim, 1998, Obstfeld and Taylor, 1998, and Officer, 1996), where the bands are determined by the gold points. It was also a system in which monetary authorities in the core countries of Western Europe, on occasion, used their policy tools to influence domestic objectives. Although the monetary authorities were supposed to follow the "rules of the game" in their use of monetary policy to speed adjustment to a balance-of-payments shock, the evidence in many cases is that the rules were violated (Bloomfield, 1959, and the literature cited in Bordo and MacDonald, 1997).

That violations of the rules of the game occurred, in the sense that central banks often sterilized gold flows (Bloomfield, 1959) and had variables other than gold convertibility in their short-run reaction functions (Davaytan and Parke, 1995; Dutton, 1984; Giovannini, 1986; Jeanne, 1995) whilst at the same time adhering to gold convertibility as a long-run objective, is consistent with the view that the gold standard operated as a well-behaved target zone. Indeed, evidence that the classical gold standard system represented a credible target zone within the gold bands is contained in a number of recent studies (Officer, 1996). According to Svensson's (1994) view, the monetary authorities potentially had the scope to conduct independent monetary policies within the gold points. However, the scope for violation was limited by the size of the bands and could only be temporary because the exchange rate must eventually revert towards central parity (Svensson, 1994).

This chapter attempts to test Svennson's hypothesis for the monetary policy conducted by the central banks of the three core countries of the classical gold standard – England, France and Germany – over the period between 1880 and 1913. The outline of the remainder of the chapter is as follows. The second section provides a motivation for our empirical results. In the third section, we describe the data set. The econometric results are contained in the fourth section. The fifth section gives our conclusions and discusses suggestions for future research.

MOTIVATION AND METHODOLOGY

Under rigidly fixed exchange rates, the condition of interest-rate parity may be expressed as:

$$i_t = i_t^* \tag{3.1}$$

where i_t and i_t^* denote, respectively, the domestic and foreign currency interest rates. Equation 3.1 indicates that the domestic interest rate cannot deviate from the foreign rate even momentarily across all maturities. This is the standard assumption in many "textbook" versions of the Mundell-Fleming model and it implies, of course, that domestic monetary policy can only have an effect on domestic variables, such as output and inflation, to the extent that the home country is "large" (i.e. the United States). For a small open economy, Equation 3.1 implies that its monetary policy is determined in the foreign country or, more realistically, the rest of the world. Condition in Equation 3.1 is often taken as a representation of perfect capital mobility (see, for example, Frenkel, 1994).

However, as Svensson (1994) indicates, there are few, if any, regimes of the international monetary system in which it can be said that exchange rates have been rigidly fixed. The classical gold standard, which is often cited as an example par excellence of a rigidly fixed exchange rate regime, in fact had (time-varying) exchange rate bands in the form of the gold export and import points (this is discussed in greater detail later in the chapter). The existence of such bands introduces a wedge between the domestic and foreign interest rate in the form of a non-zero expected exchange rate change, and this, in turn, means that domestic monetary policy will have some independence vis- à-vis foreign interest-rate policy, even for a small open economy. This may be illustrated in the following way.

The ability of the domestic rate to deviate from the foreign rate is clearest when exchange rates are freely flexible. In this case, the interest parity condition given in Equation 3.1 has to be modified to:

$$i_t = i_t^* + \Delta s_{t+k}^e \qquad (3.2)$$

where Δs_{t+k}^e represents the k period expected exchange rate change, where k represents the maturity period of the interest rates. Two assumptions are necessary to interpret Equation 3.2 as a representation of perfect capital mobility (see, for example, Frenkel, 1994): (1) an absence of impediments to capital movements and (2) the assumption that agents are risk neutral. If Δs_{t+k}^e is negative in Equation 3.2, the domestic currency is expected to appreciate and the domestic interest rate can fall below the foreign interest rate by the extent of the expected appreciation. One way this can happen is if expectations are determined by a simple regressive expectations mechanism, such as that exploited in the classic Dornbusch (1976) model. The existence of exchange rate bands can have similar implications for interest rates under certain assumptions (discussed below). As noted in Chapter 1, in the presence of an exchange rate band, s_t may be split into two components:

$$s_t \equiv c_t + x_t \qquad (3.3)$$

where c_t denotes the central parity rate and x_t denotes the exchange rate's deviation from central parity. It follows from Equation 3.3 that the expected currency depreciation in a fixed rate regime may be defined as:

$$\Delta s^e_{t+k} = \Delta c^e_{t+k} + \Delta x^e_{t+k}. \tag{3.4}$$

Substituting Equation 3.4 into Equation 3.2, we obtain:

$$i_t = i^*_t + \Delta c^e_{t+k} + \Delta x^e_{t+k}. \tag{3.5}$$

Now if the central rate is credible, in the sense that agents believe there will not be a devaluation or revaluation of the currency over the maturity horizon k, the Δc^e_{t+k} term will be zero and the domestic interest rate can rise above or below the foreign rate to the extent that Δx^e_{t+k} is non-zero. For example, if the domestic authorities increase the money supply, the domestic interest rate will fall below the foreign rate, and as investors switch funds from the domestic interest bearing asset to the foreign asset, the exchange rate depreciates relative to the central parity. Under the assumption that the central parity is credible, the depreciation will produce the expectation of an appreciation relative to c; that is, $\Delta x^e_{t+k} < 0$.

As Svensson (1994) emphasises, even a relatively small bandwidth can offer the monetary authorities substantial leverage over interest rates. For example, a 1 per cent deviation of the exchange rate from the central parity which is expected to be removed in three months implies an annualized expected appreciation of 4 per cent per year – a non-trivial number from a monetary policy perspective. It is worth emphasising that all of the preceding discussion presupposes that capital is perfectly mobile, in the sense that the Uncovered Interest Parity (UIP) condition holds. Therefore, one of the key empirical tests in this paper is a test of UIP for each of the country pairings considered.

There are, however, important limitations to the extent of any independence conferred by a country participating in a credible target zone. First, if the assumption that Δc^e_{t+k} is zero is violated and, in particular, if it is endogenously related to Δx^e_{t+k} and increasing in the exchange rate's deviation from central parity, then this will reduce the degree of monetary independence; in instances where Δx^e_{t+k}, moves in an equal and opposite direction to Δx^e_{t+k}, there will be no monetary independence. For certain currencies and at certain times in the existence of the Bretton Woods system, this may have been a reasonable working assumption. However, for the classical gold standard system, there is considerable evidence to suggest that the exchange rates studied in this paper were highly credible (see Officer,

1996). Second, the monetary independence can only be temporary, because unless expectations are systematically violated (which would ultimately mean the expected rate of realignment was non-zero), the exchange rate must eventually revert back to its central parity. This, in turn, implies that the monetary independence will be limited to interest rates with short-term maturities.

Svensson argues that the monetary independence remaining after taking account of the previously described limitations offers a central bank scope to attempt to stabilize output and inflation and engage in interest-smoothing objectives. Our main objective in this chapter is to test the implications of this view of a banded exchange rate system (which we refer to as a target zone in the following) for three gold standard exchange rates. The main focus of our work concentrates on three interest-rate systems (defined in what follows) which are used to assess different aspects of monetary independence in a credible target zone. Because it has been demonstrated elsewhere (see Officer, 1996; Chapter 2 in this volume) that the gold standard system was indeed credible, we take this as a given here. In particular, studies show that for the country pairings considered in this work, the classical gold standard was credible period by period. Given that such tests are constructed using a strong form of UIP, we interpret this as indirect evidence of the absence of a time-varying risk premium for our sample period.

The main focus of our work concerns the behaviour of three different interest-rate systems. These systems are designed to gauge the existence of short-run monetary independence and its relationship to the policy variables targeted by the monetary authorities. The systems are: system 1, which consists of a home short-interest rate, i_t^s, and a comparable short foreign rate, i_t^{s*}; system 2, which consists of the variables in system one plus a home long-interest rate, i_t^l; system 3 consists of the variables in system two plus the policy variables (discussed later in the chapter) targeted by the monetary authorities. We now discuss these systems in a little more detail.

The Svensson (1994) story is that in the short run, there should be some scope for the home short-interest rate to deviate from the comparable foreign rate, but in the longer term, such scope vanishes. By examining system 1, we hope to capture this essential feature of the Svensson model. In particular, if home and foreign short-term interest rates are individually non-stationary, or I(1), then for them not to persistently deviate from each other in the longer term they should form a co-integrating relationship of the form first proposed by Engle and Granger (1987).[1] That is, in the context of an estimated version of Equation 3.6

$$i_t^s = \alpha + \beta\, i_t^{s^*} + v_t \tag{3.6}$$

it would be expected that the error process, v_t, is stationary, or I(0), α would differ insignificantly from zero and β would be insignificantly different from unity (we discuss later in the chapter how we propose estimating Equation 3.6).

The expected change in the exchange rate within the band does not appear in the co-integrating relationship because it is expected to be I(0) and will not affect the long-run result (in a co-integration sense); it may be thought of as being subsumed in the error term. However, the non-zero Δx_{t+k}^e term will be captured in the short-run dynamic equations implied by Equation 3.6. In particular, if the two interest rates defined in Equation 3.6 are co-integrated, then the Granger Representation theorem implies that a dynamic error correction representation of the following form must exist:

$$\Delta i_t^s = -\varphi\,(i_{t-1}^s - i_{t-1}^{s,*}) + \sum_{i=1}^{p} \kappa_i \Delta i_{t-i}^s + \sum_{i=1}^{p} \gamma_i \Delta i_{t-i}^{s,*} \tag{3.7}$$

$$\Delta i_t^{s,*} = +\varphi\,(i_{t-1}^s - i_{t-1}^{s,*}) + \sum_{i=1}^{p} \kappa_i^* \Delta i_{t-i}^s + \sum_{i=1}^{p} \gamma_i^* \Delta i_{t-i}^{s,*} \tag{3.7'}$$

where the first term on the right-hand side of each equation represents the error correction mechanism (ECM) recovered from the co-integration tests on Equation 3.6 (in this example we have imposed the condition $\alpha = 0$ and $\beta = 1$ on the ECM relationship). The significance of this co-efficient will be informative with respect to which of the interest rates adjusts in response to a disturbance of the levels terms. It should be significantly negative in the first equation, to the extent that the home interest rate is adjusting, and significantly positive in the second, to the extent that the foreign rate does the adjusting. Additionally, the co-efficients on the dynamic terms will give a feel for the amount of short-run policy independence available to the participating countries. Essentially, the existence of significant explanatory variables in Equation 3.6 is *prima facie* evidence that the expected change within the band is non-zero. Of course this assumption relies crucially on

---

[1]   As we note in the fourth section, all of the interest rates considered in this chapter are I(1) processes.

the absence of a foreign exchange risk premium. There are two ways of assessing the importance of a risk premium for our sample period. One is to take the extant tests of credibility of the gold standard period (see Officer, 1996; Chapter 1 in this volume). Such tests suggest that the currency pairings we consider were highly credible and therefore there was no uncertainty regarding the gold parity values of the currencies. A second way of assessing credibility involves a direct test of UIP, and this is something we consider in the next section.

In addition to its implication for short rates, the Svensson model, as we have noted, also has implications for the behaviour of long-term interest rates. Therefore, the second system we consider introduces a long rate into system 1. We assume long rates are determined by a standard expectations model of the term structure formulation (see Campbell and Shiller, 1987):

$$i_t^l = (1-\delta)\sum_{j=0}^{\infty} \delta^j E_t i_{t+j}^s \qquad (3.8)$$

where δ is the discount factor and we have assumed, for simplicity, an infinite discounting horizon. From Equation 3.8 we see that a current change in short-interest rates, which is expected to be reversed, will have little impact on long bond yields. It follows, therefore, that long rates are not expected to move systematically with short rates and the yield gap, or spread (i.e. $i_t^l - i_t^s$), should open up after a shock to the short rate, but that this would be expected to be extinguished relatively quickly.

To examine the short-long interest-rate interrelationships we again intend exploiting co-integration methods. In particular, Campbell and Shiller (1987) have demonstrated that if Equation 3.8 is a valid representation of the long-short interest-rate relationship, long and short interest rates should be co-integrated with a co-integrating co-efficient equal to unity; an equivalent interpretation is that the spread should be stationary. That is, on subtracting i_t^s from both sides of Equation 3.8, we may obtain:

$$i_t^l - i_t^s = \sum_{j=1}^{\infty} \delta^j E_t \Delta i_{t+j}^s. \qquad (3.8')$$

Therefore, in a trivariate system consisting of a home and foreign short rate and a home long rate, we should observe two long-run relationships: one governing short rates, from the interest parity condition, and the other governing the relationship between the home short and long rates given by the term structure relationship. On the basis of the Granger Representation theorem, this kind of system will produce the following equation for the change in the domestic short-term interest rate:

$$\Delta i_t^s = -\varphi\,(i_{t-1}^s - i_{t-1}^{s*}) - \delta(i_{t-1}^l - i_{t-1}^s) + \sum_{i=1}^{p} \kappa_i \Delta i_{t-i}^s$$
$$+ \sum_{i=1}^{p} \gamma_i \Delta i_{t-i}^{s*} + \sum_{i=1}^{p} \mu_i \Delta i_{t-i}^l \qquad (3.9)$$

where the *l* superscript denotes a long rate, the first term on the right-hand side denotes the error correction term associated with the short-run interest parity relationship, the second term denotes the term structure effect, or "spread," and the remaining terms are the dynamic terms. In addition to Equation 3.9, there would, of course, be further two dynamic equations for the change in the foreign short rate and the change in the domestic long rate. Because with such a relatively complex system it can be difficult to interpret the co-efficients on any one variable, we propose examining the interrelationships represented in Equation 3.9, and the associated equations, using an impulse response analysis. This system will not only help to address the issue of the long-short relationship referred to previously; it will also give further insight into the degree of monetary autonomy which a credible target zone confers and the degree of mean-reversion which exists for short rates.

Our third system involves examining the interrelationships between short-term interest rates and the variables to which they are targeted. In particular, if we can establish that there is some independence for short-term interest rates, we may ask: How could this independence have been used? The Svensson story is that it should facilitate standard counter-cyclical objectives such as stabilizing the output-inflation trade-off and allowing the authorities to engage in interest-rate smoothing. More specifically, we investigate the effect on short-term interest rates of changes in output (y), prices (p), unemployment (u), variables designed to capture counter-cyclical operations, gold reserves (g), designed to capture an external objective, and the volatility of interest rates $Vol(i)$, which the authorities are assumed to want to minimize if they had an interest-rate-smoothing objective. These variables, apart from the interest-rate terms, are log transformed, and the volatility of interest rates is measured using the standard deviation from the sample mean.[2]

---

[2] In the pre-1914 era, seasonal movements in interest rates in economies still largely dependent on agriculture – where crop movements were financed by short-term commercial

Defining the vector $\mathbf{z}_t = [\Delta y_t, \Delta p_t, \Delta u_t, \Delta g_t, Vol(i)]'$, we may gauge what effect the fundamentals have on the domestic interest-rate change, over and above the influence of other interest rates, by introducing $\mathbf{z}_t$ into Equation 3.9:

$$\Delta i_t^s = -\varphi(i_{t-1}^s - i_{t-1}^{s,*}) - \delta(i_{t-1}^l - i_{t-1}^s) + \sum_{i=1}^{p} \kappa_i \Delta i_{t-i}^s$$
$$+ \sum_{i=1}^{p} \gamma_i \Delta i_{t-i}^{s,*} + \sum_{i=1}^{p} \mu_i \Delta i_{t-i}^{l,*} + \sum_{i=0}^{p} \mathbf{f} \mathbf{z}_{t-i}. \qquad (3.10)$$

More specifically, the Svensson model implies that the fundamentals can have an impact on the short-run behaviour of the interest rate, but they have no impact on the long-run equilibrium relationships. This feature of the Svensson approach is captured in Equation 3.10.

We summarise this section as follows. Central to the Svensson hypothesis of limited monetary independence under fixed exchange rates is the UIP condition. This condition, in turn, requires the absence of impediments to capital movements and risk-neutral investors. Clearly if UIP does not hold, then the kind of interest-rate dynamic equations that we have discussed in this section could equally be consistent with deviations from UIP and a time-varying risk premium. The existence of UIP is therefore central to the interpretation of our results.

DATA SOURCES

The data sample runs from January 1880 through to December 1913. The data are collected for France, Germany and the United Kingdom. For each of these countries we have collected data on bank rate and a single long rate (which is country-specific). Because the former interest rate is directly targeted by the central bank, we believe it is the most appropriate short rate to use in our analysis. Additionally, we have collected data on the spot exchange rates and, using shipping costs, insurance and an opportunity cost variable, have calculated the gold points for each country (the mean value of the gold points is taken to be our central parity rate). The fundamental variables which complete our data set (where available) are the money supply, industrial production, a consumer price index, gold reserves and

---

loans – were often associated with financial stress and sometimes financial crises. Hence, smoothing short-term interest rates was an important objective of central bank's policy and indeed was a rationale for the establishment of the Federal Reserve in 1913. See Miron (1996).

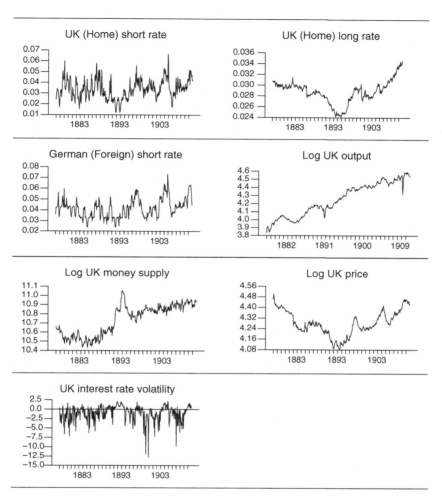

Figure 3.1. Data for the UK-German system.

unemployment. All data were originally seasonally unadjusted and have been seasonally adjusted using the X11 filter.[3] In Figure 3.1 we present the data series used to test the interest rate interactions between the United Kingdom and Germany. A complete listing of all variables, their sources

---

[3]   As Robert King has pointed out, use of the X11 filter could affect our econometric results. As a check, we re-estimated all of the relationships reported in this chapter using seasonally unadjusted data and centred seasonal dummies. The results turned out to be extremely close to those reported here and are available from the authors on request as an appendix (containing both figures and tables).

and construction are presented in the appendices of Bordo and MacDonald (1997). The calculation of the gold points follows the procedure used by Clark (1984), Giovannini (1993), and Officer (1986).

Three country pairings are examined, namely the UK-France, the UK-Germany and Germany-France. Given that the United Kingdom, and particularly London, was central to the operation of the classical gold standard, we regard the two pairings involving the United Kingdom as central to our analysis. However, we also implement our set of tests for the German-French pairing for comparative purposes; because neither of these countries can be regarded as credible as the United Kingdom, there is an expectation that this pairing will exhibit different properties to the UK-based pairings (evidence contained in Bordo and MacDonald [1997] supports this interpretation).

The calculations are based on the following formulae, for the gold import point, G_t^I, and gold export point, G_t^X, respectively:

$$G_t^I = \frac{X}{Y}\left[\frac{1}{(1+i)^{k/365}+c}\right]$$

where X is the official home currency price of an ounce of "fine" gold, Y is the official "foreign" price of an ounce of fine gold, and X/Y is therefore the official exchange rate or "mint parity"; i is the home interest rate, k is the shipping time and c denotes direct shipping costs which includes items such as freight and insurance costs, packing, loading and unloading, abrasion, charges for assay and minting and, finally, incidental expenses.

The gold export point is defined as:

$$G_t^X = \frac{X}{Y}\left[(1+i)^{k/365}+c\right]\left(\frac{1+i^*}{1+i}\right)^{k/365}$$

where, of terms not previously defined, i^* is the "foreign" or overseas interest rate. For the home and foreign interest rates we have used the market rate of discount. In computing the gold points between London and Berlin (LB) and London and Paris (LP), we follow Einzig's (1931) calculations for shipping time and costs and set $k=3$ in LB and $k=1$ in LP. We estimate the cost of shipping for LB to be $c=0.1152$ per cent and for LP $c=0.263$ per cent.[4]

---

[4] These results essentially confirm the findings of Giovannini (1993).

ECONOMETRIC RESULTS

We conducted a set of univariate root tests (both Augmented Dickey Fuller [ADF] and Kwiatkowski Phillips Schmidt Shin [KPSS] tests) on all of the variables used in this study, and the general tenor of these results was that all of the series are approximately I(1) processes (these results are available from the authors on request).

System 1 Results

In Table 3.1 we present our estimates of Equation 3.6 using the methods of Johansen (1995). Because these methods are now well known, we do not detail them here. In deciding on the deterministic specification, we have used the so-called Pantula principle (Pantula, 1989) of testing the joint hypothesis of rank order and deterministic components. The deterministic elements reported in all tables containing Johansen estimates are based on this principle.

In the short-rate system, the constant was constrained to lie in the co-integration space and evidence in favour of a single co-integration vector is fairly clear-cut across the short-rate systems. The co-efficients on the "foreign" interest rates are all positive and numerically close to unity.[5] More specifically, these values range from 0.81, for the UK-German bank rate relationship, to 1.32 for the UK-French bank rate relationship. Although the point estimates of β are numerically different from unity, on the basis of the standard errors, reported in parenthesis, none of the β co-efficients are statistically different from +1 (the numbers in the columns labeled $t\beta = 1$ are t-ratios for the null hypothesis that $\beta = 1$). Furthermore, all of the constant terms are insignificantly different from zero.[6]

We regard these results as indicating very strong support for uncovered interest-rate parity and are in marked contrast to results obtained for the recent floating period (see, for example, Frenkel, 1994 and Obstfeld, 1993). Hence a key element of the Svensson model is confirmed for our data set. The reported Lagrange Multiplier tests statistics (LM4) for up to fourth-order autocorrelation indicate that the systems all have tolerably random residuals.

---

[5] All of the systems are based on an 8-lag VAR model
[6] We also implemented a similar set of tests for market-determined short-interest rates. These results, reported in Bordo and MacDonald (1997), were qualitatively very similar, the main difference being that the constant terms in all cases were statistically significant, perhaps indicating the heterogeneity of the underlying assets.

Table 3.1. *FIML estimates of interest-rate parity*

$$i_t = \alpha + \beta i_t^* + v_t$$

Interest Rate Combination	α	β	tβ=1	lMax	Trace	LM(4)
Short Rates						
UK-France,	−0.535	1.320	1.45	24.02*	31.45*	6.67
Bank Rate	(0.68)	(0.22)		7.43	7.43	(0.15)
UK-German,	0.056	0.805	0.42	18.71*	28.88*	2.17
Bank Rate	(0.59)	(0.14)		10.17	10.17	(0.70)
German-France,	0.552	1.195	0.57	17.20*	25.26*	11.02
Bank Rate	(1.03)	(0.34)		8.06	8.06	(0.03)
Long Rates						
UK-France,	0.004	1.167	0.64	19.56**	25.41*	7.16
Long Rates	(0.01)	(0.26)		5.85	5.85	(0.13)
UK-German,	0.003	1.031	0.11	13.94**	22.80*	6.69
Long Rates	(0.02)	(0.29)		8.23	8.23	(0.15)
German-France,	0.004	0.868	0.13	18.02**	24.02*	2.21
Long Rates	(0.003)	(0.37)		6.02	6.02	(0.70)

Notes: The first column describes the interest rate/country combination. The numbers in the columns labelled α and β are the estimated constant and slope co-efficient from the interest parity regression Equation 3.6. The numbers not in parenthesis in the column headed tβ=1 are tests of the hypothesis that the slope co-efficient is unity. The numbers in the columns labelled lMax and Trace are the estimated values of Lambda Max and Trace statistics from the VAR and LM(4) is a Lagrange Multiplier test for 4-th order serial correlation. Numbers in brackets below point estimates are Fisher standard errors, whereas numbers in brackets below the LM tests are marginal significance levels. A single * denotes significance at the 5% level, whereas ** denotes significance at the 10% level.

In terms of the long-rate systems, reported in the bottom half of the table, the evidence for co-integration is also clear but only when a time trend is included in the co-integrating space (the Pantula principle indicated that both a constant and a time trend were required in the co-integrating space). The existence of a time trend could be capturing the long-run change in capital mobility occurring in our period (for example, an increase in financial market integration). However, we again note that none of the β co-efficients are statistically different from unity.[7]

Having established evidence of co-integration for all of the interest-rate combinations, the next strand in our analysis involves estimating the

---

[7] To model violations of the gold points, we experimented with including event dummies in the VECM, but this made little difference to the results.

dynamic relationships between interest rates. We do this by exploiting the Granger Representation theorem which states that if two (or more) series are co-integrated, then there must exist an error correction representation of the form in Equation 3.7 for the two variables. The resulting error correction models are reported in Tables 3.2 to 3.4 for the combinations of short-interest rates (the restriction $\beta = 1$ has been imposed in all of these systems).[8]

The results in Tables 3.2 to 3.4 may be summarised in the following way. First, in all of the systems, the ECM term enters with a negative sign in the equation for the change in the domestic interest rate and positively in the equation for the foreign rate. Given the way the ECM term is defined, this means that adjustment occurs in both markets, and given that each system has at least one significant ECM, this confirms the co-integration tests discussed earlier.

Notice that the adjustment co-efficient is always larger, in absolute terms, in the equation featuring the change in the "domestic" interest rate (i.e. in the equations for the United Kingdom – in the UK-French and UK-German systems – and for Germany in the German-French system). In the UK-French system, the co-efficient on the ECM term in the UK equation is approximately ten times larger, in absolute terms, than the corresponding number in the French equation, whereas in the UK-German system, the adjustment co-efficient in the UK equation is twice as large as the corresponding co-efficient in the German equation.

That much of the adjustment occurred in the United Kingdom is consistent with the width and depth of capital markets in the United Kingdom during this period vis-à-vis the markets in the other two countries (and also the fact that extensive bank balances were held in London by French and German nationals).[9] Using the co-efficients on the error correction terms, we calculated the implied half-lives as: 3 months, for UK-France, 6 months for UK-Germany and 7.5 months for the German-French system.

In sum, the results in Tables 3.2 to 3.4 clearly indicate that there were important and significant deviations of interest rates between countries, so that there is evidence of monetary independence for all three countries; as indicated by the relatively short half-lives, the interest-rate deviations were not purely transitory, as predicted by the Svensson model; and the large – in

---

[8] In constructing these dynamic ECMs we deleted insignificant lags, which resulted in more parsimonious models for the bank rate systems.

[9] For a further discussion on the significance of the UK financial sector during this period, see Eichengreen (1987), Giovannini (1989) and Lindert (1969).

Table 3.2. *Error correction system for UK-France*

$$\Delta i_t = \alpha + \sum_{j=1}^{n} \Delta i_{t-j} + \sum_{j=1}^{n} \Delta i^{*}_{t-j} + Error\ Correction$$

Dependent variable	ΔUK rate (t-1)	ΔUK rate (t-2)	ΔUK rate (t-3)	ΔUK rate (t-4)	ΔUK rate (t-5)	ΔUK rate (t-6)	ΔUK rate (t-7)	R^2
ΔUK Rate (t)	0.031	-0.126	-0.066	-0.070	0.0146	-0.044	-0.075	0.146
	[0.486]	[2.028]	[1.081]	[1.183]	[0.279]	[0.821]	[1.436]	
	ΔFrench Rate (t-1)	ΔFrench Rate (t-2)	ΔFrench Rate (t-3)	ΔFrench Rate (t-4)	ΔFrench Rate (t-5)	ΔFrench Rate (t-6)	ΔFrench Rate (t-7)	ECM (t-1)
	-0.139	-0.144	0.107	-0.083	-0.079	-0.174	-0.008	-0.212
	[0.870]	[0.916]	[0.691]	[0.555]	[0.572]	[1.249]	[0.057]	[4.082]

$$\Delta i^{*}_t = \alpha + \sum_{j=1}^{n} \Delta i_{t-j} + \sum_{j=1}^{n} \Delta i^{*}_{t-j} + Error\ Correction$$

Dependent variable	ΔUK rate (t-1)	ΔUK rate (t-2)	ΔUK rate (t-3)	ΔUK rate (t-4)	ΔUK rate (t-5)	ΔUK rate (t-6)	ΔUK rate (t-7)	R^2
ΔFrench Rate (t)	0.005	-0.022	0.007	-0.008	0.038	-0.012	0.011	0.087
	[0.217]	[1.062]	[0.322]	[0.415]	[2.025]	[0.698]	[0.652]	
	ΔFrench Rate (t-1)	ΔFrench Rate (t-2)	ΔFrench Rate (t-3)	ΔFrench Rate (t-4)	ΔFrench Rate (t-5)	ΔFrench Rate (t-6)	ΔFrench Rate (t-7)	ECM (t-1)
	0.067	-0.056	-0.003	-0.136	-0.051	-0.164	-0.019	0.020
	[1.260]	[1.073]	[0.049]	[2.736]	[1.115]	[3.551]	[0.414]	[1.141]

Table 3.3. *Error correction system for UK-Germany*

$$\Delta i_t = \alpha + \sum_{j=1}^{n}\Delta i_{t-j} + \sum_{j=1}^{n}\Delta i^*_{t-j} + Error\ Correction$$

Dependent variable	Δ UK rate (t-1)	Δ UK rate (t-2)	Δ UK rate (t-3)	Δ UK rate (t-4)	Δ UK rate (t-5)	Δ UK rate (t-6)	Δ UK rate (t-7)	R²
Δ UK Rate (t)	-0.051	-0.155	-0.114	-0.094	-0.015	-0.110	-0.076	0.124
	[0.471]	[2.267]	[1.689]	[1.432]	[0.239]	[1.847]	[1.293]	
	Δ German Rate (t-1)	Δ German Rate (t-2)	Δ German Rate (t-3)	Δ German Rate (t-4)	Δ German Rate (t-5)	Δ German Rate (t-6)	Δ German Rate (t-7)	ECM (t-1)
	-0.059	-0.200	-0.043	-0.063	-0.056	0.057	-0.095	-0.096
	[0.662]	[2.280]	[0.494]	[0.733]	[0.676]	[0.694]	[1.159]	[1.839]

$$\Delta i^*_t = \alpha + \sum_{j=1}^{n}\Delta i_{t-j} + \sum_{j=1}^{n}\Delta i^*_{t-j} + Error\ Correction$$

Dependent variable	Δ UK Rate (t-1)	Δ UK rate (t-2)	Δ UK rate (t-3)	Δ UK rate (t-4)	Δ UK rate (t-5)	Δ UK rate (t-6)	Δ UK rate (t-7)	R²
Δ German Rate (t)	-0.023	-0.006	0.047	0.029	0.055	-0.034	0.082	0.078
	[0.471]	[0.130]	[0.990]	[0.620]	[1.239]	[0.828]	[2.011]	
	Δ German Rate (t-1)	Δ German Rate (t-2)	Δ German Rate (t-3)	Δ German Rate (t-4)	Δ German Rate (t-5)	Δ German Rate (t-6)	Δ German Rate (t-7)	ECM (t-1)
	-0.021	-0.096	-0.066	-0.129	-0.073	-0.040	-0.110	0.082
	[0.347]	[1.569]	[1.085]	[2.169]	[1.261]	[0.695]	[1.931]	[2.238]

Table 3.4. *Error correction system for France-Germany*

$$\Delta i_t = \alpha + \sum_{j=1}^{n} \Delta i_{t-j} + \sum_{j=1}^{n} \Delta i_{t-j}^{\star} + Error\ Correction$$

Dependent variable	ΔGerman rate (t-1)	ΔGerman rate (t-2)	ΔGerman rate (t-3)	ΔGerman rate (t-4)	ΔGerman rate (t-5)	ΔGerman rate (t-6)	ΔGerman rate (t-7)	R^2
ΔGerman Rate (t)	0.020 [0.364]	-0.040 [0.726]	-0.004 [0.069]	-0.091 [1.704]	-0.021 [0.393]	-0.043 [0.809]	-0.065 [1.236]	0.066
	ΔFrench Rate (t-1)	ΔFrench Rate (t-2)	ΔFrench Rate (t-3)	ΔFrench Rate (t-4)	ΔFrench Rate (t-5)	ΔFrench Rate (t-6)	ΔFrench Rate (t-7)	ECM (t-1)
	-0.051 [0.452]	-0.022 [0.200]	0.083 [0.761]	0.076 [0.719]	0.000 [0.001]	-0.110 [1.119]	0.128 [1.279]	-0.086 [2.938]

$$\Delta i_t^{\star} = \alpha + \sum_{j=1}^{n} \Delta i_{t-j} + \sum_{j=1}^{n} \Delta i_{t-j}^{\star} + Error\ Correction$$

Dependent Variable	ΔGerman Rate (t-1)	ΔGerman Rate (t-2)	ΔGerman Rate (t-3)	ΔGerman Rate (t-4)	ΔGerman Rate (t-5)	ΔGerman Rate (t-6)	ΔGerman Rate (t-7)	R^2
ΔFrench Rate (t)	-0.070 [2.775]	-0.012 [0.485]	-0.004 [0.069]	0.015 [0.593]	0.008 [0.340]	0.007 [0.287]	0.006 [0.253]	0.092
	ΔFrench Rate (t-1)	ΔFrench Rate (t-2)	ΔFrench Rate (t-3)	ΔFrench Rate (t-4)	ΔFrench Rate (t-5)	ΔFrench Rate (t-6)	ΔFrench Rate (t-7)	ECM (t-1)
	0.098 [1.888]	-0.064 [1.258]	0.083 [0.761]	-0.127 [2.576]	-0.029 [0.636]	-0.174 [3.797]	-0.029 [0.615]	0.026 [1.912]

absolute terms – error correction terms in equations for UK rates suggest that London, as the primary financial centre, played a fundamental role in attracting capital to restore interest-rate parity.

System 2 Results

Having established the simplest of the three systems discussed in the previous section, we now turn to an examination of the VECM system consisting of a home and foreign short rate and a home long rate (the equation for the home short-interest rate from this system is reported as Equation 3.9). This system gives further insight into the independence conferred on monetary policy by facilitating an examination of the interaction between three interest rates, namely the domestic short and long rates and the foreign short rate.

These three rates give two potential equilibrium relationships: one an interest parity relationship, described by Equation 3.1 or 3.2, and the other a term structure relationship linking the domestic short rate to the long rate.

As in the case of the two variable interest-rate systems, we used the Johansen method to test for co-integration amongst these three rates.[10] The results are presented in Table 3.5. In all instances there is evidence of two co-integrating vectors. We attempt to interpret vector one as the interest parity relationship for short-term interest rates and vector two as the term structure relationship (i.e. the yield gap). This restriction cannot be rejected at the 5 per cent level for any of the systems involving UK rates, although it is marginally rejected in the two systems containing Germany and France (the reported χ^2 statistic is the relevant statistic, p-value in parenthesis).

Using these restricted vectors as our ECM terms, we then constructed VECM models where each equation in the system has the explanatory variables given in Equation 3.9. Rather than report the actual equations, which are difficult to interpret given the size of the system, we construct impulse response functions (with the two co-integrating vectors imposed on the system) for each of the country pairs.

The impulse response functions, along with the 95 per cent confidence intervals, are reported in Figure 3.2, and the country combination is indicated at the top of each column. The first two impulse pictures in each column represent the effects of a 1 per cent increase in the "domestic" rate on

---

[10] The Hannan-Quinn lag length selection criterion was used to test the optimal lag length, which was 2 for each system.

Bordo and MacDonald

Table 3.5. *Trivariate systems*

$$i_t^s = \alpha + \beta \, i_t^{s,*} + \phi \, i_t^L + v_t$$
$$i_t^s = \delta + \gamma \, i_t^{s,*} + \eta \, i_t^L + w_t$$

Interest Rate				χ^2	L-Max	Trace	LM(4)
Combination							$\chi^2_{(9)}$
	α	β	ϕ				
UK Short Bank (i_t^s)	−1.434	0.652	0.729	1.72	73.36*	104.5*	4.155
German Short Bank($i_t^{s,*}$)	δ	γ	η	(0.42)	30.56*	31.22*	(0.90)
UK Long (i_t^L)	86.461	−34.07	20.007		0.66	0.66	
	α	β	ϕ				
UK Short Bank (i_t^s)	2.141	1.391	−0.997	3.94	68.91*	94.57*	11.335
French Short Bank ($i_t^{s,*}$)	δ	γ	η	(0.14)	25.18*	25.66*	(0.25)
UK Long (i_t^L)	−13.470	−8.762	14.815		0.49	0.49	
	α	β	ϕ				
German Short Bank (i_t^s)	−3.956	−0.496	2.603	8.15	86.00*	120.4*	13.081
French Short Bank ($i_t^{s,*}$)	δ	γ	η	(0.02)	31.92*	34.40*	(0.16)
German Long (i_t^L)	12.202	3.758	−5.195		2.49	2.49	

Note: See Table 3.1 for definitions. χ^2 refers to a joint test that $\beta = 1$, $\phi = 0$, $\gamma = 0$, and $\eta = 1$ and has two degrees of freedom.

the "foreign" short rate and the "domestic" long rate, respectively. The third and fourth impulses in each column display a similar set of reactions (for the domestic short and long) to a 1 per cent increase in the "foreign" short rate. The variables are entered into the moving average representation in the following order: long rate, foreign short rate and domestic short rate. This ordering indicates that the long rate is regarded as the most exogenous followed by the foreign short, with the domestic short being the most endogenous.

The impulse plots all have the same general pattern and may be illustrated by focussing on the results for the UK-French system. This figure clearly demonstrates that in the short run, there is not a one-to-one lock between UK and French short-interest rates: a 1 per cent increase in the UK short rate produces a very small – two basis points – increase in the French rate, which is then rapidly offset (by about month 6). The UK long rate actually falls, which, through the term structure relationship, indicates that investors expect the current rise in short rates to be offset in the near future;

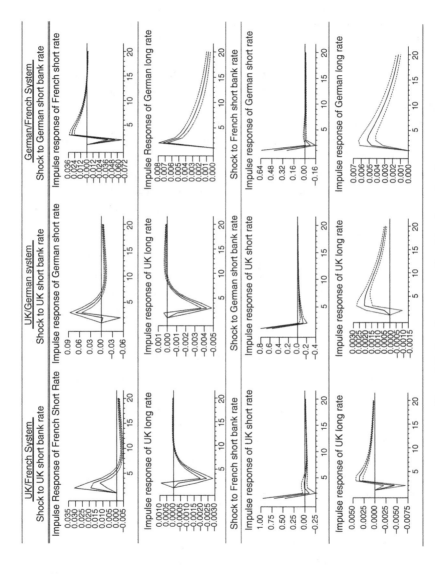

Figure 3.2. Impulse response functions for system 2.

however, notice that the long rate change is very small (less than one basis point) and the dynamics die out very rapidly. Interestingly, the corresponding French shock has a much bigger impact on the short UK bank rate (seventy-five basis points), and the effect on UK rates is very rapidly offset.

We attribute this contrasting adjustment of the UK and French rates to the importance of London as a financial centre during the period.[11] The kind of patterns that we observe in Figure 3.2 are, in general terms, repeated for the other interest-rate combinations, although we note that the German-French system (final column in Figure 3.2) is not as well behaved as the two UK systems; this is consistent with the view expressed earlier that the UK played an important role in tying down interest relationships for the period. In general, then, interest rates seem to behave in the way predicted by the Svensson model.

In sum, the existence of a credible target zone means that in the short run, domestic interest rates can deviate from foreign rates and the yield gap opens up as short rates change. However, such changes are purely transitory and are offset relatively rapidly.

System 3 Results

The final system estimated is the most general one in which the fundamentals that the monetary authorities are presumed to be using their monetary independence to target, enter the VAR. These fundamentals are defined in the previous section and are the change in the logarithm of gold reserves, the change in the logarithm of the money supply, the change in the logarithm of industrial production, the change in the logarithm of the price level and an interest-rate volatility term.[12] As we stressed in that section, these variables do not enter the long-run relationships; rather, the authorities change short-term interest rates in response to undesirable shocks to these variables, and therefore these variables only feature in the dynamic component of the VECM.

The impulse response functions corresponding to the systems with the vector of fundamentals and bank rates are reported in Figure 3.3. The ordering used to construct the Choleski decompositions is: output, money,

---

[11] This result is consistent with Eichengreen's (1992) conclusion that London had considerably greater discretion than Paris to absorb interest rate shocks.

[12] Because unemployment was not available for the full sample period for any of the countries, it does not feature in the results reported here. Robustness checks for shorter sample periods indicate that its absence from the full sample systems does not affect the results in any significant way.

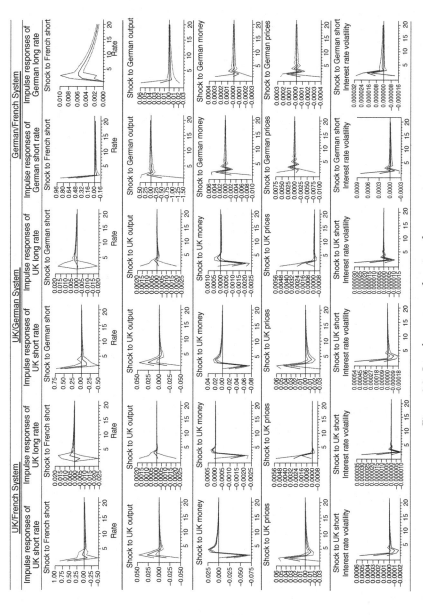

Figure 3.3. Impulse response functions for system 3.

67

prices, interest-rate volatility and the "foreign" short rate. This ordering is intended to capture the relative exogeneity of the different variables. The column headings again indicate the country combinations. The first column under each country heading indicates the response to the short rate, whereas the second the corresponding response to the long rate.

The UK-French system is representative of the two UK-based systems, and we concentrate on it here. We note that for both short and long rates, there is a significant response to fundamentals, but that this is, as predicted by the Svennson model, much smaller for long rates (indeed the impact on long rates is miniscule). Through the term structure relationship, short and long rates move in the same direction in response to the shocks, and the sign pattern is intuitively plausible.

For example, a positive shock to both output and prices generates an initial increase in the domestic interest rate, presumably through the demand for money channel, and this is rapidly offset. An increase in the domestic money supply produces a fall in interest rates of six basis points, which is reversed by month 4. A 1 per cent increase in volatility initially produces a fall in the domestic interest rate, but by a miniscule amount. There is no evidence of interest-rate overshooting, and indeed, the required interest-rate adjustment is relatively small in each instance. The magnitude of the response of the domestic rate to a foreign interest-rate shock is essentially unchanged relative to system 2. In common with system 2, we note that the independence conferred on domestic monetary policy is purely transitory and evaporates after approximately twelve months.

The UK-Germany system displays very similar properties to the UK-France system, both in terms of sign and also magnitude; the main difference occurs in the persistently positive (although extremely small) effect a shock to German rates has on UK long rates.

The impulse response functions for the German-French impulse system has some similarities to the two UK-based systems but also some important differences. In particular, the shocks to German output, money and prices have, in the majority of cases, an insignificant effect on German short rates (indeed, the output and money shocks have a perverse sign), although note that a positive shock to gold reserves (which was not available for the other two systems) produces a three-basis-points fall in the domestic short rate. Such a small fall in the interest rate tends to confirm the view that central banks did not play by the "rules of the game" during this period.

It is perhaps worth contrasting some of the interest-rate adjustments contained in Figure 3.3 with those sometimes required at crisis points during the ERM experience. Thus, the majority of adjustments in the figures amount only to a few basis points and this was sufficient to give independence for a number of months. In contrast, the Swedish example of a 75 per cent increase in interest rates in September 1992 only gave the authorities several days at most.

SUMMARY AND CONCLUDING COMMENTS

In this chapter we have used a target zone framework to analyze the behaviour of interest rates and exchange rates for France, Germany and the United Kingdom during the classical gold standard period. Our particular focus was to test a hypothesis proposed by Svensson (1994), that the existence of a credible target zone should confer on a country some independence in the operation of its monetary policy. This hypothesis is of particular interest for the classical gold standard period, because it is well known that countries did not play by the rules of the game, in the sense that they did not direct monetary policy to external objectives, yet the system seemed to operate effectively (in contrast to other regimes of the international monetary systems in which governments directed monetary policy to domestic objectives). We devised a number of tests to assess the Svensson hypothesis.

Central to our testing methods is the existence of UIP for our sample period. We confirmed that the strong-form version of this hypothesis held for all of the short- and long-rate systems considered in this chapter. Using these long-run relationships we moved to two sets of dynamic (i.e. short-run) systems to explore if there was in fact any leeway for independent monetary policies during the classical period. In the absence of a strong-form of UIP, these dynamic systems could be consistent with other interpretations, such as indicating a time-varying risk premium. However, we believe that our finding of strong-form UIP means they can be used to quantify the degree of monetary independence conferred on the currencies due to their participation in a credible target zone. The dynamic systems showed significant evidence of independence, although this proved, as expected, to be transitory and was significantly related to certain key fundamentals. This finding is in agreement with the historical literature (e.g. Sayers, 1957) that the Bank of England (as well as other central banks) were on occasion concerned with the behaviour of domestic macroeconomic variables.

Another aspect of our work was the finding that the particular combination of countries had a bearing on the results. Thus, the two bilateral systems which featured the United Kingdom worked well in the sense that adjustment was relatively rapid and fundamental variables bore a predictable relationship with interest rates; this was not, however, the case for the system which did not feature the United Kingdom (i.e. the German-French system). We believe this finding reinforces the view already prevalent in the literature that the United Kingdom, and particularly London, played a key role in the operation of the classical gold standard system.

We conclude by noting that our findings have a bearing on the kind of institutional framework required for a modern day target zone to function effectively and, in particular, to weather speculative attacks. For example, there is currently much discussion about reforming the international monetary system (IMS) and, in particular, the institutional arrangements governing the tripolar three exchange rates – the dollar, euro and yen. A number of politicians and economists have argued that the tripolar three should be governed by a target zone structure. The results presented in this chapter suggest that for such a structure to be effective requires that credibility ultimately anchors both short-term interest-rate policy and the term structure of interest rates and it has at its centre an anchor country.

Acknowledgements

Reprinted from the *Journal of Monetary Economics*, 52 (2), Michael D. Bordo and Ronald MacDonald, "Interest Rate Interactions in the Classical Gold Standard, 1880–1914: Was There Any Monetary Independence?" pp. 307–327, Copyright (2005), with permission from Elsevier. The authors are grateful to Jose Campa, Marc Flandreau, Peter Garber, Bruce Mizrach, Lawrence Officer, Pierre Sicsic, Lars Svensson and Alan Taylor, participants at the 1996 AFSE (Paris) conference, the 1997 NBER IFM conference and the Quantitative Economic History Seminar, Rutgers University, an anonymous referee and Robert King for their valuable comments on an earlier draft of this paper. We are also grateful to Andrew Davies and Gillian Maciver for their excellent research assistance.

FOUR

Realignment Expectations and the U.S. Dollar, 1890–1897

Was There a "Peso Problem"?

C. Paul Hallwood, Ronald MacDonald, and Ian W. Marsh

INTRODUCTION

A number of works have demonstrated that an important feature of the classical gold standard period (circa 1875 to 1914) was the credibility it seemed to confer on the currencies of participating countries, especially the United Kingdom, France, and Germany (Bordo and MacDonald, 1997; Giovannini, 1993; Hallwood, MacDonald, and Marsh, 1997a, 1997b, Chapter 2 of this volume; Officer, 1996). The U.S. dollar, however, was persistently weak against the UK sterling during much of the 1890s and its credibility appears to have been violated. It was not until after 1896 that the dollar's gold peg was fully trusted in the financial markets. In this chapter, we use data spanning the period between 1890 and 1908 to illuminate the causes of dollar weakness and its subsequent strengthening. Using newly available theoretical advances in the modeling of pegged exchange rates, we unravel the different possible explanations, namely economic fundamentals, political effects, expectational failures, and time-varying risk premiums.

Friedman and Schwartz (1963) state that the reason for the persistent dollar weakness during the period between 1879 and 1896 was founded on economic fundamentals rather than on political factors. At this time, strong political forces were pushing for change from the gold standard to a bimetallic gold-silver standard. Such a change was expected to raise the U.S. rate of inflation (Calomiris, 1992; Friedman, 1990a, 1990b; Mitchell, 1913). Schwartz (1987) estimates that, on average, until 1897, because of higher expected inflation in the United States than in the United Kingdom, U.S. nominal interest rates were about 2 percent higher than they would have been had America's adherence to the gold standard not been in question. As soon as it was settled in the presidential election of November 1896 that the United States would continue to adhere to the gold standard, American nominal interest rates abruptly fell to a 1 percent markup over the equivalent UK rates – a differential that reflected the actual higher American inflation rate. The juxtaposition during the 1890–1896 period of frequent expected dollar devaluation and no actual devaluation suggests a "Peso problem" (Krasker, 1980). Even though investors may have formed their expectations rationally, they still made persistently biased forecasting errors.

In this chapter we show that for the dollar-sterling exchange rate, the Peso effect is an important explanation for the biased forecast errors that did, in fact, persistently occur. However, we also find that a time-varying risk premium has a role to play. Our approach allows us to quantify the relative importance of these factors. Other contributions of this chapter to existing knowledge of U.S. monetary history relate to the effectiveness of the Morgan-Belmont syndicate in supporting the dollar in 1895; a finding that the size of an expected dollar devaluation, had it occurred, was large, supporting some contemporary opinion; and the fact that after 1896, there was a strong shift in sentiment in favor of the dollar, which helps explain why the Fisher equation failed to hold – a point of contention ever since Fisher (1907).

EXCHANGE RATES AND INTEREST RATES – THE FIRST PASS THROUGH THE DATA

Interpreting exchange rates in the classical gold standard period in the context of the target zone literature is now widespread and follows Svensson's (1992) suggestion that all of the important regimes of the international monetary system in which exchange rate fixity was the modus operandi may be analyzed using a target zone framework. Because this framework is now well known, and has already been discussed in Chapter 1, we do not give a blow-by-blow account here. As noted in Chapter 1, the so-called 100 percent confidence interval can be calculated using Equation 1.5.

A way of gaining further insight into the issue of credibility during the period, one examined in some detail in the next section, is to focus on the interest-parity condition. By assuming additionally that expectations are formed rationally and that agents are risk-neutral, the interest differential can be interpreted as representing the market's expectation of the exchange rate change. For the sample period between 1890 and 1908, our estimate of this equation is:

$$\Delta s_{t+k} = 0.0002355 - 0.04513\left(i_t - i_t^*\right) \tag{4.1}$$

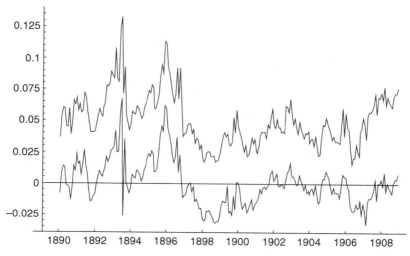

Figure 4.1. One hundred percent confidence interval.

and hence, in common with many studies for the interwar and postwar periods, the slope coefficient is closer to −1 than +1. Much of the rest of this chapter can be interpreted as an attempt to explain this finding.

In summing up political-economic developments in the 1890s, Friedman and Schwartz (1963) write that "agitation over silver reached its peak, and the political forces in favor of free silver came closest to victory. The effect was to create a lack of confidence both at home and abroad in the maintenance of the gold standard and to lead to something of a flight from the dollar – or rather a series of flights and returns as views altered" (p. 104). The target zone theory outlined earlier can add quantification to this insight. A plot of the 100 percent confidence band, given in Figure 4.1, clearly indicates that there are credibility problems for the period between 1890 and 1897, but that thereafter, the violations of credibility are few and far between.

Between 1890 and 1897, the rate of inflation was lower in the United States than in the United Kingdom, and yet U.S. interest rates were higher. Friedman and Schwartz (1963, chapter 3) explain this in terms of a perceived lack of confidence in the value of the dollar against gold and, hence, sterling. In particular, they point out that "political agitation for an expansion of the money stock ... continued from 1879 to the end of the century" (p. 91). The loci of this agitation were the labor movement and agricultural interests suffering from the depression of trade brought about by a falling U.S. price level. Both groups supported the re-monetization of silver (which had been demonetized in 1873) and were supported in this by the silver-producing states. As bimetallism was also strongly supported by a faction in the Democratic Party, it was a live political issue throughout this period until 1896 when, in the presidential election, the Democratic candidate and strong silver supporter, William Jennings Bryan, was defeated by the pro–gold standard Republican candidate William McKinley. Friedman (1990a) calculated that if the United States had re-monetized silver, the U.S. price level would indeed have been higher. A higher U.S. price level suggests that, ultimately, the dollar would have had to be devalued. Thus, given the political agitation, the devaluation expectations revealed in Figure 4.1 are understandable.

Table 4.1 lists eleven major monetary or other events that probably impacted exchange rate expectations during the 1878–1897 period.[1] We will not enter into a full historical discussion, as this is very adequately covered by Friedman and Schwartz (1963); instead, a few points will suffice.

Events 1 and 2, taken together, ambiguously committed the U.S. Treasury to buy large amounts of silver and to adhere to the gold standard, respectively. Event 3 is a straightforward financial panic that caused some flight from the dollar. Event 4, the Sherman Silver Purchase Act, introduced silver in large amounts into the U.S. money supply and could have been interpreted as heralding a regime change should the United States abandon the monometallic gold standard. Passed in July 1890, the Act was immediately followed by significant realignment expectations (Figure 4.1). These subsided temporarily after August for the next three months. But from December 1890 (after several financial firms failed in New York – event 5) until the repeal of the silver purchase clause on November 1, 1893, the only major fall in devaluation expectations coincided with the record crop exports between the fall of 1891 and the summer of 1892 (event 7). In the spring of 1891, large gold outflows were recorded (event 6), apparently confirming the pressure on the dollar.

Upon repeal of the Sherman Act (event 8), realignment expectations again fell dramatically, but this did not last long, as the approaching presidential election held the possibility of the return of a president, in William Jennings Bryan, committed to the abandonment of monometallism. The January 1895 record low for Treasury gold reserves (event 9) falls within the long run of dollar weakness. Event 10, the Belmont-Morgan syndicate providing gold reserves to the U.S. Treasury, brought temporary relief, but it

---

[1] We follow Calomiris (1992) in not including Treasury deficits in Table 4.1, as Bohn (1991) suggests that these would not have been expected to impact the U.S. money supply.

Table 4.1. *U.S. monetary and other "events" impacting exchange rate expectations, 1878–1897*

	Year	Event
1	1878	Bland-Allison Act
2	1879	The United States de facto on gold standard
3	1884	Financial panic in the United States
4	1890, July	Sherman Silver Purchase Act
5	1890, November	Financial strain in the United States
6	1891, spring	Abnormally large gold outflows from New York
7	1891, fall to summer 1892	Record U.S. crop exports
8	1893, November	End of silver purchases under the Sherman Act
9	1895, January	U.S. Treasury's gold reserve falls to record low
10	1895, February to September	Morgan-Belmont syndicate
11	1896, November	Defeat of free-silver forces in presidential election

Source: Friedman and Schwartz (1963).

was not until Bryan's defeat in the election that speculations that the United States would abandon the gold standard were more or less stilled.

From then on to the end of our data in 1908, there are relatively few, scattered months of significant realignment expectations, and these expectations were more weakly held than they had been before November 1896. The fact that these realignment expectations are rather scattered is important because it means that the long runs of biased forecasting errors had come to an end. There is no consistent explanation for the bouts of perceived dollar weakness that did occur after 1897; rather, there is a series of ad hoc explanations. The behavior of U.S. capital exports during this period would seem to be relevant to an explanation of changes in exchange rate expectations. However, examination of them does not take us very far as for the period between 1897 and 1906. Friedman and Schwartz (1963) comment that the "course of events [as pertaining to U.S. capital exports] is most puzzling" (p. 142). The significant realignment expectations toward the end of 1901 may well have been caused by the stock market collapse in May, and those of the summer of 1902 may have been a reflection of tight money supply in New York as the U.S. business cycle was moving to its peak in September. We have no explanation for the significant realignment expectations of the spring of 1903, but those of the summer of 1907 foreshadowed the severe financial panic of October of 1907.

In the rest of this chapter, we analyze expectations of exchange rate realignments in more detail. Specifically, we examine whether the biasedness findings in Equation 4.1 are explained by a time-varying risk premium, or whether the silver forces caused investors seriously to doubt the dollar's link with gold and hence led to consistent expectational errors and a classic manifestation of the Peso problem.

EXPECTATIONAL MODEL AND ECONOMETRIC METHODS

In attempting to unravel the sources of expectational bias during the period, we give the data as many "degrees of freedom" as possible. We rely on a model that highlights expectational factors but that also has a role for time-varying risk premiums that have often been suggested as an explanation of apparently biased exchange rate expectations. We therefore focus on the following equation in our econometric analysis:

$$i_t - i_t^* = \left[\left(1 - p_t^k\right) E_t \left[\Delta s_{t+k} \mid no\ deval.\right] + p_t^k E_t \left[\Delta s_{t+k} \mid deval.\right] + RP_t\right] / k \quad (4.2)$$

where the dependent variable is the interest rate differential (U.S. minus UK) on instruments of maturity k years, p_t^k denotes the time t probability of a realignment (U.S. dollar devaluation) during the subsequent k years, s_t denotes the spot exchange rate, and RP_t is a time-varying risk premium. Equation 4.2 states that the interest differential equals the risk premium plus the probability-weighted change in the spot exchange rate under the alternative scenarios of a devaluation and no devaluation.

The various components in Equation 4.2 may be identified in the following ways. Consider first the magnitude of the expected change in the spot exchange rate. If there is no devaluation, the expected change in the spot rate is equivalent to the expected change in the deviation from the "center" of the band. This center of the band could be the mint parity level, but the mean spot rate over this period was higher than the \$4.866 parity level, and the gold import and export points were asymmetric about parity. Further, unlike today, the spot exchange rate shows substantial seasonality during this period, possibly due to the greater proportion of seasonal goods (e.g., agriculture) in U.S. exports and the greater influence of international trade on foreign exchange trading. Following Bordo and MacDonald (1997), we first deseasonalize the spot exchange rate[2] and subsequently model the time-varying levels to which it regresses as the fitted values from the regression:

$$s_t = \alpha_0 + \alpha_1 t + \alpha_1 s_{t-12} + \varepsilon_t \quad (4.3)$$

where the lagged dependent variable is introduced to capture stochastic seasonality effects, and the fitted values are denoted $\bar{s}_t$. Finally, if x_t denotes

---

[2] The interest differential is also deseasonalized to avoid imposing spurious dynamics.

the deviation of the spot rate from fitted levels, $x_t = s_t - \bar{s}_t$, following Rose and Svensson (1995), we model Δx_t as

$$E_t\left[\Delta s_{t+k} \,|\, no\ deval.\right] = E_t\left[\Delta x_{t+k} \,|\, no\ deval.\right] = \beta_1 x_t. \qquad (4.4)$$

Deriving the expected change in the spot rate at a devaluation is more problematic. Mizrach (1995) models the expected size of a devaluation of key ERM exchange rates as a linear function of the previous devaluation, but this is not an option in the classical gold standard, because the dollar never actually devalued. For simplicity, we model the size of devaluation as a constant (denoted β_2).

The probability of a devaluation, p_t^k, is modeled as a function of several (seasonally adjusted) economic fundamentals, two dummies designed to take account of expectations of a return to silver, a trend, and a constant. The fundamentals are the relative (U.S. minus UK) month-on-month money supply and income growth rates, the deviation of the real exchange rate from trend, the change in U.S. cotton exports (also detrended), the change in the Standard and Poor's (S&P) stock market index, and the change in the U.S. Treasury's gold and silver holdings. These variables were chosen to highlight the importance of the events listed in Table 4.1. Thus, financial strains and panics are proxied by the S&P index, gold flows are captured by changes in Treasury reserves, and the performance of U.S. exports is proxied by cotton exports. All fundamentals are included in the model with a one-period lag to avoid endogeneity problems. Sources are detailed in the Data Appendix.

The two dummies proxy the effect of political pressures to move to silver. The first takes a value of 1 if the Sherman Silver Purchase Act is on the U.S. statutes (July 1890 to October 1893) and a value of zero otherwise. The second dummy takes a value of 1 if the bimetallism debate is still active in the United States, defined as the period from the start of our sample until the defeat of Bryan in 1896 (January 1890 to October 1896). Writing the variables in vector form (z) and denoting the coefficient vector by γ, we make a probit transformation so that $p_t^k = \Phi\left(\gamma z_t\right)$, which is bounded [0, 1].

The risk premium is modeled with an asymmetric GARCH(1,1)-in mean specification such that it varies with both the magnitude and sign of past surprises (Glosten, Jagannathan, and Runkle, 1993). Because of the number of constant terms in the model, the risk premium has the following slightly unusual specification:

$$RP_t = \delta\, h_t$$
$$h_t = v_1 + v_2\, \varepsilon_{t-1}^2 + v_3\left(\varepsilon_{t-1}^2 \,|\, \varepsilon_{t-1} < 0\right) + v_4 h_{t-1} \qquad (4.5)$$

Table 4.2. *FIML estimation results, 1890–1902 to 1908–1912*[a]

Variable	Coefficient	Std Error	T–Statistic
1. Mean Reversion, β_1	−0.260	0.122	−2.132
Size of devaluation			
2. Devaluation Size, β_2	0.581	0.020	29.741
Probability of devaluation, γ			
3. Constant	−4.380	0.439	−9.972
4. Money	1.609	1.660	0.969
5. Income	0.060	0.459	0.131
6. Real Exchange Rate	3.356	0.529	6.345
7. Cotton Exports	−0.038	0.024	−1.586
8. S&P Index	−1.557	0.341	−4.571
9. Gold Reserves	0.009	0.057	0.166
10. Sherman Dummy	0.163	0.039	4.234
11. Silver Debate Dummy	0.686	0.147	4.652
12. Trend	0.004	0.001	4.389
Risk premium			
13. Variance in Mean, δ	1.218	0.312	3.907
14. Variance Constant, v_1	0.048	0.016	2.915
15. ARCH, v_2	1.196	0.507	2.362
16. Asymmetric ARCH, v_3	−0.907	0.406	−2.232
17. GARCH, v_4	0.331	0.151	2.188

[a] The general form of the model is
$i_t - i_t^* = [(prob.\ of\ deval.)\,(size\ of\ deval.) + (1 - prob.\ of\ deval.)\,(mean\ reversion) + risk\ premium]/k$
$mean\ reversion = \beta_1\,x_t$
$size\ of\ deval. = \beta_1$
$prob\ of\ deval. = \Phi(\gamma z_t)$
$risk\ premium = \delta h_t$
$h_t = v_1 + v_2\varepsilon_{t-1}^2 + v_3\left(\varepsilon_{t-1}^2|\varepsilon_{t-1} < 0\right) + v_4 h_{t-1}$

There is no constant risk premium. Instead, the constant element of the risk premium is subsumed into the constant Peso effect.

Substitution leads to the final econometric specification:

$$i_t - i_t^* = \left[\beta_1 x_1\left(1 - \Phi\left(\gamma z_t\right)\right) + \beta_2 \Phi\left(\gamma z_t\right) + \delta h_t + \varepsilon_t\right]/k$$
$$h_t = v_1 + v_2\varepsilon_{t-1}^2 + v_3\left(\varepsilon_{t-1}^2|\varepsilon_{t-1} < 0\right) + v_4 h_{t-1}. \tag{4.6}$$

This system is estimated using maximum likelihood methods (Broyden-Fletcher-Goldfab-Shanno algorithm), with standard errors robust to heteroscedasticity and the serial correlation induced by the overlapping dependent variables. Estimation results are presented in Table 4.2.

We believe the estimated equation has a number of attractive properties that reveal the sources of the biasedness reported in Equation 4.3. First, note that the estimated coefficient of mean reversion is negative, as predicted. This suggests that the dollar was expected to close around one-fourth of the distance from its time-varying mean level each quarter.

The size of the expected devaluation is 58 percent and is strongly significant. Although this seems a relatively large value, the crucial thing in terms of our modeling is the weight placed on this number by the probability of devaluation. We provide a more detailed discussion of the magnitude of the devaluation in the next section.

The probability of a devaluation is determined by coefficients 3 through 12. Six of these ten coefficients are statistically significant (and bear the correct theoretical sign). The effect of relative money supplies is correctly signed but insignificant, and even though both relative income changes and gold reserves are incorrectly signed, they are also insignificant. The deviation of the real exchange rate from trend and changes in the S&P index are significant at reasonable levels, and cotton exports are marginally so.

Importantly, the two dummy variables are significantly positive, indicating that the political pressures to monetize silver raised the probability that the dollar would devalue. In terms of both magnitude and significance level, the continued debate over silver exerted a greater influence over expectations than the presence of pro-silver clauses in the statute book. This is consistent with Calomiris (1992), who also argued that it was unlikely that the extant silver legislation would have been responsible for pushing the United States off the gold standard. The probability of a devaluation, which captures the joint effect of the previously noted elements, is given in Figure 4.2. Typically less than 0.5 percent in the tranquil post-silver period, it was more than 1.5 percent during the two peak crisis points. Crucially, removing the effect of the silver debate results in very small devaluation probabilities. In fact, devaluation expectations based on fundamentals alone are higher in the relatively tranquil twentieth-century portion of the period under question than in the volatile 1890s. The fact that the silver debate was active had a statistically and economically significant negative effect on the credibility of the dollar's link with gold.

The variance-in-mean term, δ, is positive and statistically significant, implying that, in contrast to the assumption of the basic target zone model, the interest differential does appear to contain a time-varying risk premium. Furthermore, this is well captured by the asymmetric GARCH(1,1) model employed. The asymmetry is particularly important; a positive error leads to very persistent risk effects, but a negative error much less so.

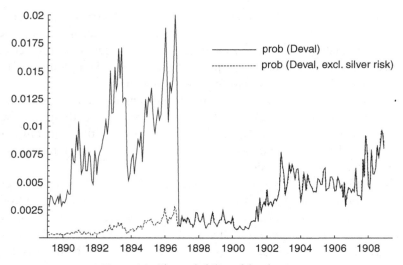

Figure 4.2. The probability of devaluation.

The relative importance of the risk premium and the Peso effect in the interest differential may be gauged from Figure 4.3, where all three series are plotted. Note that the Peso effect (the expected probability of devaluation times the expected size of the devaluation) explains the majority of the interest differential in the early years and then drops effectively to zero in 1900, before rising slightly in the run-up to the end of our data sample (which coincides with the financial panic of 1907). The risk premium is positive and significant in the estimated equation. Figure 4.3 reveals that it is quite small on average (0.25%) but with occasional large peaks in volatile periods. Nevertheless, we would argue that the Peso problem explains noticeably more of the interest differential during the silver-crisis period, and that the likelihood of devaluation was dominated by political and not economic performance.

MORE COMMENTARY

Our findings do not support Grilli's (1990) claim that the probability of a dollar devaluation built up only gradually following the passage of the Sherman Silver Purchase Act in July 1890. We show in Figure 4.2 an immediate jump in the probability of devaluation. This is consistent with warnings appearing in the financial press at the time, for example, in *The Economist* (December 20, 1890; May 16, 1891; November 21, 1891; and December 26, 1891) and Mitchell (1913, p. 52). Nor do we support Grilli's calculation that

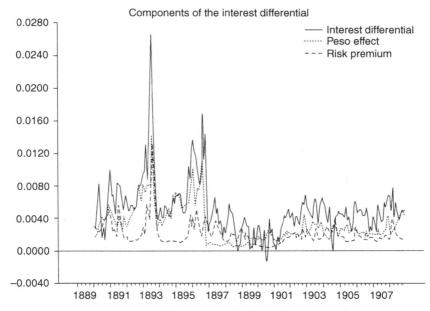

Figure 4.3. Decomposition of the interest differential into a risk premium and Peso effect.

the probability of speculative attack declined step by step in the two years leading up to the 1896 election. Rather, our findings support the opposite proposition that failure to deal with the overhang of paper money (note in Figure 4.2 that the probability of devaluation excluding the effects of the silver dummies tends to *increase* after 1893) and the gathering momentum of the free-silver movement were a threat to the United States' adherence to the gold standard.[3]

Our results allow us to comment on the February 1895 Morgan-Belmont contract with the U.S. government to support the dollar. We show the devaluation probability fell as soon as the syndicate began supporting the dollar, but in the second quarter of that year, the probability increased somewhat. This ordering squares with the discussion in Simon (1968). He claims that

---

[3] There were frequent detailed reports in *The Economist* on the overhang (from November 1895 through June 1896) and on the deleterious effects of potential new silver legislation (May through October 1896). Other foreign publications, such as the *Spectator*, also addressed the problems of the American currency in 1895 and 1896. These and received academic wisdom leave no doubt that weakness of the U.S. dollar troubled investors so much that it influenced both the propensity to invest in U.S. securities and international gold flows between the United States and the United Kingdom.

the Morgan-Belmont syndicate met with initial success in reducing external pressure on the dollar (i.e., February–April 1895). However, increased capital exports (which Simon associates with renewed silver agitation in the United States, net sales by European investors of American railroad securities, and advice in the British financial press to avoid American shares) then undermined the dollar from May through August 1895.

We also find that once the Morgan-Belmont syndicate ceased its supportive operations, in September 1895, dollar devaluation prospects dramatically increased and, though fluctuating, were to remain high until November 1896. We ascribe this course of events over these particular fourteen months to both a slight worsening of economic fundamentals affecting exchange rates and especially to the agitation for free silver.

On the basis of our evidence, the prediction by the Morgan-Belmont syndicate – as recounted by Simon (1968, p. 406) – that its support would be needed only until September 1895 (when U.S. agricultural exports, especially cotton and wheat, should have picked up) is not supported, possibly because the harvests of both major export crops were disappointing. We find a sharp increase in the probability of dollar devaluation in the later months of 1895. From this it is impossible to say whether the Morgan-Belmont syndicate saved the gold standard, because we do not know both how realignment expectations would have developed in its absence in early 1895 and what would have happened had the harvests turned out to be good. However, a dummy variable for the operational existence of the syndicate in that part of Equation 4.6, which determines devaluation probabilities, although bearing the theoretically correct negative sign, is far from significant (t-statistic equals -0.946).

An issue of interest to contemporary investors was the combination of the probability of a dollar devaluation and its likely size should it have occurred. Our estimates of these variables support the judgment of the *Economist* (July 11, 1896, p. 891) that (1) the danger of devaluation was remote (presumably because even if Bryan had won he would still have had Congress against him), and (2) if the devaluation had come, it would have been large, because the price of silver had fallen so low relative to gold. On the size of the devaluation, should it occur, *The Economist* wrote: "[O]ne of the two great parties in the States has deliberately adopted a policy of repudiation. The Democratic Party stands pledged to the most predatory set of proposals for dealing with the public currency ever set forth by a body of public men. They in effect demand that the debtor shall be allowed to pay his creditor ten shillings in the pound and demand a discharge in full"

(July 11, 1896, p. 890).[4] Confidence in our findings of a potentially large devaluation is supported by other recent work using different methodologies. Garber (1986) treats a bimetallic standard as an implicit option contract to deliver silver or gold in settlement of debts. He shows that with the sharp fall in the price of silver relative to gold in the years between 1890 and 1896, an option to deliver silver "was very much in the money" (p. 1027). Further, some calculations by Friedman (1992) suggest that if the United States had adopted bimetallism rather than the gold standard, the U.S. price level would have increased very sharply compared with that in the UK.

Our findings are relevant to a debate on the apparent failure of the intertemporal purchasing power parity, the so-called Fisher equation, to hold after about 1896. As an empirical fact, for many years after this date, while the rate of inflation in the United States increased relative to that in the United Kingdom, U.S. interest rates – also relative to those in the UK – failed to do so. This apparently confounded Irving Fisher's theory that, via uncovered interest parity, changes in relative price levels and interest rates should be positively related. As prior unsatisfactory attempts to explain the failure of the Fisher equation to hold, including Fisher (1907, p. 278), are summarized in Barsky and De Long (1989), we will not rehearse them here. However, it is worth mentioning that our findings do not support Barsky and De Long's own explanation, namely that although investors could have used publicly available information to predict inflation (hence moving interest rates in the appropriate direction), they failed to do so because they did not know how to process the relevant information into an inflation prediction. Rather, our econometric results give strong support to an explanation rejected in Barsky and De Long (1989, p. 819, fn. 5) that after 1896 and the decline in influence of the free-silver movement, there was, unsurprisingly, a strong shift in sentiment in favor of the dollar. That is, the interest differential could narrow as either the risk premium or the probability-weighted expected change in the exchange rate declined. This change in sentiment, we show, is due to a sharp reduction in the Peso effect as the probability of expected devaluation fell.

SUMMARY AND CONCLUSIONS

In this chapter, we have examined an early example of a Peso problem – the U.S. dollar between 1890 and 1897 – defined as investors holding apparently

---

[4] "Ten shillings in the pound" is a 50% devaluation.

persistently biased forecasts of exchange rate changes. For many months prior to November 1896, financial markets were forecasting a dollar devaluation against gold (and sterling) that never came. In fact the dollar was not devalued against gold until March 1933.

Our explanation of this phenomenon is that financial markets were predicting a regime change – specifically the monetization of silver alongside gold – that would have increased both the U.S. money supply and rate of inflation relative to the gold standard's "core" country, the United Kingdom. The specific events that gave rise to the belief in a regime change were the Bland-Allison Act of 1878; the prolonged agitation for the free coinage of silver, which lasted at least from 1879 until its weakening in late 1896; the Sherman Silver Purchase Act of 1890; the draining of U.S. gold reserves during the 1890s; and the support given to the free-silver movement by influential elements in the Democratic Party. Our finding of the dollar's significant Peso problem quantifies the keen insights of Friedman and Schwartz (1963) and adds to the quantitative findings of some other investigators.

Acknowledgments

Reprinted from the *Journal of Monetary Economics*, 46 (3), C. Paul Hallwood, Ronald MacDonald, and Ian W. Marsh, "Realignment Expectations and the US Dollar, 1890–1897: Was There a 'Peso problem'?" pp. 605–620, Copyright (2000), with permission from Elsevier. Ronald MacDonald is grateful to the ESRC's Global Economic Institutions Programme for financial support (Grant No. L120251023). The authors would like to thank Michael Bordo, Keith Cuthbertson, Robert King, and David Miles for useful comments.

DATA APPENDIX

Spot exchange rates for the last Saturday of each month were taken from table 13 of National Monetary Commission (1910). For the years between 1890 and 1895, the rates are the posted rates of sight exchange in New York on London for bankers' bills. After 1895, we use the actual rates of exchange.

The U.S. interest rates are those available on choice sixty- to ninety-day double-name commercial paper, taken from table 29 of National Monetary Commission (1910). The rates pertain to the last Saturday of each month.

The UK interest rates are prime bank bill rates for the last working day of each month from table III.(10) of Capie and Webber (1985).

The U.S. price level is proxied by the index of the general price level (NBER series 04051).

The UK price level is proxied by the wholesale price index of all commodities (NBER series 04053).

The U.S. money supply data are from NBER series 14135 of total circulation outside the U.S. Treasury.

The UK money supply data are from NBER series 14081 of total circulation in the United Kingdom.

U.S. income is proxied by the index of the physical volume of business activity (NBER series 01001).

UK income data are proxied by an interpolated monthly series of annual railway receipt data (NBER series 04053).

As a proxy for the export performance of U.S. agricultural interests we use physical U.S. exports of raw cotton (NBER series 07043).

As a proxy for the health of the U.S. financial system we use Standard & Poor's index of all common stock prices (NBER series 11025).

Treasury gold and silver stocks are computed as the sum of gold and silver held in the Treasury and Federal Reserve Banks at the end of each month (NBER series 14137 and 14133, respectively).

PART THREE

THE INTER-WAR PERIOD

FIVE

The Inter-War Gold Exchange Standard

Credibility and Monetary Independence

Michael D. Bordo and Ronald MacDonald

A number of previous works have demonstrated that the classical gold-standard regime represented a highly credible system, despite the fact that participating countries often did not play by the so-called rules of the game (see, for example, Chapter 2 in this volume and Officer, 1996). The reconciliation of these two apparently conflicting aspects (see Bordo and MacDonald, 1997 and Chapter 3 in this volume) appears to lie in the fact that currencies participating in the classical system were highly credible (in the sense of obeying the predictions of a target zone system [Svensson, 1994]), which allowed them limited scope to deviate from strict adherence to gold-standard rules. In contrast, certain key characteristics of the inter-war gold exchange standard would lead one to expect this system to have little credibility and therefore not offer participating countries the freedom to adopt measures which were at variance with the rules of the game. Several important factors may be cited in this regard.

First, the inter-war gold standard had evolved into a gold exchange standard in which member countries held their reserves in gold bullion and (with the exception of the reserve centre countries, the United Kingdom and the United States, and later France) in foreign exchange. This increase in the ratio of central bank liabilities to the gold base increased the fragility of the international monetary system. It also reduced the disciplinary power of gold movements by increasing the possibility of sterilisation operations.

Second, the inter-war gold exchange standard suffered from a serious maldistribution of gold between debtor and creditor nations. This reflected the Banque de France's pro-gold policies after restoring convertibility in 1926 at an undervalued parity and persistent sterilisation of gold inflows by the Federal Reserve.

Moreover in the inter-war period, the United Kingdom, which many observers believe returned to gold parity at an overvalued rate, suffered a persistent balance-of-payments deficit and a chronic shortage of gold reserves. Sterling's perennial weakness created further tension in the system.

Still, despite the apparent failings of the inter-war gold standard, there is evidence to suggest that it also appeared to be a highly credible system at least up to 1931 when the system began to unravel.

The purpose of the present chapter is to re-examine the inter-war gold standard with the objective of trying to reconcile the apparent credibility of the system, as found in a number of econometric studies, with its very evident failings. Our approach essentially extends the testing framework of Bordo and MacDonald (1997 and Chapter 3 in this volume), where the policy independence afforded to central banks operating in a credible system, namely the classical gold standard, was examined using two key arbitrage conditions. In our previous work we demonstrated that this credibility *could* have conferred on central banks the ability to pursue independent monetary policies. The emphasis on the word "could" is designed to stress the fact that before World War I, central banks used their policy tools to influence domestic goals in an episodic manner, without guiding principles or well-specified objectives.

After the war, the degree and nature of economic management changed, in particular, monetary policy became more systematic and was increasingly based on guiding principles. Thus domestic economic stability and objectives other than gold convertibility became specific arguments in a central bank reaction function. The purpose in the present chapter is to show not only the possibilities for monetary independence in a credible target zone, but also *how* central banks used this credibility to adopt independent monetary policies.

The outline of the remainder of the chapter is as follows. In the next section, we present an historical perspective on the characteristics and operation of the inter-war gold standard. In the third section, we present our modelling framework which is in the spirit of the traditional reaction function literature, although it has some important distinguishing characteristics. A discussion of our data set and econometric results are contained in the fourth section. The final section contains some concluding comments.

HISTORICAL BACKGROUND: CENTRAL BANK POLICIES AND THE INTER-WAR GOLD EXCHANGE STANDARD

The Gold Exchange Standard

Before World War I, most countries of the world adhered to the classical gold standard, with its commitment by monetary authorities to convertibility of their currencies at a fixed parity. The gold-standard era for the advanced countries was also characterized by limited central bank intervention in foreign exchange and money markets, as well as free mobility of capital.

The gold standard dissolved during World War I as all major countries, with the exception of the United States, suspended gold convertibility de facto, if not de jure. The United States imposed an embargo on gold exports from 1917 to 1919. After the war, the United Kingdom and other countries expressed a strong preference to return to gold at the original parity (Cunliffe, 1918).

Plans for reconstructing the international gold standard were laid at the Genoa Conference of 1922, where the Financial Commission, under British leadership, urged that the world return to a gold exchange standard under which member countries would make their currencies convertible into gold, but use foreign exchange – the currencies of key reserve countries, the United Kingdom and the United States – as a substitute for gold.

The gold exchange standard was restored worldwide in the period between 1924 and 1927, on the basis of the recommendations of Genoa. Central bank statutes typically required a cover ratio for currencies of between 30 per cent and 40 per cent, divided between gold and foreign exchange. Central reserve countries (the United States and the United Kingdom) were to hold reserves only in the form of gold.

The key event which restored the system was the United Kingdom's return to its original gold parity on April 28, 1925. The United Kingdom was quickly followed by the British Commonwealth and other nations, so that by the end of 1928, thirty-five countries had their currencies officially convertible into gold. Restoration was virtually completed when France declared de facto convertibility (at a parity which depreciated the franc by 80 per cent) in July 1926. De jure French convertibility occurred in June 1928.

Many believed that the gold exchange standard was established based on incorrect parities. It is widely held that sterling returned to gold at an overvalued rate of between 5 per cent and 15 per cent depending on the price index used (Keynes, 1925; Redmond, 1984). Consequently the United Kingdom suffered a competitive disadvantage with its trading partners and a chronic balance-of-payments deficit which forced the Bank of England to continuously follow contradictory monetary policies to maintain gold convertibility. The United Kingdom's weak position threatened the stability of one of the key reserve countries and hence the system itself. At the same time France restored gold at a vastly overvalued parity. Hence it ran persistent balance-of-payments surpluses and gold inflows.

This maladjustment involving two key members was greatly aggravated by inappropriate monetary policies pursued by France and the United States (see Eichengreen, 1990; Friedman and Schwartz, 1963; Meltzer, 2002). Each nation, as well as other countries (Nurkse, 1944),[1] consistently sterilized gold inflows, which reduced gold reserves available to the rest of the world and enhanced deflationary pressure.

The global gold exchange standard lasted until the United Kingdom abandoned it in September 1931. It collapsed in the face of the shocks of the Great Depression. Tight monetary policy by the Federal Reserve in 1928 to deflate the stock market boom and France's pro-gold policies precipitated a downturn in the United States and the rest of the world in 1929. Subsequent monetary collapse in the United States following a series of banking panics transmitted deflationary and contractionary pressures to the rest of the world on the gold standard.

As soon as doubts began to surface about the stability of the reserve currencies, central banks scrambled to liquidate their exchange reserves and replace them with gold. The share of foreign exchange in global central bank reserves plummeted from 37 per cent at the end of 1930 to 13 per cent at the end of 1931 and 11 per cent at the end of 1932 (Nurkse, 1944, appendix II). The implosion of the foreign-exchange component of the global reserve base exerted strong deflationary pressure on the world economy. Although there was only so much gold to go around, central banks around the world wanted more. To attract it they jacked up interest rates in the face of an unprecedented slump.

The Role of Central Bank Policies

Within this background of a strained international monetary system, central bank policy played a big role. As under the prewar gold standard, central banks were supposed to follow the rules of the game – that is, to maintain their fundamental goal of gold convertibility. They were supposed to use their policy tools to speed up adjustments to balance-of-payments disequilibria.

Considerable empirical evidence for the prewar gold standard suggests that most central banks violated the rules of the game in the sense that they did not allow gold flows to influence the domestic money supply (i.e. they engaged in sterilization), and that on occasion they geared their policy tools

---

[1]   For example, the German Reichsbank followed policies to accumulate gold and rebuild its reserve position following the German hyperinflation.

to domestic economic goals (see Bordo and MacDonald, 1997 for a survey of the evidence). Yet the violations were never serious enough to force countries to abandon convertibility. This, it is argued, may be explained by the basic credibility of the prewar gold standard which allowed monetary authorities in the short run to pursue domestic objectives without inducing capital flight.

In the inter-war regime, faced with a changed and less credible environment, one would expect violations of the rules to be more serious than before World War I. Factors suggesting that monetary authorities would attach a greater role to goals other than maintaining gold convertibility include: the rising power of organized labour and the movement towards universal suffrage, which would force central banks to be concerned over the employment and output consequences of tight monetary policy used to prevent gold outflows (Eichengreen, 1992; Simmons, 1994); and improved understanding, following advances in economic theory, of the impact of monetary policy on the real economy (Eichengreen, 1992). The changed environment would both alter the weights monetary authorities attach to convertibility versus domestic objectives and the credibility that the markets would attach to successful adherence to gold.

The evidence suggests that violations of the rules were at least as serious if not more so, in the inter-war as they were under the gold standard. According to Nurkse's (1944, p. 69) famous sign test, the correlations between domestic credit expansion and changes in international reserves were negative 60 per cent of the time for twenty-six countries from 1922 to 1938.[2]

For the individual core countries in the inter-war period, there is important evidence from econometric studies that monetary authorities attached considerable weight to domestic variables in reaction functions and that they engaged in sterilization.[3]

Was this experience of persistent violations of the rules sufficient to threaten the stability of the international monetary system, or, like the prewar gold standard, did the system possess sufficient credibility to allow the

---

[2]   These results are quite similar to those found by Bloomfield (1959) for the classical gold standard period of 1880–1914 for a smaller sample of countries. However, the evidence for the individual core countries for the prewar gold standard is mixed on violations of the rules (see Bordo and MacDonald, 1997) depending on the country, the methodology used and the time period.

[3]   For the United Kingdom, see Eichengreen, Grossman and Watson (1985); for France, see Eichengreen (1990); for the United States, see Wheelock (1991); for Germany, see Eschweiler and Bordo (1994).

monetary authorities the leeway to pursue domestic goals? In what follows we attempt to provide an answer to this question.

MOTIVATION AND MODELLING FRAMEWORK.

Because a central component of our work concerns credibility issues, we adopt a target zone framework as our modus operandi. In particular, we follow the testing methods of Bordo and MacDonald (1997 and Chapter 3 in this volume), who proposed using two key parity conditions to examine the potential for independent monetary policy in the classical gold-standard period. More specifically, this involves sequentially testing a simple interest parity equation for short-term interest rates, an interest parity equation augmented by a term structure relationship, and a system consisting of short and long interest rates and a vector of fundamentals, such as prices, output and gold reserves. These are systems 1 to 3 from Bordo and MacDonald (1997) and Chapter 3 in this volume. In contrast to that chapter, however, the structure of system 3 does not constrain the fundamental variables to have their influence solely through the short-run dynamics. Rather, the reaction function perspective which we adopt means that the fundamentals feature directly in the long-run equilibrium relationships, and this is justified on the basis of our empirical results. Our approach may therefore be interpreted as in the spirit of the traditional reaction function literature, although it differs significantly from this literature in that we approach the issue from the perspective of a target zone modelling framework.

The discussion and motivation of the three systems is the same as that given in the second section of Chapter 3 and is therefore not repeated here. The key difference in our modelling strategy here is that our third system, which involves examining the inter-relationships between interest rates and some fundamentals which could potentially have been targeted by the authorities, is modified to reflect the fact that the policy makers pursued much more proactive macroeconomic policies in the inter-war period relative to the Classical gold-standard period. The z vector for system 3 is defined as: $z_t = [i_t^s, i_t^{s*} i_t^l, y_t, p_t, g_t]'$, where, of variables not previously defined, y_t denotes the logarithm of output, p_t denotes the logarithm of prices and g_t denotes the logarithm of gold reserves. In Bordo and MacDonald's analysis of the classical gold-standard period, this vector was manipulated in such a way that only the interest rates enter the long-run equilibrium relationships (as in system 2), whereas the remaining variables were limited to having only a short-run impact through the dynamics. The justification for this follows from the prediction of the Svensson model that because interest rates can only differ transitorally across financial centres, they can only have a temporary role in absorbing shocks to, say, output or prices. As we shall see in what follows, the empirical results for the inter-war period suggest that the fundamental variables should enter the long-run co-integrating set along with the interest rate terms. We return to this point in the next section.

ECONOMETRIC METHODS AND RESULTS

Our econometric methods rely on the co-integrated VAR framework of Johansen (1988, 1991). Because this methodology is now well known, we do not discuss it further here (see Chapter 3 in this volume for further discussion). Our econometric analysis relates to six country pairings, namely the United Kingdom against, France, Germany and the United States, France relative to Germany and the United States and, finally, Germany-United States. The longest sample period is for the UK-US combination and runs from May 1925 to August 1931. Other sample periods are defined in Table 5.1. The sample periods used in this chapter may be deemed rather short for a study which exploits co-integration methods, which are generally thought to be most suited to long time spans of data. However, Granger (1986) has argued that co-integration methods can be applied to relatively short spans of high-frequency data if the concept of equilibrium studied is relevant for such a sample period. Given that the equilibrium conditions considered in this work relate to interest rate arbitrage conditions, we believe that this is indeed the case. Furthermore, because co-integration methods have relatively low power to reject the null hypothesis of no co-integration in small samples, our findings (discussed later in the chapter) of convincing evidence of co-integration for each interest rate pairing would seem to support our use of such methods.

For each of the countries we collected data on a money market short-term interest rates and a (country-specific) single long rate.[4] The non-interest-rate data are industrial production, a consumer price index and

[4]   In calculating an interest parity relationship, it is now common to use offshore interest differentials because the latter are free of so-called political risk. Unfortunately, such rates are not available for our sample period. However, we do not believe that the existence of such rates would affect the tenor of the results reported in this chapter. This is because with one or two minor exceptions, the period studied in this paper was one of remarkable political stability, a feature borne out by our credibility tests. Furthermore, our findings of credibility also mean that the short-term interest differentials examined in this chapter do not contain a significant time-varying risk premium, thereby further enhancing their usefulness in the kinds of tests we undertake.

Table 5.1. *Co-integration tests of UIP*

$$i_t = \beta_0 + \beta_1 i_t^\star + \varepsilon_t$$

System	Lags	Sample	Dummies	β_0	β_1	Trace	χ^2	α	Half Life	LM(1)	LM(4)	NM(6)
UK-France	8	1927(8) to 1931	1927(11)	1.207 (0.11)	1.00 (0.00)	20.60 / 0.67	1.59 (0.21)	-0.26 (2.63)	2.3	3.13 (0.54)	3.52 (0.54)	32.76 (0.00)
UK-Germany	12	1926(2) to 1931(6)	1929(11) 1930(2) 1930(3)	1.814 (0.07)	1.00 (0.00)	26.89 / 0.52	1.18 (0.28)	-0.03 (0.33)	23	1.27 (0.87)	12.42 (0.01)	28.13 (0.00)
UK-U.S.	12	1925(5) to 1931(8)	1929(11) 1930(2) 1930(3)	0.378 (0.16)	1.00 (0.00)	36.25 / 4.39	0.72 (0.40)	-0.03 (1.19)	23	2.75 (0.60)	0.41 (0.98)	33.68 (0.00)
France-Germany	12	1927(2) to 1931(6)	-	-3.265 (0.02)	1.00 (0.00)	59.93 / 16.56	4.96 (0.03)	-0.18 (6.43)	3.45	7.60 (0.11)	3.31 (0.51)	17.05 (0.00)
France-U.S.	6	1927(2) to 1933(1)	1929(3) 1929(10)	-1.308 (0.00)	1.00 (0.28)	33.87 / 4.36	2.71 (0.10)	-0.006 (0.72)	69	3.63 (0.46)	2.18 (0.70)	71.22 (0.00)
Germany-U.S.	12	1926(2) to 1931(6)	-	0.714 (0.14)	1.00 (0.00)	23.38 / 10.42	0.00 (0.99)	-0.01 (0.16)	69	3.51 (0.48)	13.195 (0.01)	10.63 (0.03)

gold reserves. All data were originally seasonally unadjusted and have been seasonally adjusted for this study using the X11 filter. A complete listing of all variables and their sources is presented in the Data Appendix. As noted earlier, one key assumption underpinning our work concerns the credibility of the inter-war gold standard. Recent literature suggests that the gold exchange standard was credible until 1931 (see Chapter 2 in this volume, and Officer, 1996). Therefore we do not test for credibility explicitly in this paper but build upon the earlier results.

Our estimates of the uncovered interest parity condition are presented in Table 5.1. The Akaike information criterion was used to determine the order of the lag length in the VAR, and the chosen lag length is reported in the second column of the table. The standardized residuals from the VAR were checked for outliers and appropriate intervention dummies were incorporated to account for these. The dates of the different dummies are reported in the fourth column of the table. The columns headed LM(1), LM(4) and Normality are portmanteau statistics for residual correlation and normality. In particular, LM(1 and 4) are multivariate Godfrey (1988) LM-type statistics for first- and fourth-order auto-correlation and NM(6) is a Doornik and Hansen's (1994) multivariate normality test. Reported numbers in brackets are p-values and indicate, in general, an absence of serial correlation, although there is some evidence of non-normality in all of the systems (the latter seems to be a standard finding in these kinds of systems).

On the basis of the estimated Trace statistics, all of the systems reported in Table 5.1 produce evidence of one significant co-integrating vector using a 95 per cent significance level. Normalizing these significant vectors on the "home" interest rate, we find that the restriction that $\beta=1$ cannot be rejected for any of the interest rate pairings (these restrictions tests are reported in the column labeled χ^2, with marginal significance levels in brackets). This result is consistent with the findings of Bordo and MacDonald (1997) for the Classical Gold-standard period. However, in contrast to the latter period, we note that here all of the constant terms are statistically significant (the estimated co-efficients are reported in the column labelled β_0, with standard errors in brackets). For example, the constant in the UK-US relationship is 0.38, suggesting that, on average, UK rates were higher than U.S. rates by 38 basis points for this period.

The finding of significant constants could perhaps be taken as *prima facie* evidence that the system was non-credible because it implies that, on average, over the sample, the domestic rate could differ from the foreign rate. However, if it is non-credibility driving the result, this would conflict with the extant empirical tests which focus directly on the credibility of the system (see Officer, 1996). Such tests rely on constructing 95 per cent confidence intervals using interest differentials and the deviation of the exchange rate from the centre point of the band. However, in a period, such as the inter-war period, when it was known that central banks were targeting interest rates, these 95 per cent intervals may not truly be reflecting the credibility of the system. So it may be that the inter-war system was credible, up to a constant term, and that this credibility was exploited by central banks to pursue the kinds of objectives referred to earlier. Alternatively, the system was non-credible and this was reflected in a constant risk premium. However, the existence of the latter could again have allowed the monetary authorities some leeway in the operation of monetary policy, although this would, of course, be inconsistent with credibility. Given that the independent credibility tests for this period are so clear-cut (see Officer, 1996), we are inclined towards the view that these significant constants are consistent with a credible system. This is especially so given that our sample period is shorter than that used to construct the credibility tests (our sample periods are constrained by the availability of the fundamental series).

As noted in the second section of this chapter, the key element in the independence conferred by a target zone relates to the non-zero expected change in the exchange rate in the short run. A feel for how important this was may be gleaned from the adjustment co-efficients – the α's – and the implied half-lives. These are reported in Table 5.1 in the labelled columns. The results for UK-France and France-Germany are very fast (adjustment is complete in approximately four and seven months, respectively), whereas those for UK-Germany and France-Germany are slower, suggesting policy independence of this form of around four years. The two remaining systems, France-U.S. and Germany-U.S., are slowest and would seem to be too slow to be consistent with the basic model. However, again this may be a sampling problem. We know, for example, from the recent Purchasing Power Parity (PPP) literature that half-lives are dramatically affected by the sample period (see MacDonald, 1995 and Rogoff, 1995). For example, using only data from the recent floating period, there is essentially no mean reversion in real exchange rates. However, when approximately 100 years of data are used, the half-life is a much more reasonable 4 years. Our half-life results, therefore, seem to underscore the conclusion reached earlier, that the inter-war gold-standard regime behaved very differently to the classical system, and this reinforces the point that we made regarding the significant constant terms. We now turn to our trivariate systems to gain a further perspective on these results.

In Table 5.2 we present our results from estimating system 2, that is, the trivariate systems with two short rates and a single long interest rate. The same intervention dummies used in the bivariate systems are used for the comparable trivariate systems. In each system we find, as expected, two significant co-integrating vectors, although in some instances the second vector is only marginally significant. Furthermore, we are able to interpret these vectors consistently as open interest parity and term structure relationships, and this is evidenced by the fact that the β and γ co-efficients are both unity, and the restrictions tests that they are statistically indistinguishable from plus and minus one (reported in the column labeled χ^2) are all statistically insignificant. One particularly interesting feature of these results is that all but one of the systems passed the portmanteau normality test at the 1 per cent level or better. This contrasts with our findings for the simpler systems where non-normality was a persistent problem and suggests, perhaps, that the simplest system is incomplete.

We note again that the constant terms are statistically significant in the majority of open parity conditions in Table 5.2. Furthermore, in three systems there is evidence that the constant is significant in the yield gap expressions, thereby implying that the pure form of the expectations hypothesis does not hold. These results therefore confirm that in the inter-war period, there was a "long-run" wedge separating short rates across financial centres.

In Figure 5.1, we present the impulse responses of the home short rates from the various systems reported in Table 5.2 to, respectively, a standardized 1 per cent shock in the UK long rate (part a.) and the "foreign" short rate (part b.). These impulses are designed to capture the dynamic interactions between the short interest rates across countries and the short and long rates within countries, subject to the long-run constraints given in Table 5.2. The ordering of the variables used for the Choleski decomposition is noted at the top of the figures, and we believe this accords with economic intuition. Thus the foreign rate is the most exogenous and the home rate the least exogenous (we also experimented with systems which had the orderings of i^l and i^* reversed, but these produced very similar results and are therefore not reported here). The impulse responses are calculated with the long-run relationships imposed. Following Hendry and Mizon (1993), this involves re-parameterising the error correction component of the VECM and then proceeding with the standard Choleski factorization.[5]

---

[5] In particular, this approach involves re-parameterising the error correction term into a term in first differences and a lagged levels term.

Table 5.2. *Co-integration tests of UIP and term structure*

$$i_t = \alpha + \beta i^*_t + \gamma i_{L,t} + \varepsilon_t$$

System	Lags	Sample period	Intervention dummies	i_t	α	β	γ	χ^2	Trace	Auto-correlation tests		
										LM(1)	LM(4)	NM(6)
UK-France	8	1927(2)	1927(11)	1.000	1.203 (0.092)	1.000	0	0.00 (0.97)	36.63	3.550 (0.94)	7.812 (0.55)	4.712 (0.58)
Short Rates,		to							17.24			
UK Long Rate		1931(6)		0.156	3.837 (0.095)	0	1.000		6.28			
UK-Germany	8	1926(2)	1929(11)	1.000	-1.255 (0.209)	1.000	0	3.67 (0.06)	76.63	13.173 (0.15)	4.844 (0.85)	17.245 (0.01)
Short Rates,		to	1930(2)	0.050		0	1.000		18.22			
UK Long Rate		1931(4)	1930(3)	(0.004)	4.301 (0.017)				2.57			
UK-U.S.	12	1925(5)	1928(12)	1.000	-0.533 (0.179)	1.000	0		52.28	13.553 (0.14)	11.766 (0.23)	10.062 (0.12)
Short Rates,		to	1929(3)	0.150		0	1.000		24.04			
UK Long Rate		1931(6)		(0.015)	3.890 (0.063)				3.57			
France-Germany	8	1927(2)		1.000	-0.525 (0.532)	1.000	0	0.03 (0.86)	47.06	20.492 (0.02)	6.209 (0.72)	13.599 (0.03)
Short Rates,		to		0.183		0	1.000		21.12			
France Long Rate		1931(6)		(0.191)	5.372 (0.710)				6.98			
France-U.S.	8	1927(2)	1929(3)	1.000	-0.992 (0.322)	1.000	0	1.07 (0.30)	47.19	18.695 (0.03)	4.637 (0.86)	35.286 (0.00)
Short Rates,		to	1929(10)	0.347		0	1.000		21.38			
France Long Rate		1932(11)		(0.130)	3.073 (0.309)				8.27			
U.S.-Germany	8	1926(2)		1.000	-0.783 (0.293)	1.000	0	6.86 (0.01)	47.36	5.574 (0.78)	11.414 (0.25)	17.505 (0.01)
Short Rates,		to		0.055		0	1.000		25.36			
U.S. Long Rate		1931(6)		(0.013)	3.100 (0.070)				8.89			

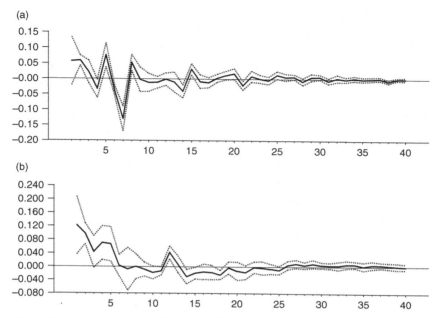

Figure 5.1. Impulse responses for $i_t = \alpha + \beta \, i^*_t + \gamma \, i_{L,t} + \varepsilon_t$.

Ordering: $i^*_t, i_{L,t}, i_t$.

System 1: UK-France short rates, UK long rate.
a. Response of UK short rate to shock in UK long rate.
b. Response of UK short rate to shock in French short rate.

System 2: UK-Germany short rates, UK long rate.
a. Response of UK short rate to shock in UK long rate.
b. Response of UK short rate to shock in German short rate.

System 3: UK-U.S. short rates, UK long rate.
a. Response of UK short rate to shock in UK long rate.
b. Response of UK short rate to shock in U.S. short rate.

System 4: France-Germany short rates, France long rate.
a. Response of French short rate to shock in French long rate.
b. Response of French short rate to shock in German long rate.

System 5: France-U.S. short rates, France long rate.
a. Response of French short rate to shock in French long rate.
b. Response of French short rate to shock in U.S. short rate.

System 6: U.S.-German short rates, U.S. long rate.
a. Response of U.S. short rate to shock in U.S. long rate.
b. Response of U.S. short rate to shock in German short rate.

In all cases bar one (iv, part a), these shocks produce an immediate increase in the short rate and in the majority of these the rise is significant. The magnitude of the shocks is similar across the countries. In the case of the UK-U.S. system, for example, the increase in the U.S. short rate produces an immediate three-basis-point increase in the UK short rate, which rises to about eight basis points after three months. Although the response is insignificantly different from zero after about sixteen months, there is still some significant persistence after that time. Other interest rate pairings tend to have a similar general profile, although the degree of significance varies. These dynamic profiles indicate that the credibility of the inter-war gold standard conferred on participating countries the ability to have interest rate dynamics which were deviant from those in the foreign country.

Our evidence so far seems to indicate two things. First, there was a "long-run" wedge separating interest rates across financial centres. Second there were different adjustment speeds towards these wedge-adjusted equilibria, with adjustment being fastest for UK-France and France-Germany and slowest for France-U.S. and Germany-U.S. We interpret the significant wedges as reflecting the fact that in the inter-war period, monetary policy became more systematic and was increasingly based on guiding principles. However, it is our contention that it was the credibility bestowed on central banks by participating in the gold standard which facilitated the independence of monetary policies during the period. Our third system is designed to shed further light on the independence of monetary policy during the period by explicitly introducing the kinds of variables likely to be the target of monetary policy.

As noted in third section, our third system is defined by the vector:

$$z_t = [i_t^s, i_t^{s^*} i_t^l, y_t, p_t, g_t]'$$

The results from systems 1 and 2 suggest that there was a "long-run" wedge between interest rates in different financial centres for our sample period. It is therefore possible that the authorities could have exploited this wedge in order to pursue standard counter-cyclical objectives which differed, on average, from their partners over the sample period. Therefore, in contrast to Bordo and MacDonald (1997) and Chapter 3 in this volume, the fundamental variables here enter the long-run relationship rather than being restricted solely to having a short-run influence. Our estimates are therefore more in the spirit of the traditional reaction function literature, discussed in the second section. However, in contrast to much of that literature, the econometric framework here explicitly recognizes both the potential nonstationarity of the variables and also any long-run co-integrating relationships. As we demonstrated, in the system with three interest rates, there may be up to two co-integrating relationships, comprising the two interest rate parity conditions. However, because system 3 has additional three variables, each of which is potentially non-stationary, there may be up to two more co-integrating vectors in this more general system.

The rank of each system 3 is reported in Table 5.3. It is clear that the addition of the extra fundamental variables has changed the long-run properties; there are now either three or four significant vectors, depending on the particular country combination. The existence of multiple co-integrating vectors in any system can prove problematic in the sense that it is unclear which vector, say, represents the intervention function. Often in such a situation a researcher will simply focus on the first eigenvector, or the one which has co-efficients corresponding most closely with a given set of priors. Here, however, we attempt to interpret all of the vectors using the structure we have already introduced. In particular, our general system contains the two short rates and long rate referred to earlier and, additionally, the variables relating to intervention. As in the trivariate systems, we interpret the first two vectors as the open interest parity relationship and the term structure relationship, respectively, whereas any other significant vectors are interpreted as relating to intervention. More formally, and following Johansen and Juselius (1994), we attempted to estimate fully specified systems of the form $\beta = \{H\phi_1, H\phi_2, H\phi_2, H\phi_2\}$ (for a four-vector system). We consider the results for the UK-France system for illustrative purposes.

In the UK-France system, reported in Table 5.3a, we have, in addition to the two parity conditions, a long-run relationship between the short rate, output and gold, and a further relationship between the short rate, prices and output. The signs on these variables seem correct in terms of a standard macro-model: Output is positively associated with the interest rate in both cases, and gold and the price level are negatively related. We note that all of the freely estimated co-efficients are statistically significant in terms of the reported standard errors. Note that the restrictions imposed on the co-integrating space of the UK-France system are accepted at the 5 per cent level. Other systems may be interpreted in a similar way, although the fact that the data generating processes differ across countries means that the form of the restricted vectors are not always the same and, indeed, when they are the same, wrongly signed co-efficients sometimes appear. However, across all of the systems, the vast majority of co-efficients are plausibly signed and significant, and the restrictions go through at the 1 per cent level or better in each case. We interpret the finding that the fundamentals are significant in the long-run relationships as consistent with our

Table 5.3a. *Long-run estimates for system 3*

System	Lags	Sample Period	Intervention Dummies	i_t	α	β	γ	δ	η	ϕ	$\chi^2_{(5)}$	Trace	Auto-correlation L-B	LM(1)	LM(4)	NM(6)
UK-French Short Rates,	6	1927(2) to 1931(6)	1927(11)	1.000	1.734 (0.150)	1.000	0	0	0	0	7.78 (0.05)	304.91	497.7 (0.00)	28.969 (0.79)	36.700 (0.44)	26.218 (0.01)
UK Long Rate,				-0.190 (0.002)	5.490 (0.030)	0	1.000	0	0	0		187.63				
UK Fundamental				0	31.045 (0.949)	0	0	0	-7.853 (0.186)	2.149 (0.050)		86.28				
				0	39.063 (0.914)	0	0	2.644 (0.083)	-9.042 (0.189)			30.81				
												12.51				
												2.15				
UK-German Short Rates,	6	1926(2) to 1931(4)		1.000	-1.955 (0.106)	1.000	0	0	0	0	6.30 (0.18)	265.91	525.6 (0.00)	46.550 (0.11)	39.999 (0.30)	20.971 (0.05)
UK Long Rate,				1.000	463.79 (17.375)	0	0	0	0	92.793 (3.450)		156.33				
UK Fundamental				0.051 (0.003)	4.286 (0.016)	0	1.000	0	0	0		111.48				
				1.000	-58.907 (4.518)	0	0	17.206 (1.198)	1.940 (0.232)	0		67.77				
												30.97				
												11.23				
UK-U.S. Short Rates,	6	1925(5) to 1931(6)		1.000	-0.481 (0.318)	1.000	0	0	0	0	11.19 (0.08)	147.04	559.4 (0.00)	49.774 (0.06)	19.580 (0.99)	7.990 (0.79)
UK Long Rate,				1.017 (0.008)	0	0	1.000	0	0	0		90.02				
UK Fundamental				1.000	0	0	0	0	0	0.891 (0.008)		58.59				
				1.000	5.636 (0.353)	0	0	-0.301 (0.091)	-0.045 (0.022)	0		36.87				
												17.98				
												7.51				

Table 5.3b. *Long-run estimates for system 3*

System	Lags	Sample Period	Intervention Dummies	i_t	α	β	γ	δ	η	ϕ	$\chi^2_{(5)}$	Trace	Auto-correlation L-B	LM(1)	LM(4)	NM(6)
French-German Short Rates	4	1927(2) to 1931(4)	1927(11) 1928(3) 1928(6)	1.000	17.050 (2.106)	1.000	0	0	0	0	6.77 (0.24)	186.52	418.6 (0.00)	47.026 (0.10)	25.539 (0.90)	44.300 (0.00)
France Long Rate,				-0.083 (0.125)	19.263 (1.591)	0	1.000	0	0	0		114.86				
France Fundamental				1.000	275.64 (25.107)	0	0	-56.093 (3.986)	2.175 (2.056)	4.039 (0.427)		58.68 / 26.03 / 7.30 / 2.07				
French-U.S. Short Rates,	4	1927(2) to 1932(11)	1928(6)	1.000	0.545 (0.620)	1.000	0	0	0	0	8.04 (0.15)	131.54	542.1 (0.00)	47.601 (0.09)	69.967 (0.00)	90.509 (0.00)
French Long Rate,				0.490 (0.092)	3.011 (0.253)	0	1.000	0	0	0		84.60				
French Fundamental				1.000	32.079 (6.960)	0	0	-12.818 (1.593)	10.505 (0.875)	0.062 (0.078)		56.77 / 29.49 / 6.80 / 0.07				
U.S.-German Short Rates,	2	1926(2) to 1931(4)	1928(12) 1929(3)	1.000	-0.452 (0.208)	1.000	0	0	0	0	12.95 (0.04)	151.21	603.6 (0.00)	26.902 (0.86)	50.563 (0.05)	33.947 (0.00)
U.S. Long Rate				0.576 (0.014)	0	0	1.000	0	0	0		92.40				
U.S. Fundamental				1.000	0	0	0	0	0	0		57.18				
				1.000	4.124 (0.471)	0	0	-0.501 (0.110)	1.079 (0.036)	0.747 (0.019)		30.69 / 18.07 / 6.79				

finding of significant constant terms in the interest rate systems. Having established the existence of sensible long-run relationships for each of our system 3 combinations, we now use an impulse response analysis to gauge the interactions of the variables.

In Figures 5.2 to 5.7 we report the impulse responses for our complete systems. These figures show the response of the home short rate – the rate assumed to be the target rate of the home central bank – to standardized 1 per cent shocks of all the other variables. Consider first the UK-France system. The profiles of the UK short rate in response to the French short rate and the UK long rate are similar to those contained in system 2. For example, the UK short rate rises by thirty basis points in response to a shock to the French rate and then oscillates between positive and negative values, with the difference becoming insignificant from zero by around twenty months. The initial response of the short rate to the long rate is negative here (although insignificant), but the dynamic profile of the rate is very similar to that for system 2, returning to zero after twenty months. The UK short rate clearly also has a shock absorber role with respect to the three "fundamental," or reaction function, variables. For example, its participation in a target zone system allows the UK rate to accommodate a positive income shock by having its short-term rate below the corresponding short-term French rate. It takes approximately thirty months for the UK short rate to return to the non-interest rate fundamentals.

The impression of domestic interest rates acting as a shock absorber with respect to changes in fundamentals is confirmed in the other systems contained in Figures 5.3 to 5.7. For example, in the two other pairings containing the French short rate (Figures 5.5 and 5.6), adjustment of the home rate back to equilibrium occurs after about one year. In the case of the French-German system, there would appear to be more significant deviations of the home short rate than in the French-U.S. system. In the two remaining pairings containing the UK short rate (Figures 5.3 and 5.4), adjustment back to equilibrium is approximately the same as in the UK-French system, namely about two years. Perhaps the greater ability of the UK rate to deviate from the foreign rate reflects the continuing importance of the UK as a financial centre in the inter-war despite the transference of hegemony to the United States in long-term lending (Bordo, Edelstein and Rockoff [1999] document the shift in the importance of the United Kingdom as a financial centre in the classical gold-standard period to the United States in the inter-war period). Again, the shock absorber role of the United Kingdom short rate is evident .

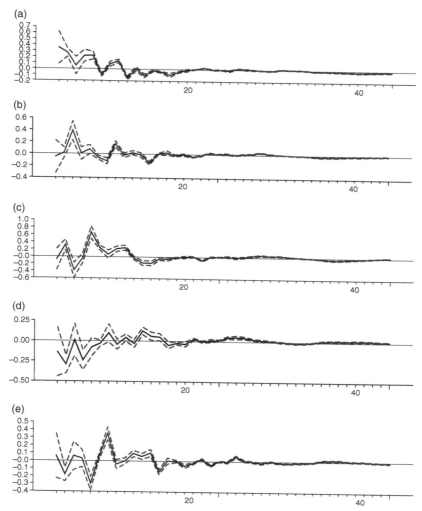

Figure 5.2. Impulse responses for $i_t = \alpha + \beta i^*_t + \gamma i_{L,t} + \delta$ Prices$_t$ + η Output$_t$ + ϕ Gold$_t$ + ε_t.
Ordering: Prices, Output, Gold Reserves, $i_{L,t}$, i^*_t, i_t.
UK-French short rates, UK long rate, UK prices, output and gold reserves.
a. Response of UK short rate to shock in French short rate.
b. Response of UK short rate to shock in UK long rate.
c. Response of UK short rate to shock in UK gold reserves.
d. Response of UK short rate to shock in UK output.
e. Response of UK short rate to shock in UK prices.

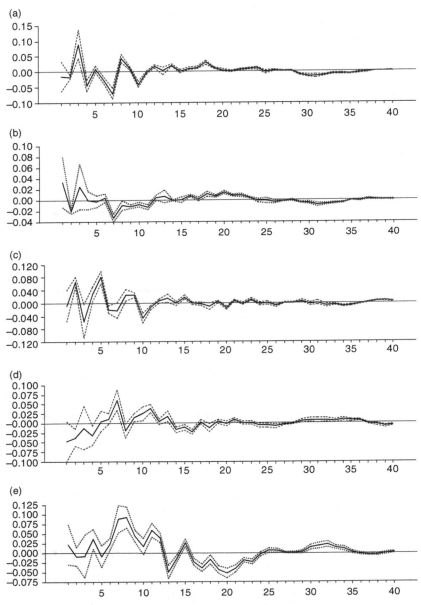

(a)

(b)

(c)

(d)

(e)

Figure 5.3. Impulse responses for $i_t = \alpha + \beta i^*_t + \gamma i_{L,t} + \delta \, \text{Prices}_t + \eta \, \text{Output}_t + \phi \, \text{Gold}_t + \varepsilon_t$.

Ordering: Prices, Output, Gold Reserves, $i_{L,t}$, i^*_t, i_t.

UK-U.S. short rates, UK long rate, UK prices, output and gold reserves.

a. Response of UK short rate to shock in U.S. short rate.

b. Response of UK short rate to shock in UK long rate.

c. Response of UK short rate to shock in UK gold reserves.

d. Response of UK short rate to shock in UK output.

e. Response of UK short rate to shock in UK prices.

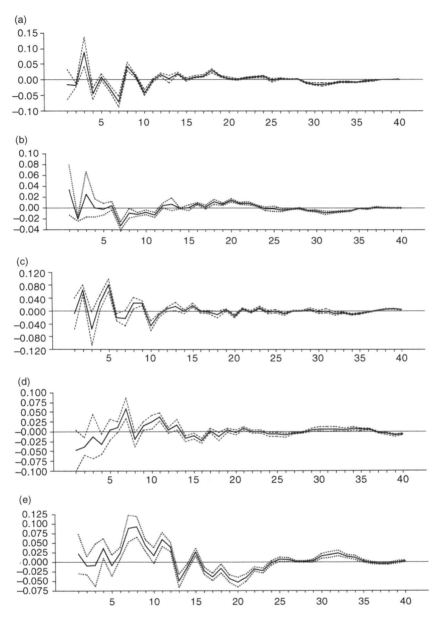

Figure 5.4. Impulse responses for $i_t = \alpha + \beta i^*_t + \gamma i_{L,t} + \delta\,\text{Prices}_t + \eta\,\text{Output}_t + \phi\,\text{Gold}_t + \varepsilon_t$.
Ordering: Prices, Output, Gold Reserves, $i_{L,t}$, i^*_t, i_t.
UK-German short rates, UK long rate, UK prices, output and gold reserves.
a. Response of UK short rate to shock in German short rate.
b. Response of UK short rate to shock in UK long rate.
c. Response of UK short rate to shock in UK gold reserves.
d. Response of UK short rate to shock in UK output.
e. Response of UK short rate to shock in UK prices.

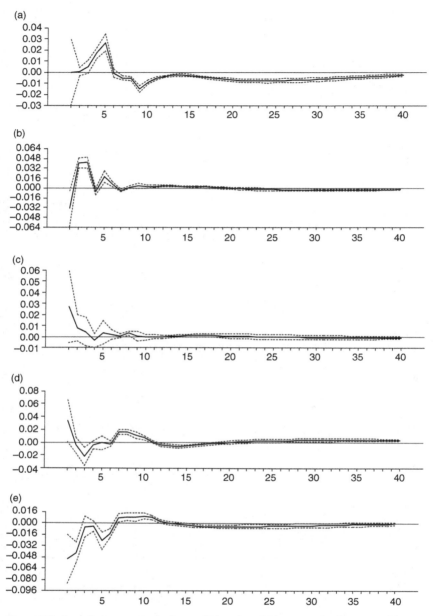

Figure 5.5. Impulse responses for $i_t = \alpha + \beta i^*_t + \gamma i_{L,t} + \delta \, \text{Prices}_t + \eta \, \text{Output}_t + \phi \, \text{Gold}_t + \varepsilon_t$.

Ordering: Prices, Output, Gold Reserves, $i_{L,t}$, i^*_t, i_t.

System 9: French-U.S. short rates, French long rate, French prices, output and gold reserves.

a. Response of French short rate to shock in U.S. short rate.

b. Response of French short rate to shock in French long rate.

c. Response of French short rate to shock in French gold reserves.

d. Response of French short rate to shock in French output.

e. Response of French short rate to shock in French prices.

110

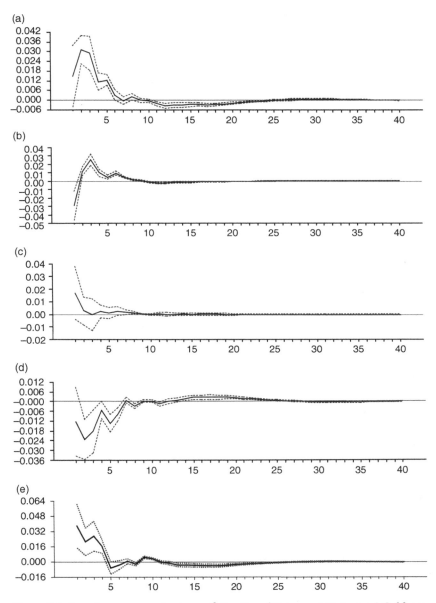

Figure 5.6. Impulse responses for $i_t = \alpha + \beta\, i^*_t + \gamma\, i_{L,t} + \delta\, \text{Prices}_t + \eta\, \text{Output}_t + \phi\, \text{Gold}_t + \varepsilon_t$

Ordering: Prices, Output, Gold Reserves, $i_{L,t}$, i^*_t, i_t.

French-German short rates, French long rate, French prices, output and gold reserves.

a. Response of French short rate to shock in German short rate.
b. Response of French short rate to shock in French long rate.
c. Response of French short rate to shock in French gold reserves.
d. Response of French short rate to shock in French output.
e. Response of French short rate to shock in French prices.

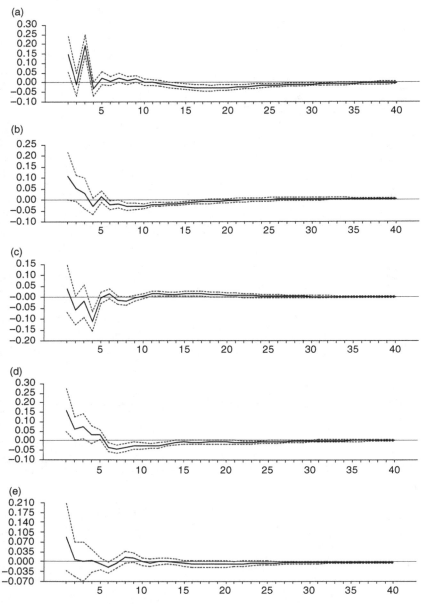

Figure 5.7. Impulse responses for $i_t = \alpha + \beta\, i^*_t + \gamma\, i_{L,t} + \delta\, \text{Prices}_t + \eta\, \text{Output}_t + \phi\, \text{Gold}_t + \varepsilon_t$.

Ordering: Prices, Output, Gold Reserves, i^*_t, $i_{L,t}$, i_t.

U.S.-German short rates, U.S. long rate, U.S. prices, output and gold reserves.

a. Response of U.S. short rate to shock in German short rate.

b. Response of U.S. short rate to shock in U.S. long rate.

c. Response of U.S. short rate to shock in U.S. gold reserves.

d. Response of U.S. short rate to shock in U.S. output.

e. Response of U.S. short rate to shock in U.S. prices.

SUMMARY AND CONCLUSION

Recently a number of studies have indicated that, despite all its evident failings, the inter-war gold standard appeared to represent a highly credible fixed exchange rate regime. Svensson (1994) has argued that the existence of such a regime should confer on the participating countries some flexibility in the use of their monetary policy. In particular, they should be able to exploit the credibility to pursue objectives like interest rate smoothing and some (albeit limited) counter-cyclical policies. In this chapter we have attempted to quantify econometrically the extent to which countries could engage in interest rate policies which were at variance with their partners. Our approach involved exploiting an uncovered interest parity relationship and a simple term structure relationship between long and short interest rates. Although we confirm that the slope co-efficient in a co-integrating regression of a domestic interest rate on its trading partner is insignificantly different from unity for all combinations, the included constant term is always significantly different from zero. This contrasts with the findings of Bordo and MacDonald (1997) (see Chapter 3 in this volume) for the classical gold-standard period, where such constants were always insignificant. Here we have argued that the existence of such significant constants does not necessarily conflict with the interpretation of the inter-war gold standard as a credible target zone regime, because it may simply be a function of the limited observations available. However, the existence of a significant wedge between interest rates implies that countries could, on average, have pursued interest rate policies which were at variance with those in their trading partners, and we believe that this is consistent with the fact that domestic economic stabilization objectives became important arguments in central bank's reaction functions during the period.

To further gauge the extent of monetary independence for the inter-war gold exchange standard we jointly modelled the parity conditions with a set of fundamental variables suggested by the reaction function literature. In contrast to much of that literature, however, we explicitly recognize the non-stationary nature of these variables and model the levels relationships using co-integration methods, whereas the dynamic interactions are captured using dynamic vector error correction models. The co-integration results produced evidence of statistically significant long-run relationships over and above those contained in the parity conditions considered on their own. Additionally, the signs on the relationship between the interest rates and fundamentals seemed appealing from a theoretical perspective. The dynamic systems produced further evidence that short-term interest rates in the inter-war period could have been used to engage in independent monetary policies, either in terms of interest rates being able to move to absorb shocks to variables like output, gold reserves and prices, or by the authorities deliberately manipulating interest rates to influence these kind of variables. Our findings therefore reinforce those of Bordo and MacDonald (1997) (see Chapter 3 in this volume) who noted the importance of the institutional aspects of the gold-standard regime in creating a credible international monetary system.

Acknowledgements

Reprinted from the *Journal of International Money and Finance* 22 (1), Michael D. Bordo and Ronald MacDonald, "The Inter-War Gold Exchange Standard: Credibility and Monetary Independence," pp. 1–32, Copyright (2003), with permission from Elsevier. The authors are grateful to an anonymous referee and Jim Lothian for helpful comments on an earlier draft of the chapter and to the ESRC for financial support under grant L120251023.

DATA APPENDIX

Data Type	Freq.	Country	Data Source
Short-term interest rate	M	United Kingdom	NBER Series 13016 (SU/SA)
		France	NBER Series 13017 (SU/SA)
		Germany	NBER Series 13018 (SU/SA)
		United States	NBER Series 13001 (SU/SA)
Long-term bond rate	M	United Kingdom	NBER Series 13041 (SU/SA)
		France	NBER Series 11021 (SU)
		Germany	NBER Series 13028 and 11020
		United States	NBER Series 13033 (SU/SA)
Gold Reserves	M	United Kingdom	
		France	
		Germany	
		United States	NBER Series 14062 (SU)
Retail Prices	M	United Kingdom	Capie & Webber (1985) (SU)
		France	NBER Series 04073 (SU) (1919–8/1939)
		Germany	International Abstract of Economic Statistics.
		United States	NBER Series 04128 (SU/SA*)

Data Type	Freq.	Country	Data Source
Industrial Production	M	United Kingdom	NBER Series 01133A
		France	NBER Series 01004B (1919–38 (SA) and 1928–39 (SU))
		Germany	NBER Series 01004A (SU) (only covers 1925–8/39)
		United States	NBER Series 01002
Money Supply	M	United Kingdom	Capie & Webber (1985) (SU) M1
		France	Paitat & Lutfalla (SU/SA) M2
		Germany	NBER Series 14098
		United States	NBER Series 14175 (SU/SA) M1

SIX

Crash! Expectational Aspects of the UK's and the U.S.'s Departures from the Inter-War Gold Standard

C. Paul Hallwood, Ronald MacDonald, and Ian W. Marsh

Within the space of nineteen months, beginning in September 1931 and ending in March 1933, both the United Kingdom and the United States departed from the gold-exchange standard system which had been reconstructed as an international regime following World War I. In this chapter, the commonalities of the experiences of these two central players in the "game" of the inter-war gold standard are examined, in particular the extent to which macroeconomic events were responsible for encouraging the speculative runs against the pound and the dollar that encouraged both of them to abandon the gold standard. The chapter also addresses the controversial matter of whether Federal Reserve policy was constrained by international considerations.

Target zone methods are utilized to extract time series of unobserved realignment probabilities for the British pound from actual interest rate differentials between the United Kingdom and the United States. These realignment series show that the markets did not expect devaluations of the pound until mid-1931, consistent with the hypothesis of a speculative attack. However, it also seems that the expected devaluation of the pound is related to several key economic fundamentals, including the differential between UK and U.S. money supplies and industrial production levels. The main lesson is that macroeconomic fundamentals between pairs of countries must move in tandem if exchange rate target zones are to remain credible in financial markets. Although this lesson is not new, we do offer a demonstration of it as drawn from an important part of twentieth-century experimentation with pegged exchange rates.

Using interest differentials between France and the United States, a series for dollar devaluation expectations is also generated. Again these show little sign of tension until the pound left the gold standard, whereupon the dollar was expected to appreciate against the French franc. After this short period of instability – just one month, September 1931 – there were three clear episodes: a nine-month period during which the dollar was consistently expected to depreciate, followed by seven months of tranquility when no parity changes were expected, and finally two months of renewed dollar devaluation expectations.

A variety of techniques are used to relate devaluation expectations to two key economic determinants: the widespread U.S. bank failures and gold flows into and out of the United States. The results confirm the hypothesis of Brown (1940) who argued that increases in U.S. money supply induced fears in Europe of American inflation at a time when American short-term liabilities to foreigners were still well in excess of the country's free gold. The inflation expectations gave rise to devaluation expectations and the external gold drain, as residents feared suspension of the gold standard, which was also a factor in the accelerating banking crisis of early 1932.

Our findings would seem to support the position that the Federal Reserve in this period was being hemmed in by the commitment to the gold standard. Therefore, we come down on the side of Eichengreen (1992), Kindleberger (1986), and Temin (1989) that U.S. monetary policy was constrained by international considerations – a position that Friedman and Schwartz (1963) have strongly denied. The Federal Reserve found itself in a dilemma: If it increased the money base to "save the banks" it was not playing by "the rules of the game" given the preponderance of gold outflows at this time. However, if it did nothing, which turned out to be the chosen policy, this risked the bank failures that also put pressure on the dollar. The United States' adherence to the gold standard quickly became untenable.

In short, we conclude that in both the UK and the U.S. domestic and international macroeconomic events, some of them directly or indirectly under the influence of the authorities, were responsible for both the United Kingdom and the United States leaving the gold standard during the interwar period. Furthermore, as our results indicate that economic factors can, to quite a large extent, explain the 1933 American episode, we do not agree that the election of President Roosevelt was an important causal factor in it.

We proceed as follows: in the second section, we empirically implement the target zone model to reveal realignment expectations for the pound and the dollar; in the third section, attention is turned to modeling the determinants of realignment expectations; finally, the fourth section presents our conclusions.

REALIGNMENT EXPECTATIONS: EMPIRICAL EVIDENCE

In this section, we estimate both 100 percent and 95 percent confidence intervals, as discussed in Chapter 1. We constrain our analysis of the pound-dollar rate to the interval from May 1925 to August 1931, the latter being the last full month during which the pound/gold link was maintained. To examine dollar devaluation expectations, we had to choose a currency to measure it against. The obvious choice was the French franc as France remained on the gold standard until 1936 and became the most important country remaining on gold following the American suspension. We use the franc/dollar rate from December 1926 (shortly after France had de facto settled on the gold standard) until February 1933, the last full month before the United States interfered with the gold convertibility of the dollar. The exchange rate series were abstracted from Einzig (1937a); short-term interest rates were taken from Homer (1977). Specifically, we use the three-month UK Treasury bill–U.S. commercial paper differential to provide the total expected change in the sterling-dollar exchange rate. For expectations of the franc-dollar rate, we use the three-month forward premium (taken from Einzig, 1937a) owing to a lack of comparable French interest rate data.[1]

In Table 6.1 we present estimates of Equation 1.6, which show clear evidence of mean reversion in the pound/dollar and franc/dollar rates.

Using the 95 percent confidence intervals derived from these equations, we calculate the 95 percent confidence intervals for realignment expectations. These are shown in Figures 6.1 and 6.2. As explained earlier, it is only when both the upper and lower confidence intervals are in the *positive* section that we are 95 percent confident that markets expect devaluation of the pound (against the dollar). Similarly with Figure 6.2, except in this case when both the upper and lower bounds are in the *negative* section, markets expect dollar devaluation (i.e., fewer francs per dollar). We discuss these figures in greater detail later in this chapter.

---

[1] We note that in Eichengreen (1986), an interest rate differential rather than the forward premium is used. The use of the latter should make little difference if uncovered interest parity is assumed to hold – an assumption actually made in Eichengreen (1986). Furthermore, forward premium data are more sensitive to exchange rate expectations than are some interest rate series when the later are changed only at fairly long intervals. Moreover, in other of our work on the period up to 1931 on the pound-dollar rate, we have found that it makes little difference whether we use a market interest rate or the forward premium (see Chapter 2 of this volume).

Table 6.1. *Expected change in exchange rate within the band*

	Pound/Dollar	Franc/Dollar
	1925(5)–1931(8)	1927(3)–1933(2)
Constant	0.0009	−0.0009
	(1.85)	(1.79)
x_t	−0.619	−0.758
	(3.38)	(5.14)
R^2	0.309	0.345

Notes: Figures in parentheses are *t*-statistics computed with Generalized Method of Moments standard errors.

Figure 6.1. Expected rate of realignment, 95% confidence interval, sterling-dollar.

EXPLAINING DEVALUATION EXPECTATIONS

The Experience of the United Kingdom

It is known that the United Kingdom was financing a basic (on current and long-term capital account) balance-of-payments deficit via short-term capital inflow throughout the 1925–1931 period. Furthermore, as the MacMillan Committee (1931) acknowledged, this practice was "precarious." It was precarious because its continuation depended on international

Figure 6.2. Expected rate of realignment, 95% confidence interval, franc-dollar.

investors sustaining their confidence in the value of the pound. According to our evidence in Figure 6.1, they did so until the summer of 1931.

Just when did strong speculation against the pound first start? Cairncross and Eichengreen (1983) dissect the speculative runs of 1927, 1929, and 1931, commenting that they were of increasing severity, and we find some evidence for this in Figure 6.1. In both 1927 and 1929, realignment expectations turned to favor the devaluation of the pound, but not statistically significantly so, at least at the 95 percent level. In fact, the pound was generally weak against the dollar throughout the 1925–1931 period, lying nearer to the gold export point than to the gold import point (for statistical evidence on this, see Officer, 1993), and the mean realignment expectation over the period as an entirety was positive (i.e., more pounds per dollar).

It is the final run on the pound, the one that led to Britain leaving the gold standard, that is of greater interest. It can be seen from Figure 6.1 that it was *not* a long, drawn-out affair. The market's confidence in the pound was sustained even up to the summer of 1931. Contemporary evidence (Einzig, 1937a, the *Federal Reserve Bulletin*, and *The Economist*) points to a short sharp speculative attack that cost the Bank of England about $1 billion (at £1= $4.86) over the period between July and September 1931. Cairncross and Eichengreen (1983) support this view, although they do point out that on some bourses, as early as January, the forward pound had, for a while, moved outside of the gold export point. They also point out, however, that well into summer of 1931, the financial press remained sanguine about the value of the pound. Cairncross and Eichengreen (1983) produce econometric evidence that strong speculation against the pound only began in mid-summer 1931, being provoked by the collapse of Austria's largest bank, Creditanstalt, and bank failures in Germany. These bank failures both reduced the Bank of England's accessible foreign assets held in Austria and Germany and alerted the markets to the possibility of inconvertibility crises in other countries, including the United Kingdom.

The Cairncross and Eichengreen (1983) econometric evidence is as follows: They estimate a monetary model of the balance of payments for the period from 1926 to the beginning of 1931 for the determinants of the Bank of England's gold and foreign exchange reserves. They then simulate it out-of-sample for the rest of 1931. Their main finding is that although the model predicts the behavior of reserves well during the in-sample period, in the third quarter of 1931, it overpredicts them (a case of "missing reserves"). Thus, in that quarter, on the basis of the actual monetary determinants of the UK's balance of payments, the Bank of England's gold and foreign exchange reserves should have risen when in fact they fell. As Cairncross and Eichengreen (1983) explain: "[T]he conventional view, that the 1931 crisis is properly understood as a consequence of a scramble for liquidity only indirectly related to the fundamental determinants of Britain's balance of payments position, remains the logical candidate" (pp. 76–77). This view would appear to be consistent with our own finding that realignment expectations only turned significantly (in a statistical sense) against the pound in July and August 1931; they account for the run on the UK's gold reserves as foreign investors withdrew funds from London.

Nevertheless, we may still want to investigate whether there were any motivating factors for the attack. Specifically, we ask whether realignment expectations can be explained by the behavior of macroeconomic variables that enter into standard models of balance-of-payments and exchange rate determination? The evidence in this section suggests that macroeconomic events ultimately did play a significant role in pushing the United Kingdom off the gold standard. It remains true, however, that for the six years until mid-1931, macroeconomic variables behaved well enough for financial markets to believe that the United Kingdom would remain on the gold standard.

We deploy the methods of Chen and Giovannini (1994) to reveal the determinants of realignment expectations. Their approach involves projecting the expected realignments term onto an appropriate set of explanatory variables. The regression equation we employ has the following form:

$$E_t[dc_t]/dt = \beta_0 + \beta_1(\pi - \pi^*)_{t-1} + \beta_2(m - m^*)_{t-1} + \beta_3(ca - ca^*)_{t-1}$$
$$+ \beta_4(y - y^*)_{t-1} + \beta_5(dreal)_{t-1} + \varepsilon_t \qquad (6.1)$$

where π denotes the inflation rate, m the money supply, y income (proxied by industrial production), ca the current account ratio (exports/imports), and *dreal* denotes the change in the real exchange rate. All variables are in logarithms, and an asterisk denotes a foreign variable. Seasonal dummies are also included but not reported.

The regression results for Equation 6.1, shown in Table 6.2, have good explanatory power with a highly significant chi-squared test statistics for the explanatory variables taken together, and a reasonable R^2. Encouragingly, the significant explanatory variables bear signs that would seem to accord with economic intuition. For example, the money-supply term is strongly significant and has a positive sign, suggesting that excessive domestic monetary expansion creates expectations of a devaluation (the inflation differential is perhaps insignificant because it captures the same information as the money-supply magnitudes). The strong negative effect of relative industrial production indicates that an increase in UK output relative to that in the United States reduces the expected rate of devaluation, possibly because it increases the demand for money relative to supply. Both of the other nonmonetary variables (*ca* and *dreal*) are insignificant.

We can now answer two key questions. First, how well does the model fit the experience in the crucial final few months? This is easiest shown in Figure 6.3, where we report the actual rate of realignment expectations together with the fitted value from the equation reported in Table 6.2. From this figure, it is clear that the upturn in devaluation expectations in the summer of 1931 is at least partially captured by the model based on fundamental factors. Second, which variables are driving this increased expectation of devaluation? Sequentially dropping variables from the model leads to the conclusion that differences in relative money supplies are the key cause. Plots of the money-supply series for the United Kingdom and the United States show clearly that the UK authorities were sterilizing the effects of the gold outflow, and that the U.S. authorities, as has already been well documented elsewhere, were reducing the money supply against all the "rules of the game." Thus it does seem that the United Kingdom's refusal to allow the gold outflows to reduce the money supply, coupled with the contrarian US strategy of tightening the monetary stance at a time of gold inflows,

Table 6.2. *Fundamental determinants of realignment expectations*

	Pound/Dollar
	1925(7)–1931(8)
$(\pi-\pi^*)_{t-1}$	0.1312
	(0.19)
$(m-m^*)_{t-1}$	0.1540
	(3.55)
$(y-y^*)_{t-1}$	−0.0127
	(2.79)
$(ca-ca^*)_{t-1}$	0.0102
	(1.82)
$dreal_{t-1}$	−0.1373
	(0.24)
Observations	74
R^2	0.407
Standard error of equation	0.0065
χ^2 test	17.165 [0.00]

Notes: Figures in parentheses under the coefficient estimates are *t*-statistics computed with Generalized Method of Moments standard errors. π denotes inflation, m denotes money supply (M1), *ca* denotes the current account ratio (exports/imports), *y* denotes income, and *dreal* denotes the change in the real exchange rate. All independent variables are lagged by one period and a * denotes a foreign (U.S.) variable. The χ^2 test is a test that the fundamental determinants are jointly insignificant. The figure in brackets after the test statistics is the marginal significance level.

contributed to initiating the speculative attack that ended the United Kingdom's gold link.

The Experience of the United States

Like the United Kingdom, the United States had a crucial weakness as an international financial center during the period of the inter-war gold-exchange standard: Its short-term liabilities to foreigners were much greater than its available gold reserve. Only free gold reserves could be counted as "available," as the Federal Reserve note issue required a minimum 40 percent gold backing, with the other 60 percent coming from eligible securities held by the Fed or from gold. As the Fed was short of eligible securities, free gold was even less than it otherwise might have been as gold was needed to make up the difference. By January 1930, free gold was down to $600 million

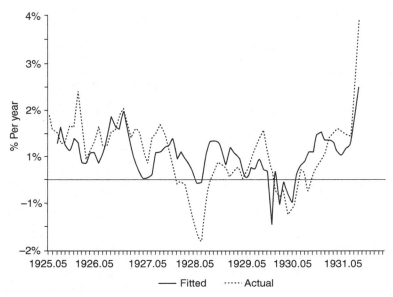

Figure 6.3. Fitted devaluation expectations, sterling-dollar.

(Friedman and Schwartz, 1963, p. 401), whereas the New York banks' short-term liabilities to foreigners were more than four times this amount (Board of Governors, 1943, p. 547). In fact, at almost $900 million, short-term liabilities to France alone exceeded the amount of free gold. About $2 billion was owed to European countries, and it was France, the Netherlands, Switzerland, and Belgium (four of the countries that were later to form the Gold Bloc, along with Poland and Italy) that were to exchange their deposits for U.S. monetary gold: $431 million in 1931, $739 million in 1932, and $219 million in 1933 (Board of Governors, 1943, p. 540). By February 1932, free gold was down to $461 million (Brown, 1940, p. 1227), and short-term liabilities to foreigners were still about 2.5 times higher.

Counting October 1931 – the first full month after the United Kingdom abandoned the gold standard – until the United States' suspension of the gold standard in April 1933, there are eighteen complete months. We can divide this period into three successive phases: the nine-month period to June 1932 of statistically significant (or almost so) dollar devaluation expectations – see Figure 6.2; the following seven months to January 1933 of relative tranquillity when no significant realignment expectations were recorded; and finally the two-month prelude-to-suspension of strong realignment expectations in February and March 1933 (see Table 6.3).

Table 6.3. *Three phases of the dollar after the UK leaving and the U.S. suspension of the gold standard*

	Mean realignment expectations (+: Dollar appreciation)	Net monthly gold flow $m. (+: inflow)	Banking crises*
1. October 1931– June 1932	−3.2%[b]	−91	October peak month of losses is second crisis.
2. July 1932– January 1933	+0.2%[c]	+91	Begins calm, ends with third crisis.
3. February 1933– March 1933	−3.6%[a]	−135	Bank holidays.[d]

* As measured by deposits at suspended commercial banks.
[a] All months having significant realignment expectations.
[b] All months significant or very close to 95% significance.
[c] No months with significant realignment expectations.
[d] The bank holiday was proclaimed March 6, 1933 as a means of stemming further bank runs and failures. (Also suspended were gold convertibility of the dollar and gold exports from the United States.)
Sources: column 2: Figure 6.2; column 3: Board of Governors (1943, p. 537); column 4: Friedman and Schwartz (1963) and Board of Governors (1943, p. 283).

The interesting aspects of these phases are:

1. The nine-month period (October 1931–June 1932): Over these months, the mean monthly realignment expectation was −3.2 percent (meaning dollar devaluation was expected – fewer francs per dollar), reaching highs of −5.1 percent in December 1931 and −6.1 percent in May 1932. These latter dollar devaluation expectations were the first to be statistically significant since the U.S. banking crisis of 1907, and the worst since 1896, when presidential candidate William Jennings Bryan campaigned to withdraw the United States from the gold standard and was only narrowly defeated.[2] Gold outflows accompanied these negative dollar realignment expectations. The gold outflow of October 1931 was a record in U.S. history to that point in time. Of these nine months, six saw net outflows of gold from the U.S. monetary gold stock, and they were especially great in May–June 1932, as well as the previous October. Brown (1940, p. 1222) saw this as

---

[2] We make the observations in this sentence on the basis of our findings published in Chapter 2 of this volume. Our monthly data for the pre–World War I period in fact ended in 1908, but our annual data is continuous from 1879 to 1913.

two separate episodes of speculative attack, but our calculations of realignment expectations suggests that the entire period was one of continuous dollar weakness: Mean realignment expectations in all nine months were negative, six of them being statistically significant at the 95 percent level and the other three almost so.

The Bank of France was the major destination of the U.S. monetary gold outflow, but by the spring of 1932, it had almost entirely withdrawn its balances from the United States. Accordingly, the French withdrawals coincided with the strong dollar devaluation expectations, and the weathering of these coincides with the cessation of French pressure against the dollar.

2. Next came the seven months to January 1933. This represented a tranquil period in the foreign exchange market – no significant monthly realignment expectations were recorded, and the mean value was very close to zero. Gold on a net basis returned to the United States in every one of these months for a monthly average of $91 million.

3. The final two full months before suspension of the gold standard by the United States saw the reemergence of strongly significant negative realignment expectations, with mean values of −2.9 percent in February, and −3.6 percent in March 1933. Suspension coincides with the third banking crisis.

There can be little doubt that gold outflows from the United States were provoked by the question of its continued adherence to the gold standard. First, as described earlier, there is the correlation between our calculations of realignment expectations and gold flows. More formally, in a linear regression, we find a significant – at the 1 percent level – and correctly signed (i.e., positive) relationship between contemporaneous changes in the U.S. gold stock and realignment expectations, although the R^2 is only 0.16. The low R^2 is only to be expected as U.S. official gold holdings would be affected by developments in its "above the line" balance of payments, as well as changes in the preferences of foreign central banks' for holding gold rather than dollars. Secondly, at least three experts on the financial history of this period suggest it. Friedman and Schwartz (1963) comment that: "France was strongly committed to staying on gold, and the French financial community, the Bank of France included, expressed the greatest concern about the United States' ability and intention to stay on the gold standard" (p. 397). Brown (1940) wrote that "[t]he uninterrupted large scale purchases of government securities [during the early months of 1932] by Federal Reserve Banks [in an effort to stimulate the economy] seemed in the eyes of foreigners to be evidence of approaching inflation [sic] in the US. The gold outflow to the continental creditor countries was consequently sharply accelerated as this policy was vigorously pressed forward" (p. 1233).

Concurrent with dollar weakness and fluctuating official gold stock was the succession of American banking crises. Over the period from December 1926 to February 1933, there is a statistically significant – at the 1 percent level – negative relationship between bank failures (measured either as number of banks or value of assets) and changes in U.S. official gold stocks.[3]

This negative relationship indicates that losses of official gold and bank failures moved together and is consistent with the argument of Brown (1940). He suggested the following line of causation (pp. 1222–1240). The Federal Reserve, attempting to raise the money supply, induced fears in Europe of American inflation at a time when American short-term liabilities to foreigners were still well in excess of the country's free gold. The inflation expectations gave rise to devaluation expectations and the external drain of gold. The external drain then stirred an internal gold drain as residents feared suspension of the gold standard. Finally, the internal gold drain was a factor in the accelerating banking crisis of early 1932.[4]

In contrast with the United Kingdom, where the lack of a clear theory to explain sterling's departure from gold forced us to rely on a reduced-form equation incorporating several economic variables, for the United States we focus on Brown's hypothesis regarding the links between realignment expectations, changes in the U.S. gold reserve, and banking crises.[5] Our first step is to set up tests of trivariate Granger-causality. That is, we

---

[3]   There is no significant correlation between bank failures and dollar realignment expectations. It is true that the first banking crisis, beginning in late 1930, had no discernable effect on dollar realignment expectations. There seems to have been no real rush by foreigners to get out of dollar deposits at this time. Then again, both the second and third banking crises were concurrent with dollar weakness, the latter, in fact, with American suspension of the gold standard.

[4]   Contrary to the view that declining gold reserves were an important factor forcing the United States off gold, Coleman (1992) argues that the United States was not forced off gold in 1933 by this factor. Rather, the new president, Roosevelt, wanted to move the United States out of depression and to do this saw raising the price of gold as a vital step. The fact is, however, that expectations of dollar devaluation and gold outflows were correlated.

[5]   Furthermore, although it seems reasonable to expect that U.S. developments would have an important influence on the United Kingdom's decision to leave gold, the size of the U.S. economy compared to that of France (the only reasonable choice as partner country) and the United States' relatively closed nature mean that the reduced-form approach of Equation 6.1 is less applicable here.

Table 6.4. *Granger causality between devaluation expectations, gold flows, and banking crises*

Direction of causality	Test statistic	Marginal significance
Gold → Devaluation	3.9412	0.0067
Bankfail → Devaluation	7.4624	0.0001
Devaluation → Gold	0.6155	0.6560
Bankfail → Gold	1.1327	0.3501
Devaluation → Bankfail	1.2050	0.3185
Gold → Bankfail	2.6849	0.0401

Notes: The test statistics reported in column 2 are distributed as $F(4,58)$.
The marginal significance of these statistics is reported in column 3.

estimated the following set of equations for the period from December 1926 to February 1933[6]:

$$E_t[dc_t]/dt = \sum_{i=1}^{4}\alpha_i\ E_{t-i}[dc_{t-i}]/dt + \sum_{j=1}^{4}\beta_j\ gold_{t-j} + \sum_{k=1}^{4}\gamma_k\ bankfail_{t-k} + \varepsilon_t$$

$$gold_t = \sum_{i=1}^{4}\delta_i\ gold_{t-i} + \sum_{j=1}^{4}\eta_j\ E_{t-j}[dc_{t-j}]/dt + \sum_{k=1}^{4}\theta_k\ bankfail_{t-k} + \mu_t \qquad (6.2)$$

$$bankfail_t = \sum_{i=1}^{4}\psi_i\ bankfail_{t-i} + \sum_{j=1}^{4}\lambda_j\ E_{t-j}[dc_{t-j}]/dt + \sum_{k=1}^{4}\varphi_k\ gold_{t-k} + \varsigma_t$$

where banking crises were proxied by the deposits of suspended commercial banks. The lag length of four was determined by *LM*-tests from a more general model, although alternative lag lengths produce very similar results. Gold flows would be deemed Granger causal to devaluation expectations (denoted gold → devaluation) if the restrictions $\beta_j = 0$ ($j = 1$ to 4) could be rejected using a standard F-test. The results of the six combinations of Granger-causality tests are given in Table 6.4.

The results of estimating Equation 6.2 suggest three significant casual relationships. The most significant is between bank failures and devaluation. However, gold flows are also a significant determinant of devaluation expectations and of bank failures. This causality pattern does not fit particularly well the story put forward by Brown, but it is important to recognize that Granger-causality tests are not designed to highlight contemporaneous causality. If foreign investors moved sufficiently quickly

---

[6] The sample is terminated in February 1933 because of the declaration of bank holidays in March 1933.

to ship gold out of the United States because of their devaluation fears, lagged expected realignment expectations may not explain gold flows in a monthly database.

To investigate this point further, we calculate the impulse responses of the VAR expressed in Equation 6.2. These are graphed in Figure 6.4, together with ±2 standard error bars. Ignoring the autoregressive tendencies given by the graphs on the leading diagonal, we interpret the results as follows. A shock to realignment expectations causes a purely contemporaneous gold flow in the expected direction but has no impact on bank failures (row 1). Similarly, gold flows have a contemporaneous impact on bank failures, together with a lagged effect on realignment expectations (row 2). Finally, in row 3, bank failures have a lagged effect on realignment expectations but no independent impact on gold flows. These results are fully compatible with Brown's hypothesis. An increase in devaluation expectations causes gold to flow out of the United States, which in turn causes bank failures to rise. Both the gold flows and bank failures serve to strengthen devaluation expectations with a lag.[7]

Our findings throw light on what has been a disputed international aspect of the Great Depression: Was the United States, in particular the Federal Reserve, hampered by its international commitments? Put differently, did the United States' commitment to the gold standard constrain expansionary monetary policy during the Depression up until March 1933 when the United States suspended the gold standard? Kindleberger (1986) takes the view that the key constraints were international ones, but he does not analyze statistically the matter of international monetary constraints on Federal Reserve policy. Eichengreen (1990) has demonstrated international interactions between *global* money supply, key currency backing of non-key currencies, and the maldistribution of gold toward the United States and France. But this is not the same thing as demonstrating that the leading key currency country itself, the United States, was constrained by international monetary events. Eichengreen (1992), *inter alia*, does show a keen awareness of the notion that U.S. monetary policy was most probably constrained by the fear of "endangering the gold parity" (p. 295). However, it has never been demonstrated statistically that this was the case. In contrast, Friedman and Schwartz (1963) take the contrary position, arguing that the Federal Reserve could have undertaken substantial

---

[7] It is well known that the ordering of variables in a VAR may change the properties of the impulse responses, and this is true in our case. Because we specifically chose the ordering to be in line with Brown's hypothesis, the strongest statement we can make is that the impulse responses provide evidence consistent with his story.

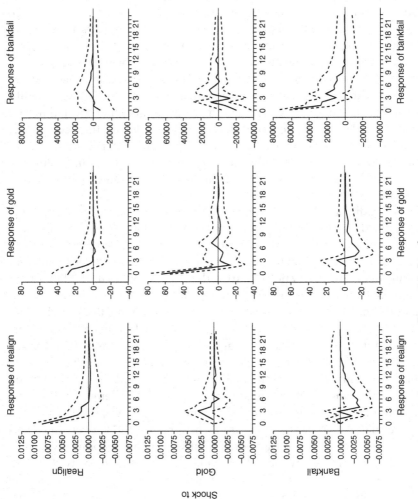

Figure 6.4. Impulse responses.

130

open-market purchases if it had really wanted to.[8] Epstein and Ferguson (1984) have challenged the latter's position using data on the Fed's open-market operations.[9]

Our evidence on U.S. monetary policy and international interactions supports the argument that the Federal Reserve's monetary policy was constrained by international considerations. The evidence is as follows. First, the fact that bank failures cause with a lag (on both the Granger causality and VAR tests) devaluation expectations suggests a domestic cause of the weakening of the United States' adherence to the gold standard. In other words, even more stringent monetary contraction and resulting bank failures would have caused even greater fragility of the dollar on the foreign exchanges. Even more significantly for our argument, we also find positive feedback from gold outflows to bank failures (a lagged effect on the Granger-causality tests and a contemporaneous effect from the VAR). That is, an international interaction was adversely affecting the U.S. banking system. Furthermore, gold outflows were having a lagged effect on dollar devaluation expectations (this time from both of our tests), which must also have been a worry for the Fed. These findings would seem to support the position of Kindleberger and Eichengreen rather than that of Friedman and Schwartz. The Federal Reserve was indeed being hemmed in by the United States' commitment to the gold standard. The Federal Reserve found itself in a dilemma: If it increased the money base to "save the banks," which it did try to do with open-market purchases in the spring and early summer of 1932, it was not playing by the rules of the game given the preponderance of gold outflows between September 1931 – when sterling left gold – and June 1932. However, if it did nothing, which turned out to be the preferred policy, this risked the bank failures that, as we have shown, also put pressure on the dollar. Under these circumstances, the United States' adherence to the gold standard was becoming untenable.

---

[8] Friedman and Schwartz (1963) wrote "that a shortage of free gold did not in fact seriously limit the alternatives open to the [Federal Reserve] System. The amount was at all times ample to support large open market purchases.... The problem of free gold was largely an *ex post* justification for policies followed, not an *ex ante* reason for them (p. 406).

[9] However, one may want to treat the Epstein and Ferguson (1984) results with caution for two reasons: (1) many of the significance levels are low even for one-tailed tests; (2) such tests are not appropriate when the hypothesized sign could be reversed (e.g., their hypothesis is for a negative relationship between currency inflow and open-market purchases, but if the Fed were to take inflows as a sign of confidence in the dollar, the sign would be reversed).

CONCLUSIONS

The pound was subjected to a short sharp speculative attack, which, owing to the precariousness of its gold reserves and balance of payments, it was able to weather for less than three months. After the fall of the pound, the attention of speculators turned to the U.S. dollar. But, largely owing to the greater strength of the U.S. balance of payments and gold reserve, it took nineteen months for the dollar to fall. A nine-month phase to June 1932 of speculative attack was overcome and gold began to return to the United States for the seven months to and including January 1933. Finally, however, another speculative attack, combined with the third banking crisis, lead to the United States suspending adherence to the gold standard.

What was driving exchange rate realignment expectations seem to be explained well by the relationships we have examined. We find support in our UK regression for the hypotheses that perverse monetary policies in the United Kingdom relative to the United States increased devaluation expectations. For the United States, we focus on the huge gold flows and bank failures that characterized the run-up to gold suspension. We provided results from a VAR analysis, which were fully consistent with the hypothesis of Brown (1940) that devaluation expectations caused a withdrawal of gold, which in turn precipitated waves of bank failures. In short, macroeconomic events, some of them directly or indirectly under the influence of the authorities, were ultimately responsible for both the United Kingdom and the United States leaving the gold standard during the inter-war period. But this is not necessarily to say that the authorities approximately played by "the rules of the game" for most of the inter-war experience with the gold standard. Only toward the end did they deviate sufficiently to bring the system down.

Acknowledgments

Reprinted from the *Explorations in Economic History*, 34 (2), C. Paul Hallwood, Ronald MacDonald, and Ian W. Marsh, "Crash! Expectational Aspects of the Departures of the United Kingdom and the United States from the Inter-War Gold Standard," pp. 174–194, Copyright (2003), with permission from Elsevier. MacDonald and Marsh gratefully acknowledge funding from the ESRC's Global Economic Institutions program (grant number L120–25–1014). The authors would like to thank Peter Temin and two anonymous referees for their comments on an earlier draft of this paper.

SEVEN

Did Impending War in Europe Help Destroy the Gold Bloc in 1936? An Internal Inconsistency Hypothesis

C. Paul Hallwood, Ronald MacDonald, and Ian W. Marsh

This chapter investigates how the Gold Bloc operated between France, the Netherlands, Switzerland, and Belgium, especially over the period after the United States left the gold standard in March 1933 to its end in September 1936. It inquires into the effect of military developments in Germany and Italy's Abyssinian incursion on the sustainability of the Gold Bloc between its members. We juxtaposed the views of some political scientists who see impending war in Europe as deeply and adversely affecting psychology in Europe, particularly France, and what may be called the "economic historians' view" that sees the demise of the Gold Bloc as being caused almost exclusively by economic factors. Developing concepts of internal (to the Gold Bloc) and external (or relative international price level) inconsistency, this chapter draws the conclusion that asymmetric military shocks impacting France were probably a factor in destroying the last vestiges of the gold standard.

To set the scene, it was not until Raymond Poincare formed a government in July 1926 based on conservative principles – no capital levy, reduced burden of taxes on the rich, and tight budgets – that capital returned to France and expectations of franc devaluation subsided. Thus began the "Franc Poincare," or strong-franc policy (Hautcoeur and Sicsic, 1999; Moure, 1991, 2002; Patat and Lutfalla, 1990). Stabilization was at 124 francs per pound in December 1926, with formal restoration of the gold standard in June 1928. Of the other main Gold Bloc members, Netherlands continued with the policy of *gulden financiereringregel* or "golden rule of finance," and remained very committed to maintaining the gold parity of the guilder ('t Hart, Jonker, and van Zanden, 1997, p. 151). Belgium uneasily adhered to the gold standard until problems in its banking system led to its ejection in March 1935 (Shepherd, 1936). Switzerland had for decades been committed to a pegged exchange rate regime, having been a founder member of the Latin Monetary Union. Following the latter's breakup, the Swiss National Bank declared in June 1925 that it would hold the Swiss franc between gold import and export points.

The credibility of the franc's gold peg was quickly established, as is shown in Hallwood, MacDonald, and Marsh (Chapter 2 of this volume, 2000a, 2000b), as soon as January 1927. It remained credible through the devaluations of the pound sterling in September 1931 and the U.S. dollar in March 1933 (Hallwood, MacDonald, and Marsh, 1997a, 1997b). The gold pegs of both Switzerland and Netherlands were also credible through to the end of the Gold Bloc in September 1936, largely because they applied a financial orthodoxy as strict as that as France (Bordo, Helbling, and James, 2006).

Various investigations show that adverse macroeconomic developments adequately explain the timing of the devaluations of the pound sterling in September 1931 and the U.S. dollar in March 1933. Perhaps because the franc was devalued only three and a half years later, also amid adverse economic circumstances – high unemployment, falling money supply, weak balance of payments – much of the economic history literature also points to macroeconomic causes as being responsible for the devaluation of the franc and the end of the Gold Bloc.[1] The other remaining players in the Gold Bloc, Switzerland and the Netherlands, announced that they too would devalue – because, according to Bordo, Helbling, and James (2006), they feared that their currencies would be next in line for speculative attack. In fact, as financial diplomacy at the Bank for International Settlements in early September 2006 reveals, both countries had prepared themselves for a devaluation of the French franc. L. J. A. Trip, President of the Netherlands Bank, said that "when action comes it will consist of the Netherlands leaving the gold standard and then holding the guilder around a certain rate vis a vis sterling." And the President of the Governing Board of the Swiss National Bank, G. Bachmann, said that he would "tie the Swiss franc to sterling in the event the French franc leaves the gold standard" (both quotations from Toniolo, 2005, p. 178).

However, we argue that shocks to confidence in an international monetary system may originate from outside the purely economic sphere, especially when war with a larger neighbor is in prospect. Contemporary sources referenced later in the chapter recognized that this was the case in the months prior to the devaluation of the French franc and the end of the

---

[1]   See Bernanke (1995), Cassiers (1995), Eichengreen (1992), Eichengreen and Temin (2000), Hautcoeur and Sicsic (1999), Hogg (1987), Sauvy (1984), Wandschneider (2008).

Gold Bloc on September 26, 1936, as do Homer (1963), Kirshner (2007), and Moure (1991).

Thus, beginning, at the latest, in the autumn of 1935, France faced foreign competition on two fronts: economic, due to the earlier devaluations of the pound sterling and the U.S. dollar; and military, due to developments in Germany, as well as adverse political developments for France stemming from the Italian invasion of Abyssinia. Deflationary budgetary policies could not simultaneously achieve increased international economic competitiveness *and* increased national security. This was clearly recognized by the government of Leon Blum when it came to power in June 1936. It changed French priorities from being the primacy of increasing international economic competitiveness through deflation, encouraged by successively tighter budgets and tight monetary policy, to the primacy of increasing national security through increased government spending on the military. Certainly military developments in Germany did have clear budgetary implications for France. Castillo, Lowell, Tellis, Munoz, and Zycher (2001), Conetta (2006), Einzig (1937b), Kirshner (2007), and Posen (1986) suggest that before this change in priorities, the French government had refused to finance a general military mobilization called for by France's own military because of its budgetary cost. Unfortunately, failure to spend on rearmament only deepened the contradiction between maintenance of the gold standard and national security.

It is relevant to our thesis that, according to Thomas (1992), prominent French historians of the Popular Front, such as Kergoat (1986), Lacouture (1982), and Renouvin (1981), emphasize the social programs introduced by the Popular Front. However, these were mainly completed as early as July 1936 and that "only Robert Frank's (1982) study of French rearmament in the five years prior to war acknowledges that the cost of the 1936 re-equipment program set the parameters for funding in all other fields" (Thomas, 1992, p. 659). It is possible, therefore, that the external inconsistency hypothesis expounded by economic historians is based on less than the broadest appreciation of the history of the Popular Front.

Considering military spending, Thomas (1992) explains that "[t]he process by which the French government turned from social reform to preoccupation with national defense was remarkably swift, having largely taken place by the time Finance Minister Vincent Auriol announced a heavy devaluation of the franc in September" (pp. 659–660). Moreover, it was also clear in the summer of 1936 that "the government was committed to re-equipment on an unprecedentedly large and *long-term scale*" (p. 667, italics added).

It cannot be said, therefore, that the departure of France from the gold standard in September 1936 was only to give it the freedom to reduce its price level so as to improve its domestic economic circumstances. It just as well can be argued that France became prepared to increase defense spending even if it meant abandoning the gold peg to meet the growing military threat. As an expert on inter-war French defense spending, Robert Frank said the government of Leon Blum did more for guns than butter.[2] And as Moure (1991, p. 256) points out, following the huge increase in French defense spending announced on September 7, 1936, two weeks *before* the devaluation of the French franc, gold losses rose sharply, taking in nearly a billion francs from September 11 to September 18 and 2.5 billion the following week. Our contention is that from some time in 1935, French capital recognized this contradiction between French economic and security policies and moved abroad. We find some empirical support for this contention in our event analysis.

France, in fact, faced several adverse non-economic developments in the international sphere in the few years before the devaluation of the franc. To pick out some of these, in the plebiscite of August 24, 1934, Hitler was allowed to combine the roles of President and Reich Chancellor – indicating a gathering threat to French security. Several foreign policy matters also did not go well for France: the London Naval Disarmament Conference (October 23–December 19, 1934) failed to achieve its objectives, and the Anglo-French Conference (February 1–3, 1935) failed to obtain German agreement on a pact of mutual assistance with governments in Eastern Europe. Shortly afterward, in March 1935, Germany announced that it would rearm and reintroduce conscription, thus abrogating both the Versailles and Locarno Treaties. It was on the former that France had based its postwar foreign and security policies (Schuker, 1976), but these had now been badly undermined. In October 1935, Italy invaded Abyssinia, which was a serious foreign policy setback for France. And in March 1936, German troops marched into the Rhineland – another abrogation of the Versailles Treaty, bringing German troops to the border with France.

We dub the view that the collapse of the Gold Bloc was caused by failure to reduce the French price level sufficiently quickly to the level of those countries that had already devalued against gold as the external inconsistency hypothesis.[3] In contrast, we present an alternative to the Gold Bloc inconsistency

---

[2] Quoted in Jackson (1988), p. 180.
[3] A dissenting contribution is Beaudry and Portier (2002), who argue that overvaluation of the French franc was not a major factor causing the Great Depression in France, because

hypothesis based on the historical fact that Germany posed an asymmetric military threat against France to a greater extent than it did against Switzerland or even the Netherlands. The neutrality of Switzerland is well known, that of the Netherlands is less so. The Dutch had, in fact, followed a policy of neutrality, or a "passive role in international politics," for a hundred years before the outbreak of World War I (Vandenbosch, 1927, 1959) and had been neutral during World War I. Moreover, "when international tensions began to increase after Germany reoccupied the Rhineland, Germany repeatedly reassured the Netherlands that it would respect its neutrality, an assurance that was repeated as late as August 1939" (Warmbrunn, 1963, p. 5).

On the assumption of an asymmetric military threat to France, the Gold Bloc broke under the strain of gold losses from France, in some measure to other Gold Bloc countries. Ultimately the French could not sustain these gold losses and had to abandon gold.

We proceed as follows: the first section sets out the international military-political context in which the franc was devalued. The second section discusses the economic context. The third section extends the discussion of the economic context with a statistical investigation of the internal consistency of the Gold Bloc's exchange rate regime. We find that exchange rate commitments between the members were not viewed in financial markets as being consistent with one another, implying that the Gold Bloc was not a credible target zone. An implication of this is that asymmetric shocks stemming from the military-political context were all the more potent. The fourth section discusses how short- and long-term interest rate behavior among the Gold Bloc four relates to our thesis of asymmetric military-political shocks playing a role in the Bloc's destruction. We find support for the notion that France's commitment to gold was adversely affected by Italy's invasion of Abyssinia, as well as Germany's reoccupation of the Rhineland. The fifth section examines post-gold bloc capital flows. It is pointed out that capital that had left the Netherlands and Switzerland in the run-up to their abandonment of gold returned to these countries during 1937, as it had to Belgium following its devaluation in March–April 1935. However, neither foreign capital nor French capital returned to France during the same year. This set of observations is consistent with the asymmetric military-political shock hypothesis: In financial markets, German remilitarization was seen as more of a problem for France than for the other Gold Bloc members. The sixth section contains our conclusions.

---

international trade was too small a percentage of GDP (p. 86). However, that line of analysis is quite different to ours.

Table 7.1. *Four major events used in the event analysis*

1. March 16, 1935	Germany reintroduces conscription, which was against the Versailles Treaty.
2. October 1935	Italy invades Abyssinia – a foreign policy disaster for France.
3. March 7, 1936	Germany reoccupies the Rhineland, which was against the Versailles Treaty and Locarno Pact, and was a military and another foreign policy disaster for France.
4. June 1936	The Popular Front forms a government – a challenge to the financial orthodoxy.

THE INTERNATIONAL MILITARY-POLITICAL CONTEXT

Table 7.1 picks out four major events that could be expected to affect the credibility of the franc's gold peg. The first three are major foreign military-political developments; the fourth is the formation of a government by the left-wing Popular Front that is widely accepted as challenging the financial orthodoxy of the Bank of Franc.

Event 1 was a serious setback for France as it indicated both that the Treaty of Versailles had become unworkable and Germany was certainly moving to remilitarize. Event 2, Mussolini's invasion of Abyssinia in October 1935, was also a debacle for French foreign policy. In the vain hope of drawing up an alliance with Italy against Germany, France had acted to thwart the League of Nations' sanctions against Italy, imposed because of the latter's invasion. Shirer sums up this failure of French foreign policy: "Because of its hesitations and the devious policies of [Prime Minister] Laval, the French government had lost all: Italy as an ally against Germany, the military backing of Russia, Great Britain as a close partner, the League of Nations as a potential force in halting aggression" (Shirer, 1969, p. 250).

Most disastrous of all for French security, however, was Event 3, the German reoccupation of the Rhineland in March 1936. German military forces moved closer to France, and French foreign policy in Eastern Europe was virtually destroyed – both because French land forces were blocked from moving eastward, and because the East Europeans, realizing this, began to look elsewhere for their own security. Of the Rhineland invasion Shirer writes, "The whole structure of European peace and security set up in 1919 collapsed (Shirer, 1969, p. 281). Capital immediately began to leave France, as the Bank of France confirmed.[4] Paul Einzig (1937b) reports a

---

[4] *Annual Report* of the Bank of France, p. 309 in Federal Reserve *Bulletin*, April 1937.

run on the banks in northern and northeastern France in March 1936, thus linking financial disturbances in France to German military events. Einzig also reports wealthy French streaming across the English Channel to London carrying currency and gold for deposit in British banks, which were so swamped that they ran out of safe deposit boxes. In England, this gold was safe from an occupying German army.

It is possible to argue, therefore, that military developments in Germany and Italy, combined with French failures to combat them, undermined the confidence of the French not so much in the franc as in the survival of France itself. This is especially so as surely more people than just Pierre Flandin, the Foreign Minister in March 1936, had the prescience to say that "once Germany had fortified the Rhineland, Czechoslovakia would be lost and that, soon after, general war would become unavoidable."[5]

Thus, when one considers the international military and political position of France in the spring of 1936, there is a clear inconsistency between crumbling confidence in national security and a strong franc. This inconsistency should be contrasted with the oft-stated inconsistency between reflation and a strong franc.

ECONOMIC FACTORS

When Britain and the United States devalued, along with other countries in their respective currency areas, France and the Gold Bloc countries were adversely affected. As they were set against devaluation to compete internationally, they had to reduce their own price levels through a process of disinflation – which was advocated by the financial orthodoxy of the Bank of France and the governments that it supported politically.[6] In fact, all leading political parties in France, including the Popular Front, were set against devaluation.

Unfortunately, the process of price deflation in the Gold Bloc was drawn out and incurred huge costs in terms of lost output.[7] French industrial

---

[5]   Quoted by Kissinger (1994), p. 305.
[6]   A fuller analysis of the French economic predicament would be on the lines of the monetary approach to the balance of payment (Dornbusch, 1973; Johnson and Frenkel, 1976). McCloskey and Zecher (1976) apply this theory to the classical gold standard. Thus, devaluations by the United Kingdom and the United States in the early 1930s raised their price levels and encouraged hoarding (in excess of domestic credit creation). This was satisfied by increases in base money through their balance of payments, the Gold Bloc countries being a source of dishoarding.
[7]   See Eichengreen (1992), chapter 12 for a description of the prolonged Depression in France.

production in May 1935 was 36 percent below its peak in May 1930 and had fallen quite steadily over the interval. The wholesale price level halved between early 1929 and August 1935. The merchandise balance was negative from 1928 to the end of our period in 1936. Gold and foreign exchange reserves were 37 percent lower in December 1936 than they had been in early 1931. The aggregate monetary measure M2 was 10 percent lower in September 1936 than it had been in February 1933. Deposits at commercial banks fell by much more.[8] Still, the Bank of France continued staunchly to defend the franc with tight money. Indeed, from 1931, the French real money base increased least among the four Gold Bloc countries. Successive deflationary packages were implemented (the last of them in July and November 1935). With the French public wearied of the depression but still set against devaluation, they increasingly turned to the Popular Front, which stood for the contradictory policy of reflation without devaluation (Eichengreen, 1992).

EXCHANGE RATE BEHAVIOR

We begin our analysis of the Gold Bloc and its collapse with a consideration of how soundly the four members were viewed in financial markets as being wedded to the gold standard. If a country is thought by financial markets to be securely tied to gold, its exchange rate should be mean-reverting (Krugman, 1991). That is, if an exchange rate is near either of the gold points, especially the gold export point where the currency is weak, it should tend to revert toward the center of the band rather than to bump along one of its edges. To test for mean reversion of Gold Bloc exchange rates, we use the variance ratio test, originally proposed in the economics literature by Cochrane (1988) and previously used to test for mean reversion of exchange rates under the classical gold standard by Hallwood, MacDonald, and Marsh (Chapter 1 of this volume).[9] For that period, the French franc was found to be a mean-reverting currency, securely on the gold standard. The variance ratio test is discussed in Chapter 1.

The results of our variance ratio tests for the Gold Bloc period are reported in Table 7.2, for lag lengths K = 2 through to K = 30. In sum, and in contrast to the results reported for other gold standard periods, the results here show no sign of exchange rate mean reversion for any of the four currencies

---

[8] Source of this data is League of Nations, *Monthly Bulletin of Statistics*, various issues.
[9] Exchange rate data abstracted from Board of Governors of the Federal Reserve System (1943), *Banking and Monetary Statistics*, Washington, DC.

Table 7.2. *Variance ratio test for mean reversion of Gold Bloc exchange rates, December 1926–September 1936*

Lag length	K = 2	K = 5	K = 10	K = 30
Currency				
V1 Be Franc	1.73	3.21	4.48	2.57
	(0.08)	(0.00)	(0.00)	(0.01)
V2 Be Franc	1.52	2.70	3.37	0.63
	(0.12)	(0.00)	(0.00)	(0.52)
V1 Fr Franc	1.88	1.81	2.23	4.22
	(0.06)	(0.07)	(0.03)	(0.00)
V2 Fr Franc	1.69	1.41	1.44	1.34
	(0.09)	(0.16)	(0.15)	(0.18)
V1 Sw Franc	1.68	1.59	1.24	3.50
	(0.09)	(0.11)	(0.21)	(0.00)
V2 Sw Franc	1.52	1.24	1.95	1.15
	(0.13)	(0.21)	(0.05)	(0.25)
V1 Ne Guilder	1.52	2.09	2.72	4.08
	(0.13)	(0.04)	(0.01)	(0.00)
V2 Ne Guilder	1.80	1.79	2.09	1.88
	(0.07)	(0.07)	(0.04)	(0.06)

Notes: V1 denotes the variance ratio calculated with a finite sample correction, and V2 is the corresponding ratio without such a correction (see Wright, 2000). Numbers in parenthesis are heteroscedasticity robust p-values.

against each other. The results are read in the following way. For each currency we present two variants of the variance ratio test – V1 and V2. The former is calculated using a small sample correction, which is likely to be important in the current application, whereas the latter is not. The column headings K = 2 to K = 30 denote the lag lengths (number of months) used to calculate the variance ratio test. Numbers in parenthesis denote p-values. The results are unambiguous because all apart from one cell entry (V2 and K = 30 for the Belgian franc) exhibit super persistence and an absence of mean reversion.

We conclude from this that in the inter-war period, the Gold Bloc countries were never securely based on gold, and the system was therefore vulnerable to either economic or military shocks. Interestingly, Ritschl and Wolf (2003) throw light as to why Gold Bloc countries' cross exchange rates were not strongly mean-reverting: The Gold Bloc members were not well trade-integrated with each other. Specifically, the 1928 trade patterns did not "predict" membership of the Gold Bloc, whereas they did so for the Reichsmark bloc and the sterling bloc, which were both formed after sterling was knocked off gold in September 1931. We move on to see whether internal inconsistency was indeed a factor in causing the collapse of the Gold Bloc.

INTEREST RATES

We use Switzerland as a "base" country as it was much less likely to become embroiled in a new world war than was France. Indeed, "Switzerland enjoyed unusual political and economic stability for almost a century and a half. Beleaguered but untouched by two world wars, the small nation became a symbol of neutrality and a safe haven for refugee capital" (Homer, 1963, p. 470). The Netherlands too is used as a base country as it had for long been a neutral country, as previously mentioned. We assume that changes in French interest rates relative to Swiss and Dutch rates capture at least some of the asymmetric shock of German remilitarization on the internal coherence of the Gold Bloc.

To pick out the effect of military-political events on the internal inconsistency of the Gold Bloc, we turn to a discussion of:

1. Behavior of short-term interest rates of other Gold Bloc countries against France.[10] From the theory of uncovered interest rate parity, a rise in French short-term interest rates relative to those of another member indicates expected depreciation of the French franc.[11]
2. Yield gap analysis – a rise in short-term rates relative to long rates generally indicates worsening economic conditions.[12]

Short-Term Interest Rates in the Gold Bloc

Figure 7.1 shows the short-term interest rate spread (private discount rates). Negative values indicate higher French short-term rates. The four events listed in Table 7.1 are marked in calendar order in Figure 7.1.

The behavior of relative interest rates after Event 1 does not support the internal inconsistency hypothesis, as French rates tended to fall rather than

---

[10] Short-term interest rate data for France, the Netherlands, and Switzerland was collected from the Board of Governors of the Federal Reserve System (1943), *Banking and Monetary Statistics*, Washington, DC.

[11] Given the estimates by Officer (1993), a rise in relative interest rates of about 0.5% is enough to move expectations outside of the gold points.

[12] France: long bond, 3% irredeemable government bond; the Netherlands: 2.5%–3% irredeemable government bond; Switzerland: State and Federal 3.5% railways bond. Data collected from League of Nations Statistical Yearbook, various issues.

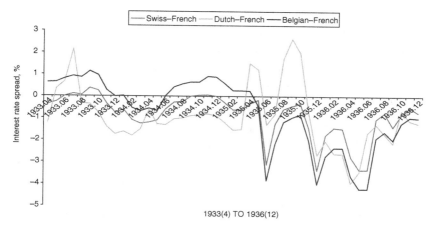

Figure 7.1. Short-term interest rate spread, %.

rise compared with those in the other three countries. However, the behavior of French short-term interest rates following Event 2, Italy's Abyssinian adventure, with its serious consequences for French foreign policy, does conform to the internal inconsistency hypothesis.[13] So too does Event 3 – the Rhineland reoccupation by German forces. Thus, there is evidence here supporting the internal inconsistency of the gold bloc beginning in the autumn of 1935, but not before.

Yield Gaps

Another way to indicate the effect of German remilitarization on the internal consistency of the Gold Bloc is to compare French and Swiss interest rate gaps (long minus short rates)[14]. A rise in the short-term interest rate

[13] Thus, "When the tension in Europe over the Ethiopian situation reached a critical point last autumn [1935], there was a heavy transfer of funds from London to New York, and other times international political developments abroad appear to have stimulated the flow of capital" (Federal Reserve *Bulletin*, July 1936, p. 511). The Swiss National Bank in its *Annual Report* for 1935 also linked the Abyssinian situation to interest rate developments. Thus, "Economic sanctions decreed by the League of Nations against Italy and made effective on November 18th, 1935, created a new barrier to international trade" (*Annual Report* reprinted in Federal Reserve *Bulletin*, May 1935, p. 344). These last two quotations from central bank reports make a clear link between the Abyssinia invasion, constrained international trade, and speculation against the French franc – occurring in the same month as the League of Nations sanctions.

[14] French yield curve: 3% irredeemable government bonds minus one-month private discount rate. Swiss yield curve: 3.5% federal and state railway bonds less one-month private discount rate. Source: League of Nations, various issues.

relative to the long rate is often taken as a sign of economic and/or financial weakness (Dotsey, 1998; Mishkin, 1995, and references therein). Under a pegged exchange rate regime such as the gold standard, a rise in short-term interest rates indicates a lack of trust in the stability of the value in foreign currency of short-dated securities. Lower interest rates on long-term securities, or at least a rise in short rates relative to long rates, may indicate the expectation of a long-term weakening in the real economy. That is, a steeper yield curve – for which the yield gap proxies – is associated with increased levels of economic activity and a flattening of it with reduced activity. In particular, a yield curve flattening may occur with a combination of a rise in short-term interest rates and a negative shock to expected real economic activity. We argue that military-political shocks (emanating from Germany and Italy) on France would indeed cause short-term interest rates to rise relative to long rates. In 1936, French short-term interest rates did rise – to stem a capital outflow – while it is arguable that prospects for the French real economy would also have been adversely affected.

Of interest, therefore, is how the French yield gap (French long-rate minus French short-rate) behaved relative to the comparable Swiss yield gap (Swiss long-rate minus Swiss short-rate). Figure 7.2 shows time series of French-Swiss short-term and long-term interest rate differentials.

Figure 7.3 indicates the extent of the relative shifts in French-Swiss yield gaps.[15] All three military-political Events listed in Table 7.1 are followed one month later by a worsening of the French position – a relative flattening of its yield curve – a behavior conforming to the internal inconsistency hypothesis. Moreover, Event 4 – the coming to power of the Popular Front, with its supposed challenge to the financial orthodoxy – did not lead to a worsening of the French relative situation; indeed, its relative yield gap steepened in July and August, only to worsen in September following the announcement of a huge increase in French defense spending.

The yield gap picture is similar when comparing France with the Netherlands. Figure 7.4 shows French minus Dutch short and long interest differentials from March 1933 to December 1936.[16] Figure 7.5 shows the French yield gap minus that of the Netherlands. The event analysis

---

[15] The time series in Figure 7.3 is calculated using the following interest rates (French long–French short) – (Swiss long–Swiss short).

[16] The shorter period for Dutch data compared with that of France or Switzerland is due to the Netherland Bank temporarily publishing relevant interest rate data quarterly rather than monthly in the middle of our data period. The French interest rate data is as defined earlier. That of the Netherlands is the private discount rate as proxying for Dutch short-term interest rates, and government 2.5%–3% irredeemable bonds for long rates.

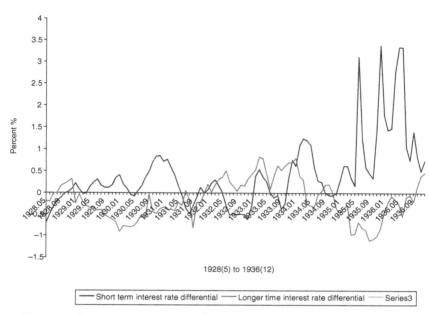

Figure 7.2. French minus Swiss monthly short and long interest rate differentials.

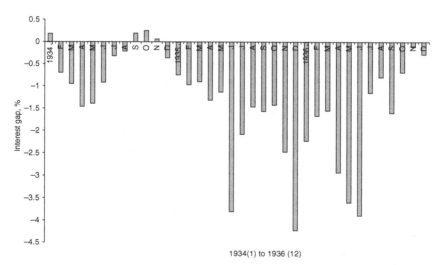

Figure 7.3. French minus Swiss interest rate gaps.

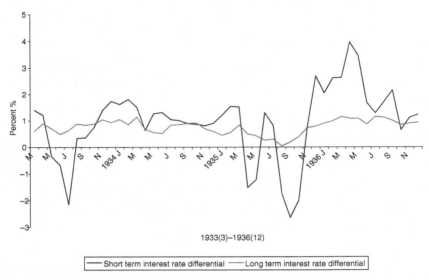

Figure 7.4. French minus Dutch short and long interest differentials.

is similar in the France-Netherlands case compared to what it is in the France-Switzerland case. Event 1 listed in Table 7.1 is not, in fact, followed by a flattening of the relative French yield gap, and thus does not conform to the internal inconsistency hypothesis. However, both Events 2 and 3 do so. Again, we see that the yield gap steepened following the election of the Popular Front, only to flatten later, beginning one month before the announcement of the large increase in French defense spending.

POST-DEVALUATION CAPITAL FLOWS

Following the currency devaluations of September 1936 and the Tripartite Agreement to stabilize the foreign exchanges between France, the United Kingdom, and the United States (in short order joined by Switzerland, the Netherlands, and Belgium), it can be argued using the external inconsistency hypothesis that capital outflows from the former Gold Bloc members would reverse themselves as investors repatriated capital from abroad to take their profits. However, if German remilitarization was a factor alarming wealth holders in equal measure in each of the Gold Bloc members, it is entirely possible that capital placed abroad would not return to them. In fact, in the final quarter of 1936, the international bullion and specie balances of the Netherlands and Switzerland (as well as Belgium, which had re-pegged to gold following its devaluation of March–April 1935) were in

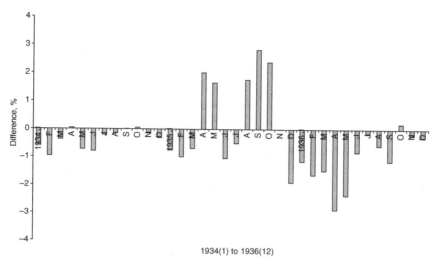

Figure 7.5. French minus Dutch interest rate gaps.

surplus as flight capital began to be repatriated to these countries. The Swiss National Bank reported "large amounts of Swiss and foreign gold coins ... as well as gold bullion reappeared at the window of the Bank" following the Swiss franc's devaluation.[17] In the last three months of 1936, following the end of the Gold Bloc, the gold holdings of the Swiss and Dutch central banks increased, respectively, by 611 million Swiss francs and 150 million florins (Bank for International Settlements, 1937, p. 46).

However, the bullion and specie balance of France remained strongly negative, signifying that net capital outflow continued despite the French devaluation. The juxtaposition of the behavior of these capital flows lends support to the hypothesis that German remilitarization did indeed have an asymmetric effect on the Gold Bloc members, with France being the one most adversely affected.

Comments in central bank annual reports also support the asymmetric military shock hypothesis. Uncertainties in France were more severe than in the other former Gold Bloc countries because, as the *Annual Report* of the Netherlands Bank, 1937–1938 noted, France was the only one of the six main gold-holding countries to lose monetary gold during 1937.[18] The

---

[17] Annual Report, 1936, p. 321, in Federal Reserve *Bulletin*, April 1937.
[18] The six main holders of gold at the end of 1937, with 82% of the world's monetary gold stock, were the United States, the United Kingdom, France, the Netherlands, Switzerland, and Belgium (Netherland Bank, p. 659).

other former Gold Bloc countries – the Netherlands, Switzerland, and Belgium – all gained gold that year. The value of gold held by the Netherland Bank increasing enormously, by 59 percent, in the year to March 31, 1938 (p. 663).[19] Moreover, so strong was the flow of funds to Switzerland in 1937, threatening both exchange rate and price level stability, that the Swiss National Bank established a "Gentlemen's Agreement" with Swiss banks to reduce the "excessive volume of foreign deposits held by the banks in Swiss currency" (Swiss National Bank, Annual Report).[20] As to France, the Netherland Bank *Annual Report, 1937–38* said that "permanent restoration of confidence in the financial and monetary position of France, with a consequent repatriation of French capital and a return flow of gold to France" was yet to occur (p. 659).

CONCLUSIONS

We distinguish two different but not necessarily mutually exclusive causes of the abandonment of gold by the Gold Bloc members (France, the Netherlands, and Switzerland) in September 1936 – the external and internal inconsistency hypotheses. The external inconsistency hypothesis, extant in the economic history literature, takes the form of an argument that economic causes – high price levels in the Gold Bloc relative to non– Gold Bloc countries (such as the United States and the United Kingdom) – exerted deflationary pressures in the Gold Bloc that eventually became intolerable. Our alternative internal inconsistency hypothesis is that the Gold Bloc became unworkable because of asymmetric military-political shocks emanating from Germany and Italy adversely affected confidence in the French franc to a greater extent than either the Swiss franc or the Dutch guilder.

Thus, France was in a bind: maintain tight budgets to defend the franc now but risk falling behind militarily vis-á-vis Germany, thus risking the franc later. The financial orthodoxy could not have it both ways – it could not have constrained military spending in the early to mid-1930s as well as greater (than it in fact had) military security in the late 1930s. The financial orthodoxy of the Bank of France was self-defeating because the threat to the franc was not just greater international economic competition, but also greater military competition from Germany. To deal with the former, financial orthodoxy demanded ever tighter budgets and deflation in France.

---

[19] Page numbers in this paragraph are those in Federal Reserve *Bulletin*, August 1938.
[20] Federal Reserve *Bulletin*, May 1938, p. 362.

However, to deal with the latter, France needed larger budgets, especially to finance the French military: more than just the fortification of the Maginot Line was needed; so was new weaponry, something that its military was starved of. The franc fell anyway, and it did so almost exactly three years before the outbreak of World War II, in part, at least, because wealth holders moved their money to places where it would be safer – outside France. It is not possible quantitatively to disentangle the relative contributions of foreign economic and military competition on the fall of the franc in September 1936 as statistically their effects confounded one another. Certainly, the Blum government abandoned financial orthodoxy but it did so not only to revive the French economy, but also to revive the French military by devoting a massive increase in government spending to it.

We find some support for the internal inconsistency hypothesis. In particular we show that short-term interest rates rose in France relative to the Netherlands, Switzerland, and Belgium concurrent with some military events in Germany that posed – at least for a time – an asymmetric threat to France. Italy's Abyssinian incursion is also found adversely to have affected the French franc. Moreover, we find that at critical moments the French yield gap flattened relative to those of both Switzerland and the Netherlands – events that we interpret as showing both declining confidence in the French franc and an expected relative worsening expected long-run economic conditions in France.

PART FOUR

BRETTON WOODS

EIGHT

Sterling in Crisis 1964–1967

Michael D. Bordo, Ronald Macdonald, and Michael J. Oliver

INTRODUCTION

The Bretton Woods agreement in July 1944 established an international monetary framework that would overcome the perceived problems of the inter-war period, especially the perceptions that floating exchange rates and capital flows (hot money movements) were a key source of the instability of the 1930s and that international co-operation had failed. The implicit goals of the system were exchange rate stability and trade liberalisation. The former was to be achieved by countries operating a pegged but adjustable exchange rate and the latter through the acceptance of current account convertibility. Once the European members declared current account convertibility in December 1958, however, the system quickly evolved into a gold dollar standard with many of the flaws of the inter-war gold exchange standard combined with some new ones: the inability of the adjustable peg to adjust because of fear of the speculative attack that would ensue if even the hint of devaluation were made; and the inability to seal off capital flows (Bordo, 1993). These flaws opened up the prospects of currency crises in the face of inconsistency between domestic financial policies and/or changing competitiveness and the declared peg.

One of the most vulnerable currencies to speculative attacks was sterling and one of the key dramas of the demise of Bretton Woods was the series of sterling crises between 1964 and 1967. The 1964–1967 period has long fascinated academics, and with the release of new papers from the archives, important new questions can be raised about the management of sterling in this period.[1] This chapter focuses on the speculative attacks of

[1] The best contemporary sources include Brandon (1966), Davis (1968), Stewart (1977) and the account in the *Sunday Times* on November 26, 1967. The standard accounts of the

the 1964–1967 period and the behaviour of reserves. Sterling acted as the second reserve currency of the international monetary system after the dollar and because of this was defended against speculative attacks by exchange-market intervention,[2] especially forward market operations by the Bank of England (henceforth "the Bank") and by the protection of the United Kingdom's foreign exchange reserves. Reserves were the key measure of the status of the defence of sterling, and understanding the management of the crises between 1964 and 1967 hinges on an analysis of reserves.

There are two analytical approaches to explaining the behaviour of international reserve inter-temporally. The first, which we may label the theory of international reserves, is essentially partial equilibrium in nature and posits that observed reserves respond to discrepancies between desired and actual reserves held by a country, and in this literature much of the focus is on the adequacy of international reserves on a global basis (Clark, 1970; Grubel, 1971). The second approach takes a macroeconomic perspective and draws on the classic monetary approach to the balance of payments (MABP), which in turn is largely a variant of the Humean price-specie-flow mechanism (Frenkel and Johnson, 1976). In summary, in this view, excessive movements in the supply of money relative to the demand for money will produce equal and offsetting reserve movements for a small open economy with a fixed exchange rate and facing perfect capital mobility. In the MABP, therefore, reserve changes are essentially a residual term, and this seems to contradict the theory of international reserves. However, the two approaches can be reconciled once it is recognised that if there is a stable demand for international reserves, domestic credit cannot be exogenous (Edwards, 1984).

On the face of it, a strict application of the MABP to the UK position in the 1960s would seem to imply that the large reserve losses sustained in the 1960s, owing to the large balance-of-payments deficit, should have led to a currency devaluation much sooner than the actuality. However, for a country which is not small, which faces less-than-perfect capital mobility, and whose currency was regarded as a reserve currency (i.e. was held for reasons other than the settlement of transactions) – which seems to be a better description of the position of the United Kingdom in the 1960s than the baseline MABP model – the link between changes in the money supply

period include Brittan (1971) and Cairncross and Eichengreen (2003). For a recent revival of interest in sterling's travails between 1964 and 1967, see Bale (1999), Dockrill (2002), Middleton (2002), Newton (2009), Roy (2000) and Schenk (2002).
[2]   In the United Kingdom as well as the United States. See Bordo, Humpage and Schwartz (2006).

and reserves would not necessary be equal and opposite, thereby postponing the inevitable day of reckoning. Nonetheless, of course, the underlying MABP relationship still existed for the United Kingdom in the 1960s, as the very large UK balance-of-payments deficit in the period demonstrate, and so understanding why the inevitable devaluation of sterling did not occur until the late 1960s indicates that the institutional structure within which the monetary-reserve relationship is embedded is important for understanding the sterling crisis in the 1960s, and that is the key focus of this chapter.

This chapter is divided into five sections. The second section provides a chronology of the sterling crises from 1964 to 1967. The third section examines evidence from credibility tests to show that the sterling peg was often not credible and that the speculative attacks were justified. The fourth section presents new daily data on sterling reserves from the archives of the Bank, which show that UK reserves were lower than official estimates at the time and in worse shape than policy makers admitted to the general public and their own creditors. The fifth section examines the relationship between reserves and the exchange rate (the expected rate of realignment) as well as the Bank's reaction function for reserves. Consistent with first-generation speculative attack models (adjusted for the presence of partial capital controls), we find that reserve movements driven by monetary and fiscal indiscipline are a key driver of the expected rate of realignment. We also show that the Bank was responsive to lagged exchange rate changes – a leaning-against-the-wind effect – and was also sensitive to movements of the exchange rate with respect to the exchange rate band. Finally, we offer some conclusions.

CHRONOLOGY OF STERLING CRISES

At the outset of this chapter we need to be clear about what constitutes a currency crisis. According to Bordo and Schwartz (1996, p. 438), a currency crisis is a "market-based attack on the exchange value of a currency. It involves a break with earlier market judgment about the exchange value of a currency. If a devaluation, which also involves a change in the peg, does not occur because of market pressure, it does not qualify as a currency crisis." A similar definition has been employed in the study by Bordo et al. (2001, p. 55), but they also add an international bailout to the list of qualifying criteria.

Based on these criteria, there were several sterling crises after 1945. Two of the most damaging to sterling's status as a reserve currency had been the ill-fated attempt at convertibility in July 1947 and the devaluation of September 1949, when the pound sterling was devalued from $4.03 to $2.80 (Cairncross, 1985, pp. 121–164; Cairncross, Eichengreen and Sterling, 2003, pp. 111–155).[3] Although the proximate cause of these and subsequent crises was due to a combination of substantial deficits in the government's international transactions (which were responsible for the weakness in the current account balance) and the scale of overseas direct and portfolio investment (which put the overall balance of payments into deficit), they also reflected some fundamental weaknesses with the British economy, such as the lack of competitiveness (Hirsch, 1965; Middleton, 2002).

Contemporaries pointed out that one of the impediments to faster growth in the 1950s was the attempt by the Conservative government to fine-tune the economy (referred to as "stop-go"), which "caused (or failed to restrain) faster growth than could be sustained, which then had later to be restrained" (Dow, 1964; Dow, 1998, p. 263). The pursuit of higher growth was undertaken with the sole objective of keeping unemployment (artificially) low using very crude macroeconomic tools. This created cyclical instability which generated additional costs and uncertainty for businesses, adversely impacting on the marginal efficiency of capital and the inducement to invest. These stop-go economic policies were also inextricably linked to the deep-seated balance-of-payments problems of the British economy, namely that weak export growth could not support the full employment level of imports (Middleton, 1996, pp. 42–43).

Although the United Kingdom held official reserves to counter a "run" on the pound sterling, these were inadequate by themselves to offset a major attack on sterling, and on occasions (e.g. 1956 and 1961) it was necessary to seek short-term central bank assistance through the Bank for International Settlements (BIS) or the International Monetary Fund (IMF). The low level of reserves became a further concern for policy makers for two reasons. First, sterling was a reserve currency and if it was forced off its parity then the U.S. dollar would likely become more vulnerable to speculative attack. Secondly, foreign banks and monetary authorities overseas held sterling-denominated reserves, known as the "sterling balances." At the end of 1945, the United Kingdom's gross sterling liabilities stood at £3,602 million and by the end of 1963 these had risen to £4,232 million. The worry for the Bank was that the value of the sterling balances exceeded its foreign exchange reserves and could have grave repercussions if these funds were repatriated

---

[3]   See also "Treasury Historical Memorandum No. 4: Convertibility crisis of 1947," The National Archives, Kew, London (hereafter TNA) T267/4.

to London and presented for exchange for U.S. dollars or other convertible currencies (Schenk, 1994).[4] This might not have been a cause for concern if the balance-of-payments deficits had not led to a persistent fear that the pound might be devalued. A devalued pound would mean that the Bank would be faced with demands for compensation from overseas sterling holders and it would most likely be co-opted to offering costly guarantees against future exchange risks.

By early 1964, the generally accepted view had been that the deficit on current account would continue to grow, the outflow of long-term capital would be above the 1963 figure and the overall balance of payments would continue to deteriorate (Blackaby, 1978, pp. 24–25; NEDC, 1964; National Institute Economic Review, 1964, p. 9). Despite this, there was no widespread call for devaluation by economists, and the Treasury and Bank were also opposed to a change in parity. They argued that devaluation would severely strain Britain's relations with other countries, particularly the Sterling Area, where the main holders of sterling would begin to withdraw their balances from London; threaten the stability of the international monetary system by throwing into question the practice of reserve currencies; and finally provoke retaliatory measures in Western Europe and a "scramble for gold" as the future of the dollar would be put into question.[5]

Upon taking office in October 1964, the Labour government announced its intention to end stop-go economic management and shifted its strategy towards an emphasis on incomes policy and selective intervention to improve the industrial structure of the economy (Tomlinson, 2004). The triumvirate of the Prime Minister, Chancellor of the Exchequer and the First Secretary of State quickly denounced devaluation as a solution to Britain's economic difficulties. However, this economic strategy – famously described by the Prime Minister's economic adviser, Thomas Balogh, as "the third way" – was ill-equipped to address the frequent short-term crises of confidence which gripped sterling in the foreign exchange markets.

The short-run prospects for the balance of payments were grim. Ten days after taking office, the government publicised that the balance-of-payments deficit for 1964 was going to be £800 million. This announcement was accompanied by some details about the government's long-term strategy for dealing with the balance of payments, but this did not go far enough to placate the deteriorating market sentiment about sterling.

---

[4] "Treasury Historical Memorandum No. 16: Sterling Balances Since the War," TNA T267/29.
[5] "Devaluation," GB (64) 61, October 15, 1964, TNA T171/758.

Following a neutral budget in November, the foreign exchange markets began to lose confidence in the ability of the government to keep the parity at $2.80, and sterling came under heavy pressure beginning November 11. There was an inordinate delay in raising the Bank Rate and by the time it was increased from 5 per cent to 7 per cent on November 23, it did not stem further heavy reserve losses over the following two days. If the Governor of the Bank, Rowley Cromer, had not managed to secure $3 billion of credits from other central banks on November 25, the Labour government would have been forced to devalue or float the pound sterling (Cairncross, 1996, p. 105).

Following this first sterling crisis, the pound remained weak throughout December 1964 and into the first few months of 1965, as doubts persisted about whether $2.80 could be defended unless further deflation was forthcoming. Sterling was undersold heavily during March 1965, although the Budget on April 6 and some tough talking by the Prime Minister in New York a week later did modify some of the pressure for the rest of the month into May. In June, however, trade figures were released for May and showed a heavy deficit. This revived doubts about whether the United Kingdom had really addressed its basic economic problems.

A second sterling crisis began in July 1965, prompted by a remark from the Chancellor on July 15 that no new measures were needed to strengthen the British economy, despite published reserves and trade figures which failed to show any real recovery (Cairncross and Eichengreen, 2003, pp. 177–178). Sterling was sold heavily on the exchanges in the week ending July 24, and further measures were announced on the July 27 to reduce public expenditure, tighten credit, and make Exchange Control more effective. The markets were not convinced that the crisis was under control, however, and two news items provoked heavy and widespread selling and renewing rumours about a possible devaluation. First, the reserve statement for the end of July was published on August 3, and although it was reported that £50 million had been lost, it was known that the United Kingdom had received a special receipt of £41 million from Germany, prompting suggestions that the true loss was more than £100 million. Secondly, it was announced that President Johnson had met with the Chairman of the Federal Reserve and had drawn pessimistic conclusions about sterling. This prompted a further run on the pound between August 3 and 6. Following the publication of July trade figures on August 10 – which showed record exports and a deficit of only £5 million – the market began to stabilise and the sentiment began to improve. New international support for sterling totalling $925 million was arranged by several European countries, the United States and Canada on September 10, 1965. Between September 1965 and March 1966, confidence returned and the spot rate strengthened.

Between March and May 1966, however, signs of weakness began to appear. First, there was some nervousness about the outcome of the general election campaign, but this disappeared with the re-election of the Labour government. Secondly, the Budget at the beginning of May had introduced some new taxes, but this failed to give sterling a significant boost and following indifferent trade figures and the outbreak of the seamen's strike, sterling was sold and confidence took a dip. The third sterling crisis occurred between June and August 1966, and it reached its peak in July when confidence in sterling collapsed and the government was forced to announce a wide-ranging package of measures. These included an increase in Bank Rate from 6 per cent to 7 per cent; tightening of Hire Purchase; travel restrictions; a six-month standstill of wages and prices; and cuts in public expenditure (Cairncross and Eichengreen, 2003, p. 180). In September 1966, another package of aid for sterling was assembled totalling $400 million, and the Federal Reserve Bank of New York increased its swap facility to $1.3 billion from $750 million which had been granted at the time of the first sterling crises in November 1964.

From September 1966 to April 1967, there was again a period of recovery in sterling. Bank Rate was gradually reduced to 5.5 per cent in early May, and policy makers began to express hopes that the balance of payments would be in surplus by the end of 1967. It was not long before this second "false dawn" came to an end. In May and June 1967, there was a sharp break in confidence, as bad trade figures were published and tensions rose in the Middle East. Both events pushed the spot rate down, and unease continued into July and August with the closure of the Suez Canal, rumours of Arab sales of sterling, the publication of further bad trade figures and rising unemployment. As sterling came under pressure, the press began to discuss the likelihood of devaluation, which was also stimulated because the government had made a formal application to enter the European Economic Community. Hire purchase restrictions were relaxed in August and social security payments increased in September, both of which were seen by the markets as a sign that the defence of sterling was not the government's chief priority, and prompted more selling of sterling. A dock strike and further bad trade figures kept the sentiment adverse, and the raising of the Bank Rate in October did little to restore confidence.

In early November, rumours continued to circulate that the pound would be devalued, and sterling came under heavy pressure. Despite a further raise in the Bank Rate on November 9, the sentiment for sterling continued to ebb. Rumours that a potentially new massive support package for sterling was being assembled began to circulate during the week commencing on November 13, and as the authorities neither confirmed nor denied this, the foreign exchange market was further destabilised. Although the Chancellor still hoped that a bailout from the IMF and the U.S. Treasury could be raised, the government agreed to devalue the pound on Thursday, November 16. No loan was forthcoming, and following unprecedented sales of sterling on Friday, November 17, the prime minister announced that the pound would be devalued from $2.80 to $2.40 on Saturday, November 18, 1967 (Cairncross and Eichengreen, 2003, pp. 186–191).

Aside from September 1965 to May 1966 and September 1966 to May 1967, the weakness of sterling between 1964 and 1967 suggests that sterling was suffering from a fundamental disequilibrium. However, this was not how contemporaries saw it. As Hutchison has argued, a myth grew up after devaluation that the majority of the economics profession was in favour of devaluation between 1964 and 1967, when there is no evidence to show that this was indeed the case (Hutchison, 1977, pp. 131–136). To be sure, there were some who did argue that the pound should be devalued (particularly after the July 1966 crisis), but many "hesitated to state publicly the case for devaluation, recognizing that, the more convincingly the case for devaluation was stated, the more difficult it would be for the government to bring it about smoothly and without speculative urges" (Cairncross and Eichengreen, 2003, pp. 159–160).

With the number of speculative attacks and reserve losses over the period, how did the United Kingdom manage to hold sterling at $2.80? Quite simply, between 1964 and 1967, the United Kingdom received lines of credit from central banks and the IMF and enjoyed the use of a swap network with the Federal Reserve Bank of New York. What is often not appreciated, however, is the scale of the assistance given to sterling throughout the period. Much of this assistance, such as the overnight swap with the United States and the Bank for International Settlements gold swap, was secret, so that the scale of the figures involved would not become public knowledge and undermine confidence in sterling. The United Kingdom was also provided with short-term central bank assistance and had medium-term facilities available under IMF drawing rights. To give some idea of the figures involved, it should be noted that in September 1964, the UK authorities had at their disposal $2 billion. At the end of September 1965, this figure had risen to $3.31 billion, rising to $4.37 billion by September 1966 and falling slightly to $4.323 billion in the weeks preceding devaluation.

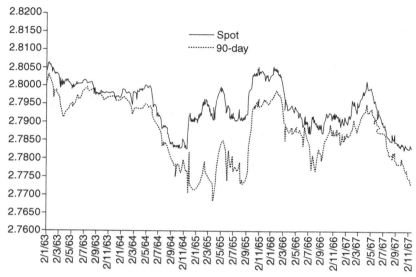

Figure 8.1. Spot and ninety-day forward exchange rate, 1963–November 17, 1967. *Source: The Times.*

TESTS OF STERLING'S CREDIBILITY

The exchange rate arrangements for sterling in the 1960s – with its central parity and margins for flexibility above and below that parity, defined by the exchange rate bands – can be interpreted as a target zone and therefore the kinds of tests for credibility of sterling this period introduced in Chapter 1 may be applied. As we saw there, perhaps the simplest test of credibility involves plotting the forward exchange rate against the upper and lower bands of the target zone (Svensson, 1993), and Figure 8.1 shows the spot and three-month forward rate from the January 2, 1963 to November 17, 1967. Data are daily exchange rates in London, collected from *The Times*. The horizontal, dashed line shows the central parity, whereas the upper and lower edges of the figure coincide with the Bretton Woods band.

As Figure 8.1 shows, the spot rate weakened during the third week of August 1963, but had recovered by March 1964. Thereafter, it fell below its $2.80 parity and came close to $2.78, the level below which, under the IMF rules, the Bank could not permit it to fall. The spot rate was then particularly weak for two periods: the first ten days after the Labour victory of October 16, 1964 and between the time of the budget and until the interest rate rise on November 23, 1964. However, aside from the first "false dawn"

(November 1965 to March 1966) and the second "false dawn" (September 1966 to July 1967), sterling remained close to the bottom of the band.

The three-month forward rate peaked on October 28, 1964 and then fell until the crisis of November 25, 1964 when it spiked above $2.78 briefly as details of the $3 billion loan were announced. However, credibility at this maturity was very short-lived and did not return until just before the 1965 crisis. There had been a very significant change made to forward market policy at the time of the first sterling crisis in 1964. Prior to November 24, 1964, it had been common ground for the Treasury and the Bank to avoid continuous intervention in the forward market at a relatively narrow margin, largely because it reduced the insurance premium which had to be paid by those who sought to cover themselves (in other words, it made the cost of speculation cheap) (Oppenheimer, 1966). From this point, operations in the forward market had the objectives of protecting the spot reserves by making forward cover cheaply available and to retain in London the large amount of arbitrage funds which had built up to the end of 1964. The intervention, which began modestly at first, strengthened and between November 1964 and November 1967, there were only two periods when forward cover was reduced by the Bank: between September 1965 to February 1966 and October 1966 to April 1967. Aside from these two periods, the forward rate was under pressure, particularly so during the choppy waters of July and August 1966 and in November 1967. The Treasury, which was not privy to the exact magnitude of the large forward positions built up by the Bank, estimated that the average size of the Exchange Equalisation Account's oversold position was between $1.8 billion and $2 billion from November 1964 until August 1966; in fact, the true position by this later date was $3 billion and by the time of the devaluation it stood at $4.6 billion.[6]

Overall, then, the behaviour of the ninety-day forward rate suggests that for much of the period, sterling was credible, although there are important exceptions such as the period September 1964 to the end of 1965, the summer of 1966 and the immediate run-up to the 1967 devaluation. Plotting the forward rate against the exchange rate bands, as we have considered in the earlier discussion, is informative but does not give an indication of the significance of the violations of credibility. To address this, we construct the so-called 95 per cent credibility confidence intervals which focus on whether the expected rate of realignment is significantly different from zero

---

[6] Bell to Workman, September 28, 1966, TNA T318/201.

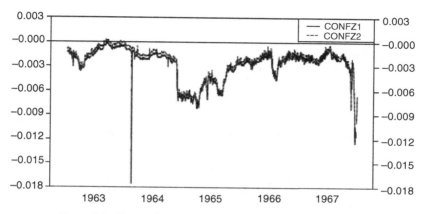

Figure 8.2. Ninety-five percent confidence interval, 1963–1967.

(which contrasts with the simplest test which focuses on the *total* expected exchange rate and does not test the significance of non-zero values of the expected rate of realignment). Svensson (1993) has argued that the 95 per cent confidence interval test is a much tighter test of credibility than simply plotting the forward exchange rate against the target zone bands, and their derivation is given in Chapter 1.[7]

The estimated 95 per cent confidence interval is presented in Figure 8.2 and the message from this figure is stark: Absent a few observations in 1963, after 1964, sterling was essentially a non-credible currency.

The figure predicts well the November 1964 crisis, with the expected rate of realignment dropping sharply in mid-1964 and credibility recovering soon after the crises, although it dipped again in early 1965. The stabilising effect of short-term central bank assistance in September 1965 seems to be clear in Figure 8.2, with the expected rate of realignment rising to a value which was almost insignificantly different from zero toward the end of 1965. However, early in 1966, credibility took a further dip, which would seem to be an anticipation of the pressure sterling was under in the summer of 1966. The recovery of sterling in the winter of 1966 and the early spring of 1967 is confirmed in these figures by the rise in the expected rate of realignment towards zero. However, this was short-lived, with credibility starting to take a hit as early as late August 1967 and then recovering somewhat in late September but then from late October credibility fell sharply.

---

[7] Siklos and Tarajos (1996) raise some econometric issues connected with such tests.

RESERVES

It was recognised in the mid-1960s that Britain had the lowest level of reserves of all the Western European countries, which was made worse because it required a considerable margin for key currency status and to provide for the outstanding liabilities of the Sterling Area (Heller, 1966, pp. 305–307). As Harold James (1996, p. 186) has noted, "the instability caused by the sterling balance overhang and the danger of liquidation . . . lay behind each of the major British crises of the second half of the 1960s."

From our earlier discussion, it was suggested that the underlying story in this period is one of macroeconomic weakness of the UK economy coupled with an unwillingness to adjust the exchange rate, which led to a growing inconsistency between the peg and the economic fundamentals. If this is the case, it might make an analysis of foreign exchange intervention of limited interest other than as a measure for the pressure on the exchange rate. However, the prevailing view of the authorities at the time was that they could finance the external deficit in the short run by using the reserves and bolster the reserves where necessary with international rescues. An analysis of the extent of changes in the reserve position is thus highly relevant to understanding how the government managed to avoid devaluation.

The extent of reserve losses over this period have never before been revealed, as the published figures by the Bank were subjected to extensive "window dressing," with swaps and Treasury bonds sales typically not reported or seen as part of the reserves. This allowed a false picture of the reserves to be presented and allowed the asset side of the reserve position to be presented and any sterling liability to be hidden. Regarded as a standby which could be activated on demand, the transaction would not affect the exchange rate directly, at least not until one or other central bank sold its holdings of the other central bank's money.

Table 8.1 shows an exact tabulation of gold and convertible currency reserves, levels at end-months, between June 1964 and December 1967.

The true position of the reserves can be seen in column 4 (the extent of the Bank's "window dressing" can be seen in column 3), which highlights the scale of the assistance given to sterling over the period. Although the figure for net reserves at the end of March 1966 was more than £1 billion, this was the result of a liquefied portion of the dollar portfolio being brought into the reserves at the beginning of February. Column 5 illustrates the enormous scale of forward sales over the period. The magnitudes of these net forward sales of sterling have been hinted at by Cairncross and Eichengreen

Table 8.1. *UK currency reserves, October 1964–December 1967 ($ millions, current prices)*

	Published Reserves	of which Gold	Convertible currencies	Reserves less assistance	Net reserves	Free reserves[a]	EEA oversold forward position
		(1)	(2)	(2)	(3)	(4)	(5)
1964							
October	2,453	2,290	162	2,038	2,038	3,357	188
November	2,344	2,240	104	1,142	1,142	2,467	249
December	2,316	2,136	179	1,789	1,789	2,033	1,319
1965							
January	2,299	2,181	118	1,498	1,448	1,714	2,052
February	2,363	2,148	216	1,658	1,607	1,879	1,982
March	2,330	2,111	218	1,389	1,282	1,560	2,083
April	2,352	2,111	241	1,254	1,148	1,431	2,122
May	2,859	2,206	652	2,710	2,604	2,892	2,027
June	2,792	2,226	566	2,282	2,257	2,551	2,094
July	2,652	2,148	504	1,977	1,952	2,251	2,173
August	2,584	2,246	339	1,445	1,420	1,725	2,584
September	2,755	2,139	616	1,756	1,708	2,019	2,394
October	2,873	2,139	734	1,924	1,876	2,192	2,097
November	2,988	2,282	706	2,089	2,041	2,374	1,826
December	3,004	2,265	739	2,232	2,184	2,520	1,778
1966							
January	3,018	2,159	860	2,481	2,422	2,775	1,523
February	3,648	2,131	1,518	3,349	3,231	2,699	1,310
March	3,573	2,036	1,537	3,273	3,156	2,632	1,327
April	3,520	2,038	1,481	3,231	3,114	2,621	1,338
May	3,413	1,966	1,448	3,133	3,016	2,523	1,352
June	3,276	2,041	1,235	2,780	2,663	2,176	1,394

(continued)

Table 8.1. (*continued*)

	Published Reserves	*of which* Gold	Convertible currencies	Reserves less assistance	Net reserves	Free reserves[a]	EEA oversold forward position
		(1)		(2)	(3)	(4)	(5)
July	3,206	2,237	969	1,935	1,672	1,184	2,260
August	3,153	2,131	1,022	1,621	1,338	854	3,108
September	3,161	1,940	1,221	1,630	1,296	812	3,175
October	3,217	1,957	1,260	1,747	1,408	930	2,688
November	3,282	1,988	1,294	1,901	1,551	1,072	2,486
December	3,100	1,940	1,159	1,770	1,420	952	2,484
1967							
January	3,130	1,932	1,198	2,327	1,901	1,436	2,643
February	3,170	1,968	1,201	2,542	2,173	1,722	2,408
March	3,259	1,677	1,582	3,058	2,786	2,391	2,066
April	3,405	1,613	1,792	3,245	2,976	2,601	1,949
May	2,954	1,714	1,240	2,666	2,366	2,512	2,134
June	2,834	1,708	1,126	2,433	2,195	2,346	2,481
July	2,792	1,694	1,098	1,982	1,562	1,714	2,584
August	2,758	1,848	910	1,389	960	1,126	2,568
September	2,733	1,831	902	1,042	644	820	2,640
October	2,808	1,781	1,028	792	244	479	3,245
November	2,935	1,066	2,181	415	−281	−281	4,332
December	2,695	1,291	1,404	−89	−775	−2,323	4,241

Notes: col. 1 official reserves (gold and convertible currencies plus special drawing rights); col. 2 less short-term central bank assistance and comprises all operations (including repayments) with overseas central banks and the BIS (excluding BIS currency deposits), initiated by the United Kingdom for the purpose of increasing the UK reserves of gold and foreign currencies; col. 3 excluding guaranteed sterling, special BIS and market swaps and deposits and Israeli deposits and Swiss loan; col. 4 excludes IMF drawing but includes the dollar portfolio; col. 5 excludes the forward aspect of assistance operations, since these liabilities are shown as deductions from the spot reserve.

Sources: col. 1, statistical annex to Bank of England *Quarterly Bulletin*, various years; cols. 2–5, "Gold and convertible currency reserves," Bank of England Archives, 4A98/1.

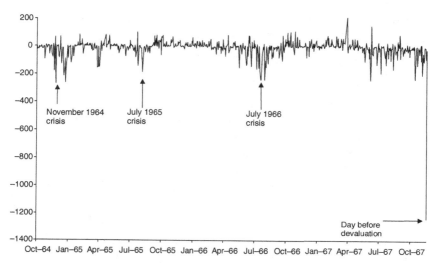

Figure 8.3. Daily changes in total reserves, October 1, 1964–November 17, 1967.
Source: Dealers reports on the foreign exchange and gold market, Bank of England Archives C8.

(2003, pp. 185–186), but the exact figures were a closely guarded secret by the Bank and are revealed here for the first time.

We have used the dealers' reports from the Bank to reconstruct changes in the reserves on a daily basis between 1964 and 1967 (Figure 8.3).[8] Positive entries represent increases in reserves, whereas negative entries represent losses of reserves. Each of the currency crises discussed in the first section of this chapter are marked on the figure.

Hamilton (2008, p. 79) has suggested that the strength of the reserves on the eve of the 1967 devaluation meant that sterling "could have weathered the storm," and that the day before devaluation "the till was still far from empty." Although this is an intriguing suggestion, the evidence does not support it. Hamilton quotes from a Treasury document which estimates that the published figure for the reserves at the end of October would be $2.78 billion. The addition of the dollar portfolio, central bank facilities and the IMF drawing rights brings the amount of assets available to $5.1 billion. However, when Britain's short- and medium-term liabilities are factored in, this figure falls to $2.5 billion. On November 16, 1967, the Treasury assumed that slightly more than $1 billion of resources would still be available at the end of November, and coupled to the IMF drawing rights, the United Kingdom had at its disposal a total of $2.2 billion with which to defend

[8] This follows the same approach as Klug and Smith (1999).

sterling.[9] However, because of window dressing, published reserve figures are misleading, and column 3 of Table 8.1 shows that at the end of October, net reserves stood at $244 million, which at that point was probably the lowest end-of-month figure ever. The dealers' report show that by November 16, a further $728 million had been spent trying to defend the parity, so in reality, the situation was much worse. Without a further massive rescue (which had been ruled out by the IMF and U.S. officials over the weekend of November 10–11, 1967), the $2.80 parity was simply untenable.

The scale of the total reserve losses during the crises between 1964 and 1967 can be compared to earlier postwar crises. Between April 1, 1949 and the devaluation of September 18, 1949, the reserves fell by $564 million (Cairncross and Eichengreen, 2003, p. 147). During the sterling crises of September 1951 to January 1952, the reserves fell by almost $900 million (Dow, 1964, p. 73). Klug and Smith (1999, p. 193) report that in the 1955 crisis (July to December), $248 million was lost and in the Suez Crisis (July 26 to December 7, 1956) $655 million was lost. During the Suez Crisis, $400 million was lost in one month alone (November 1956), which was the highest single monthly figure postwar, since a loss of $256 million in October 1951 (Boughton, 2001, pp. 434–435). The losses during the period between 1964 and 1967 were on a scale far larger than anything prior to this date, as can been seen from Table 8.2.

Table 8.2 shows how market intervention was the overwhelming cause of the reserve loss, particularly in the form of support to forward sterling. As discussed earlier, this policy was unprecedented. In November 1956, only $13 million were spent on supporting forward sterling and only $30 million were spent in the year as a whole; the totals for 1964, 1965, 1966 and 1967 were $1.6 billion, $1.7 billion, $3.7 billion and $4.8 billion, respectively. The steady loss of reserves illustrated in Table 8.2 and Figure 8.3 at the time of each currency crisis, followed by acceleration in reserve losses and intervention, are typical of the other currency crises described by economists and economic historians (Bordo and Schwartz, 1996; Bordo et al., 2001; Eichengreen, Rose and Wyplosz, 1996).

EXPECTED RATE OF REALIGNMENT, RESERVE CHANGES AND REACTION FUNCTIONS

In this section we examine the interactions between reserve changes and two measures of exchange rates: the change in the spot rate, in terms of a

---

[9] "The length of our tether as at 16 November 1967," TNA T318/183.

Table 8.2. *Market intervention to support sterling, various dates,*
1964–1967 ($ millions)

	Spot Intervention	Forward Intervention	Total Reserve Loss
	(1)	(2)	(3)
November 13–November 25, 1964	−727.30	–	−724.50
November 26–December 31, 1964	−324.80	−1,652.00	−1,629.50
March 19–April 2, 1965	122.50	−879.90	−792.40
July 8–August 13, 1965	−518.00	−539.00	−957.60
May 16–June 10, 1966	−302.40	−277.20	−575.40
July 4–July 29, 1966	−546.00	−1,380.40	−1,738.80
August 1–September 2, 1966	60.90	−793.80	−705.60
May 16–September 29, 1967	23.80	−1,654.10	−1,968.40
October 12–November 17, 1967	−1,095.81	−2,456.61	−1,409.80

Notes: col. 3 is not the total of cols. 1 and 2 because gold operations, short-term assistance, repayments and claims are not shown in the table.
Source: Dealers reports on the foreign exchange and gold market, Bank of England Archives C8.

standard reaction function, and the relationship between the expected rate of realignment and the change in reserves. The former relationship gives an indication of the interaction between two measures of financial crisis and, specifically, quantifies how reserves react to exchange rate changes. The latter relationship should shed light on how important reserve changes were during the period in driving the lack of credibility, which, as we demonstrated earlier, was the norm in the 1960s.

Reserve Changes and the Expected Rate of Realignment

In this section we examine the extent to which the evident non-zero expected rate of realignment was related to reserve changes over the period. First-generation speculative attack models emphasise the importance of poorly managed monetary and fiscal policy for the evolution of a currency crisis and the ultimate attack on a currency (Krugman, 1979; Obstfeld, 1984). Monetary/fiscal indiscipline should show up in reserves and they should be a key driver of the expected rate of realignment. Of course, there may be an important degree of endogeneity in such a relationship in the sense that if interventions are successful in transitorily raising credibility, there will be less reserve losses, thereby resulting in an inconsistent co-efficient estimate on the measure of reserves.[10] In our econometric estimates we account for such potential endogeneity using an instrumental variables estimator in which the instruments are a constant and two lagged values of both the dependent and independent variables. Additionally, because the model of Krugman is one in which capital controls are absent, we do not expect the reserves/credibility relationship to conform exactly to that predicted in the standard first-generation speculative attack model. For example, it is well known that the United Kingdom in the 1960s had partial capital controls in place and the existence of such controls allowed the UK authorities to borrow to prolong the period before sterling had to be devalued. In the baseline speculative attack model, with no capital controls, the loss of reserves is a characteristic of an attack, and when this occurs, borrowing new reserves cannot prolong the life of the peg. Nonetheless, and as Wyplosz (1986) demonstrates in a variant of the first-generation model with capital controls, the relationship between reserves and credibility should still exist in a modified form for our period.

We use three measures of reserve changes: spot (rspot), gold (rgold) and total reserve changes (rtotal), and provide two sets of co-efficient estimates: GMM is an OLS estimate in which the standard error has been corrected for heteroskedasticity and serial correlation using a standard Newey-West damp factor, and GMMIV is an Instrumental variables estimate in which the standard error has also been corrected for heteroskedasticity and serial correlation using a standard Newey-West damp factor. The results are reported in Table 8.3, and with the GMM results we see that for all three measures of reserves, there is a negative relationship (note that to make the interpretation clear we are using the sterling-dollar rate) between the expected rate of realignment and reserves, although this is statistically significant only in the cases of gold and total reserves: In terms of gold reserves, a 1 per cent worsening of UK reserves produces a 0.1 per cent increase in the expected rate of realignment of sterling (sterling-dollar). Using the IVGMM estimator, we note a much stronger relationship between the reserve measures and credibility, although again the co-efficient on spot reserves is insignificant. The correction for endogeneity, therefore, produces a much sharper relationship between reserves and credibility, with the co-efficient rising by a factor of 10 in absolute terms. These results seem intuitive enough and provide confirmation of the main message of first-generation speculative attack models, namely that poorly disciplined macroeconomic policy, particularly monetary policy, will have serious implications for reserves and

---

[10] We are grateful to Marc Flandreau for making this point.

Table 8.3. *Regressions of the expected rate of realignment on the change in reserves*

Constant	Rspot	rgold	Rtotal
3.58(30.73)	−0.002(1.35) GMM −0.194(0.67)IVGMM		
3.50(30.38)		−0.094(4.09) GMM −0.157(2.06)IVGMM	
3.56(41.31)			−0.013(3.12) GMM −0.069(3.55)IVGMM

Notes: T-ratios reported in parenthesis (the underlying standard errors are robust to heteroscedasticity and auto-correlation and a Newey-West damp factor has been used).

Figure 8.4. Recursive estimates of the co-efficient on total reserves.

the credibility of the peg (note that because the United Kingdom had capital controls in the 1960s, our results cannot be seen as confirmation of a specific first-generation speculative attack model, such as Krugman). Further light may be shed on this by looking at the evolution of the co-efficient on reserves over time – is it relatively constant or does it change as a crisis approaches?

In Figure 8.4 we report recursive estimates of the co-efficient generated from the regression of the expected rate of realignment on total reserves. The picture indicates that the weight placed on reserves declines from the early 1960s down to mid-1964 and then rises steadily until it peaks at the time of the devaluation in 1967. It would seem that the importance of reserves loomed larger and larger as devaluation approached.

Table 8.4. *Total reserve reaction functions*

Constant	RT_{t-1}	$0.360-S_{t-1}$	ΔS_{t-1}
28.37(1.88)	0.334(14.49)	−21.50(1.94)	−
−0.87(1.33)	0.310(11.32)	−	−8.68(4.86)
33.13(2.68)	0.35(15.76)	−24.82(2.31)	−16.43(10.0)

Notes: T-ratios reported in parenthesis (the underlying standard errors are robust to heteroscedasticity and auto-correlation and a Newey-West damp factor has been used).

Reaction Functions

Reserve and exchange rate movements (both spot and forward rates) are often taken as measures of financial crises, and in this sub-section we attempt to link these two measures by estimating reaction functions for sterling. A standard reaction function linking reserve changes to the exchange rate is given as:

$$\Delta r_t = \lambda_0 + \lambda_1 \Delta r_{t-1} + \lambda_2 (s_{t-1} - \bar{s}_{t-1}) + \lambda_3 \Delta s_{t-1}$$

where the lagged reserve terms is included to allow for serial correlation in the change in reserve process, the second term on the right-hand side captures the deviation of the actual exchange rate from some target or equilibrium level (as captured by s overbar) and the last term is a standard leaning-against-the-wind term. To be consistent with the extant reaction function literature, we define the exchange rate as the home currency price of a unit of foreign currency (sterling-dollar) and take as the target exchange rate the reciprocal of the dollar-sterling lower point (2.77) which is 0.360: A depreciation of the exchange rate above this point should trigger a reserve change to defend the currency.

The results from estimating variants of this reaction function are reported in Table 8.4. In the first regression we exclude the "leaning against the wind" term and find a significantly negative co-efficient on the deviation of the exchange rate from the edge of the band: a 1 per cent depreciation of the rate above the band produces a 21 per cent change in reserves. In the second specification, we drop the deviation term and include the "leaning against the wind" term. This also produces a significantly negative co-efficient, although the magnitude is not as large as for the deviation term. Finally, the last equation includes both exchange rate effects, with both appearing statistically significant: the co-efficient on the deviation term is similar to the first regression whereas the co-efficient on the "leaning against the wind" term is about double that on the same term in equation with the deviation term.

Clearly then it would appear that the Bank during the 1960s was reacting to both exchange rate pressure within the target zone bands – intra-
marginal intervention – and also intervening at the lower band itself
(marginal intervention), and that this intervention had a relatively large
effect on the reserve position.

CONCLUSION

This chapter has contributed to the literature on sterling by drawing on new
archival sources of information and fresh data on reserves and exchange-
market intervention. Our research shows that the sterling peg became
increasingly incredible in the period from 1964 to 1967 as it flirted with
and fell below the lower credibility bands we estimated. Moreover we show
that the pound sterling was propped up by international rescue loans from
the G11 and the IMF. The peg collapsed when the rescues ceased. Thus the
new reserves data reveals that the United Kingdom's international reserves
were inadequate at the same time as the credibility of the peg was low.
Indeed without the international rescues, sterling would have been forced
to devalue earlier. The addition to its reserves gave the British authorities
the breathing room to manage the inevitable exit from the sterling peg of
$2.80. At the time, the monetary authorities found it hard to admit to them-
selves that sterling was doomed.

The sterling crises represented key examples of a flaw of the Bretton
Woods adjustment mechanism under which overvalued countries reluctant to deflate were forced to adjust by devaluation. The crises were good
examples of first-generation speculative attack models driven by a growing
inconsistency between the peg and the domestic fundamentals. The crises also showed the operation of the famous trilemma which posits that
pegged rates, open capital accounts and independent financial policies cannot co-exist. Under Bretton Woods rules, the trilemma was supposed to
work because of capital controls. Like the crises of the 1940s and 1950s, the
crises of the 1960s showed that capital controls were porous.

Finally, although the crises of 1964 to 1967 were some of the most important milestones in the saga of the rise and fall of the Bretton Woods system,
devaluation also represented a climacteric for sterling. The change in parity
signalled the end of sterling as a major reserve currency, bringing to a close
a story going back to the mid-nineteenth century. The devaluation also represented a breach of the first line of defence of the dollar as the linchpin of
the gold dollar standard that Bretton Woods had evolved into by the end
of the 1960s. Moreover, worse was to follow after the 1967 devaluation, as

the gold crisis in March 1968, the rumours about an expected devaluation of the franc and possible revaluation of the Deutschmark in the autumn of 1968 all impacted on sterling with the result that there were further substantial reserve losses.

Acknowledgements

The authors would like to acknowledge the excellent research assistance of Melaine Rohat-Meheust and Claire Grimes. We wish to thank Charles Goodhart, John Hills and Bill Allen (all formerly of Bank of England) for sharing their expertise on the operation of the foreign exchange market in the 1960s. We are also grateful for the comments of participants and referees at the third Past, Present and Policy conference, held at Genoa in March 2008. Finally, the authors are indebted to the late Adam Klug for his contribution to this paper and would like to dedicate this chapter to his memory.

PART FIVE

THE EUROPEAN MONETARY SYSTEM
PERIOD

NINE

On the Mean-Reverting Properties of Target Zone Exchange Rates

Some Evidence from the ERM

Myrvin Anthony and Ronald MacDonald

INTRODUCTION

For the formulators of the Delors Committee Report (1989), one of the key elements in the process towards European monetary integration was the Exchange Rate Mechanism (ERM) of the European Monetary System (EMS). Although the ERM is now effectively in abeyance, the period of its existence in its original form has generated a very useful database on which to test the process of exchange rate determination within predetermined bands. It is now widely accepted that to understand this process, a theoretical framework which views the exchange rate as determined in a target zone should be adopted. One key prediction of the target zone literature is that if an exchange rate band is credible, the exchange rate within the band should exhibit strongly mean-reverting behaviour, thus imparting a degree of stability to an exchange rate which is absent under freely floating rates, and which may also be absent even in a conventional managed float. Although this mean-reverting attribute has been widely referred to in the literature (see, for example, Krugman, 1991; Rose and Svensson, 1994; Svensson, 1992, 1993), and perhaps even taken for granted as a natural property of a target zone system, little effort has been devoted to testing its validity. Of the work that has been done to test this hypothesis, it is our belief that it has not been correctly implemented. In this chapter we seek to rectify this important lacuna in the target zone literature.

In particular, we offer in this chapter a careful dissection of the mean-reverting properties of all seven of the participating member currencies of the ERM for the period from March 13, 1979 to April 9, 1992. Usually, discussion of ERM exchange rates concentrates on only the German mark bilateral rates. However, we believe it to be of interest to examine all of the ERM rates (i.e. all of the cross-bilateral rates in addition to the mark-bilateral) to see if the other rates have the same properties as the key central ERM rate; if the system was operating correctly, they should have. The comprehensivity of our tests necessarily implies that the chapter is rather lengthy and results-orientated; however, this comprehensivity should be a useful reference source for others on the behaviour of target zone exchange rates. For each currency we conduct our tests using data for each of the realignment periods, where the periods are modified to exclude potentially turbulent observations generated by the realignments. Our testing method consists of two sets of tests. Tests in the first set are univariate in nature and consist of standard unit root and variance ratio tests. The latter test has useful advantages over the standard unit root test, because a significance test can be computed which controls for heterosecdastic processes and non-normal errors and also gives a clear picture of any mean reversion that actually exists.

One potential disadvantage of univariate unit-root tests, such as the Dickey-Fuller class of statistics, is that they can have poor power properties in small samples. One way of increasing the power of such tests is to increase the span of the data on an historical or cross-sectional basis. In terms of the former method, it has now become fashionable in international finance research to utilise very long runs of annual data (for at least 100 years) or to construct panel data sets consisting of pooled cross-section/time-series data. Clearly, the former option is not available to a researcher analysing an historical episode with a fixed starting point, but in the context of the ERM experiment, where time-series data is available on a group of currencies, it is possible to construct panel data sets and implement panel unit root tests. This is a test which we implement in this chapter.

The outline of the remainder of this chapter is as follows. In the next section, we give a brief discussion of why exchange rates should be mean-reverting in a target zone and also outline the univariate methods we propose using to test for such mean reversion. In the third section, our univariate unit-root and variance ratio test results are presented, along with a full listing of realignment dates. In the fourth section, we discuss our panel unit-root-testing methods and results. The chapter closes with a concluding section.

MEAN REVERSION: TARGET ZONE BEHAVIOUR AND UNIVARIATE TESTING METHODS

The assumptions, and predictions, of the target zone model are now well known and are not surveyed here in any detail (see Svensson, 1992 for an excellent survey). The basic model is set out in Chapter 1. As noted in that chapter, there is a negative association between the exchange rate within the band and the expected rate of currency depreciation within the band, which implies that the exchange rate within the band displays mean reversion. To quote Svensson (1992):

[T]hat is, the expected future exchange rate within the band is closer to the long run mean of the exchange rate within the band the further away in time it is. This mean reversion is *an important general property* of target zone exchange rates that is independent of the validity of the specific Krugman model. (emphasis added)[1]

In periods of less-than-perfect credibility, and in particular in periods when agent's expected rate of realignment is non-zero, there would be no necessary requirement for the exchange rate to display a negative association with respect to the *total* expected rate of currency depreciation within the band; rather it should be negatively related to the expected rate of currency depreciation within the band, a measure derived by subtracting the expected rate of realignment from the total expected rate of currency depreciation. Hence, the importance of examining the mean-reverting properties of exchange rates within periods in which the exchange rate was not actually realigned should be obvious and is one we are careful to adopt in this study (this is discussed again in the third section). We believe that testing for mean reversion within the band is simpler than Svensson's "simplest test"; it may be appropriate to christen our approach the "simplest simple test"!

We propose using two univariate methods for testing the mean-reverting properties of our ERM exchange rates (we consider a multivariate or panel test in the fifth section): a standard Augmented Dickey-Fuller t-ratio and a variance ratio test. Both tests may be illustrated in the following way. Our null hypothesis is that an exchange rate, s_t, is generated by a random-walk process with drift

$$s_t = \phi + s_{t-1} + \gamma_t, \tag{9.1}$$

where $\gamma_t \sim NID(O, \sigma^2)$. If this is the case, the exchange rate will not exhibit any mean-reverting properties: A current shock to the exchange rate is permanent. The alternative hypotheses is that the time-series properties of s, are described by

$$s_t = \phi + \beta s_{t-1} + \gamma_t, \quad |\beta| < 1. \tag{9.2}$$

The alternative hypothesis in Equation 9.1 places the restriction on β that it should lie between −1 and 1. In this case, the exchange rate series is

[1] Svensson (1992, p. 127).

stationary and, in particular, mean-reverting. The standard way of testing the null is to estimate the following regression equation:

$$\Delta s_t = \gamma_0 + \gamma_1 t + (\beta_0 - 1)s_{t-1} + \sum_{j=1}^{n-1} \beta_{j+1}\Delta s_{t-j} + v_t, \qquad (9.3)$$

where t denotes a time trend. Given that $\phi(B)$ will contain a unit root if $\sum_{1}^{n}\phi = 1$, the presence of a unit root is formally equivalent to a test of whether $\beta_0 = 1$ or $(\beta_0 - 1) = 0$. This hypothesis may be tested using a standard t-test, although, as Dickey and Fuller (1979) and many others note, this will have a non-standard distribution, and therefore one has to use the percentiles tabulated by Fuller (1976) or MacKinnon (1991). The inclusion of the correct specification of deterministic variables in Equation 9.3 is crucial to the power of the test (see Banerjee et al., 1993). In view of this, we compute both the t_τ (based on Equation 9.3) and the t_μ test, where t_μ is obtained from a regression equation *without* the time trend, t. However, because in the context of target zones the exchange rates are expected to be stationary around the central parity, it seems more appropriate to use a regression model without t. We therefore only report the results for the t_μ test in this chapter (although the results from the t_τ, test are principally similar for all the bilateral rates).[2]

An additional practical issue which must be resolved when conducting Dickey-Fuller unit root tests is the choice of the lag parameter, n, in Equation 9.3. Given that n will usually be unknown, some procedure must be employed to ensure that the appropriate lag structure in Equation 9.3 is being applied. Failure to do this can adversely affect the validity of the test because too few lags may not eliminate serial correlation in v_t, whereas, on the contrary, too many lags can reduce the efficiency of the test because more parameters have to be estimated than is required (see Banerjee et al., 1993). To address this problem, we follow the simple model selection procedure suggested in Hall (1990) and Campbell and Perron (1991). In particular, we estimate an auto-regression as in Equation 9.4, where the lag parameter is set at $n = 20$ initially. If the co-efficient on the last included lag is statistically significant from zero we set $n = 20$ in Equation 9.4; if not, we successively reduce the order of the auto-regression until the co-efficient on the last included lag in the reduced model is statistically significant. If none of the lags is statistically significant, we set $n = 0$.

---

[2]   Unit-root tests for the first-difference of these bilateral exchange rates were also computed using both the t_n and t, tests. These results, as well those for the t, test on the level of the exchange rates, can be obtained from the authors by request.

$$s_t = \gamma_0 + \sum_{j=1}^{n} \beta_j s_{t-j} + \mu_t. \tag{9.4}$$

It is now widely accepted that standard unit-root tests based on Equation 9.4 are not very powerful in detecting whether a series is stationary or not, particularly when the series contains a root which lies close to the unit circle (see, for example, Campbell and Perron, 1991). Lo and MacKinlay (1988) have demonstrated that the variance ratio test has greater power to reject the null hypothesis of a unit root when it is in fact false than the standard Dickey-Fuller test, essentially because it is better able to capture the underlying time-series properties of the data. The variance ratio test was introduced into the relatively recent economics literature by Cochrane (1988) and has the further advantage that it offers a very straightforward interpretation of how rapidly a series reverts back to, or diverges from, its mean value. It is given in Chapter 1 by Equation 1.9, and we refer to $\hat{V}_k$ as the estimated value of the variance ratio.

If $\hat{V}_k$ is either above or below unity, the random-walk null is rejected. However, it is only in the latter case that the series exhibits mean reversion, and we therefore take values $\hat{V}_k$ for of one or above as evidence against the target zone model. How do we determine if $\hat{V}_k$ is indeed significantly different from one or not? The test statistics $z_1(k)$ and $z_2(k)$ are the two most widely used alternatives and we use them in this chapter.

To our knowledge, the only tests of the mean-reverting properties of the ERM currencies are those contained in Nieuwland et al. (1994), Svensson (1993) and Rose and Svensson (1994). Svensson (1993)[3] is, in fact, concerned to estimate the expected rate of exchange rate depreciation using the following regression equation:

$$\Delta x_{t+k} = \sum_{j} \beta_{0j} d_j + \beta_1 x_t + \beta_2 i_t^k + \beta_3 i_t^{*k} + \varepsilon_{t+k}, \tag{9.5}$$

where, of terms not previously defined, x_t is the exchange rate *within the band* (i.e., the exchange rate less the central parity), d_j is a dummy for regime p – that is, each period between realignments – i_t^k denotes an

---

[3] The equation estimated in Rose and Svensson (1994) is

$$\Delta x_{t+k} = \sum_{j} \beta_{0j} d_j + \beta_1 x_t + \beta_2 (i_t^k - i_t^{*k}) + \varepsilon_{t+k}. \tag{9.5a}$$

Because the same criticisms of Equation 9.5 are applicable to Equation 9.5a, we do not discuss the equations separately.

interest rate with maturity k and an asterisk denotes a foreign magnitude. Svensson estimates this relationship for the six German mark exchange rates used in this paper (with the same data set used in this chapter) and interprets the t-ratio on β_1 as the Dickey-Fuller statistic discussed earlier. Based on this interpretation he finds strong evidence of mean reversion in the x_t process. It is not, however, clear that this interpretation is correct.

First, the critical values calculated by Dickey and Fuller are for a regression consisting of simply the first difference of the variable on the lagged level of the variable and a constant (it does not include the other deterministic elements or the interest rate variables used by Svensson).

Second, the regressand Δx_t in Equation 9.5 is not the first difference of the exchange rate within the band (as would be the case in the standard Dickey-Fuller equation) but the *sixty-fifth difference* (when Equation 9.5 is estimated for the three-month horizon). Third, although x_t is properly adjusted to exclude observations which may reflect realignment expectations (when Equation 9.11 is estimated for the three-month horizon), and a set of dummy variables (d_j) which account for shifts in regimes is included in Equation 9.5, we do not think that this equation is a legitimate variant of the class of unit-root tests which consider deterministic breaks (or regime or structural shifts) in the time-series process (see, for example, Banerjee, Lumsdane and Stock, 1992; Perron, 1989).[4] Thus, in this context, this t-ratio is difficult to interpret as a normal Dickey-Fuller statistic used to evaluate the null hypothesis of a unit root in a time series. Indeed, in the context of constructing panel unit-root tests, Levin and Lin (1992) have demonstrated that the introduction of extra deterministic elements (that is, over and above a constant and time trend) requires very large t-ratios, in absolute terms (around 10 in value), to reject the null of a unit root.

Moreover, no lagged changes in the exchange rate (within the band) appear in the estimated version of Equation 9.3, which is desirable in the presence of serially correlated disturbances. Svensson does, however, calculate standard errors for the co-efficient based on a Newey-West correction and his t-ratio on β_1 may therefore be (broadly) interpreted as a

[4] Svensson (1993, p. 779) correctly points out that the critical values of this class of unit-root tests tend to be larger than those for the standard tests, and therefore his use of the critical values of standard Dickey-Fuller test would not invalidate his conclusions; but this is not an adequate justification for using Equation 9.11 to evaluate the unit-root hypothesis, given the other limitations of this equation which we have adumbrated above.

Phillips-Perron adjusted Dickey-Fuller statistic; but even this interpretation is questionable. Further, there is now growing evidence to suggest that Phillips-Perron type unit-root tests have "serious size distortions in finite samples when the data-generating process has a predominance of negative autocorrelations in first differences. This suggests that the Phillips-Perron tests may be less reliable than the Dickey-Fuller methodology where a parametric correction is applied."[5] As we indicated previously, a further problem with unit root tests based on the Dickey-Fuller approach is that even if they are implemented correctly, they are not, in circumstances when the null hypothesis is rejected, informative about the profile of mean-reversion.

In their study, Nieuwland et al. (1994) use weekly German mark bilateral exchange rate data (for the currencies examined by Svensson, 1993 and also the British pound and the Spanish peseta) for the period from March 15, 1979 to February 27, 1992. They utilise predominantly a variety of Phillips-Perron unit root tests (as well as the Dickey-Fuller test) to check for mean-reversion in these exchange rates, and found little evidence of it, with the exception of the Dutch guilder/German mark exchange rate. However, as these tests are conducted over the *entire sample* which contains several realignments (changing parities or means), they may be unable to detect mean reversion in these exchange rates because, as is well-known (see Perron, 1989), these standard unit-root tests perform poorly in the context of time-series with "trend- or other deterministic breaks" – a point which the authors themselves acknowledge. In order to deal with this difficulty, the authors re-compute these unit-root tests on data (for the *whole sample period*) which exclude *only* the realignments and arrive at the same conclusion. It is our opinion, however, that the deletion of *only* the realignments is not a sufficiently satisfactory way of adjusting these exchange rates to check for mean reversion, because observations which are close to (but preceding) realignment dates may reflect realignment expectations, as we explained earlier.

UNIVARIATE TESTS OF MEAN REVERSION

The Data and Realignment Dates

The data for this study were originally extracted from the BIS database and run from March 13, 1979 to April 9, 1992 (observational frequency

---

[5] Campbell and Perron (1991).

is daily).[6] All of the exchange rates are spot ecu-rates and are recorded at a daily central bank telephone conference at 2:30 P.M. Swiss time, and they are: the Belgian/Luxembourg franc (BF), the Danish krone (DK), the Deutsche mark (DM), the French franc (FF), the Italian lira (IL), the Irish punt (IP) and the Netherlands guilder (NG). The bilateral exchange rates have been calculated from these ecu-rates. All have been transformed using the natural logarithm operator, and missing values, all of which appear to correspond to holidays, have been deleted.[7]

As we noted in the second section, it is clearly important that our tests for mean reversion be conducted in periods in which there was no realignment and no expectation of such. We have therefore taken our full-sample period and sub-divided it into sub-periods corresponding to periods between realignment dates.[8] Our mean-reversion statistics are then calculated for these sub-sample periods. However, even during periods of no realignment, there may still be a non-zero expected rate of realignment which could potentially bias our results. For example, in a period immediately before a realignment, there would in all likelihood be a non-zero expected rate of realignment. In order to exclude any exchange rate turbulence associated with a realignment date, we have truncated each of these period's ten observations before the end (we experimented with other truncation periods and obtained qualitatively similar results).[9]

The Dickey-Fuller (DF) Results

German Mark Bilateral Rates

Table 9.1 contains the results of the DF (τ_μ) tests for the DM bilateral rates.

Consider first the BF/DM exchange rate. With the exception of regime 1 (79:03:13–79:09:23), we find evidence in favour of the unit-root hypothesis, and thus the absence of mean reversion in the other regimes. Similarly, the first regime (79:03:13–79:09:23) of the IP/DM exchange rate also

---

[6] The data set was kindly provided by Lars Svensson.

[7] Because of space limitations, we only present here a subset of the tables containing our Dickey-Fuller and variance ratio tests' results. Interested readers can refer to our discussion paper (see Anthony and MacDonald, 1998) to obtain the full complement of these tables for the twenty-one exchange rates we discuss. The discussion paper also contains a list of all the cross-exchange rates considered in this paper, and a complete set of realignment dates for all of the cross-rates is also provided.

[8] Using data for the full sample would not in any case be a feasible option because, as we noted in the second section, it would have to include a large number of non-standard deterministic elements for each currency (to capture realignment dates).

[9] We are grateful to an anonymous referee for suggesting this point.

Table 9.1. *Dickey-Fuller (τ_μ) test for unit roots*

Period	DM-based exchange rates					
	BFDM	DKDM	FFDM	TLDM	TPDM	NGDM
1	−3.42 (16)[a]	−1.39 (3)	−0.61 (11)	−2.56 (16)	−3.86 (18)[c]	−1.25 (0)
					1.25 (0)	
2	−1.71 (12)	−1.19 (8)	−0.70 (17)	0.05 (13)	−1.32 (1)	−3.13 (16)[a]
3	0.32 (12)	−2.79 (19)[b]	1.21 (17)	0.84 (1)	0.13 (1)	−2.78 (16)[b]
4	0.13 (19)	−2.21 (19)	0.73 (17)	0.97 (18)	0.84 (1)	
5	0.89 (19)	−2.09 (19)	−0.91 (17)	1.03 (12)	−0.36 (2)	
6	−0.55 (19)	−0.82 (19)	−0.36 (17)	−0.22 (19)	0.07 (2)	
7	−0.38 (19)	−1.78 (19)	−1.75 (17)	0.08 (12)	−0.07 (15)	
8	−1.79 (19)	−1.53 (12)		0.68 (19)	−1.57 (5)	
9		−2.83 (19)[b]		−1.38 (19)		
10				−1.88 (19)		

Notes: [a] Denotes significance at 5% level.
[b] Denotes significance at 10% level.
[c] Denotes significance at 1 % level.
Number of lags used for ADF tests is given in parentheses.

demonstrates evidence of a mean-reverting tendency; but in all the other seven regimes, we find support for the non-stationarity of the exchange rate. There is also evidence of stationarity for the DK/DM exchange rate in regimes 3 (79:11:30–81:10:04) and 9 (87:01:12–92:04:09), respectively, although in both cases the unit-root hypothesis is only rejected at the 10 per cent level of significance.

The Netherlands guilder suffered the least number of devaluations (relative to the German mark) in the ERM, and in this respect, the NG/DM exchange rate was the most "stable" rate within the system. We find no evidence in favour of mean reversion during the first regime (79:03:13–79:09:23), but cannot reject the mean-reversion hypothesis for the final two regimes (79:09:24–83:03:20 and 83:03:21–92:04:09).

Probably the more interesting cases of mean reversion cited previously relate to the final regimes of both the DK/DM and NG/DM exchange rates. Both regimes coincide with the period of relative stability in the ERM, and the evidence for mean-reverting behaviour in these instances would seem to give some credence to the theoretical postulation of the target zone literature. In particular, the result for the NG/DM exchange rate suggests that the most "stable" exchange rate in the ERM was also probably the only one to have behaved most consistently like a typical target zone exchange rate. The initial instability in the Dutch guilder (relative to the German mark) in the formative years of the ERM eventually gave way to stability in the later years. This result is, however, probably not surprising given that during the 1980s, the Netherlands had effectively ceded monetary sovereignty to Germany by pegging the guilder to the German mark. The behaviour of the NG/DM exchange rate is, therefore, merely a reflection of the de facto monetary union between these two countries.

In stark contrast to the results for the BF/DM, DK/DM, IP/DM and NG/DM exchange rates, the results for the FF/DM and IL/DM exchange rates are much stronger in their rejection of mean reversion in the sense that we cannot reject the unit-root hypothesis for these exchange rates in any of the regimes. Thus, the weight of evidence, taken over all the regimes for all the DM exchange rates, is mainly supportive of their non-stationarity, and thus the absence of a mean-reverting tendency.

In general terms, the foregoing findings are not in concordance with the results for the DM rates presented in Svensson (1993) and Rose and Svensson (1994). Unlike these works, we find that the behaviour of the DM exchange rates within most regimes is typically non-stationary: in thirty-nine out of a total of forty-five instances, we fail to reject the unit-root hypothesis for these DM exchange rates. However, this is higher than the number that would be expected to occur by chance at the 5 per cent level and, to the extent to which these tests have power to reject the null, this may imply a lack of credibility within the non-stationary periods.

Non-German Mark Exchange Rates
"Inner core" exchange rates. The ERM is a cooperative arrangement in which the participating currencies are restricted to fluctuate within bands which are defined around bilateral central par values relative to each other. Although the DM bilateral exchange rates, in practice, have been the most important exchange rates in the ERM, it is, nonetheless, worthwhile to examine the time-series properties of the other cross-exchange rates in the system because they also would be expected to demonstrate mean-reverting behaviour. But before we discuss the findings for the other bilateral exchange rates, we wish to highlight that the results for a set of bilateral rates have certain implications for the other cross-exchange rates.

Given any set of bilateral exchange rates, we can compute the relevant cross-exchange rates that exist among the various currencies. Thus, if we have $s_{i/j}$ and $s_{k/j}$, where $s_{i/j}$ is the (log) exchange rate between currency i and j (expressed as the number of units of currency i per unit of currency j), and $s_{k/j}$ is the (log) exchange rate between currency k and j (expressed as the number of units of currency k per unit of currency j), the cross-exchange rate $s_{i/k}$ is derived from the linear expression in the following:

$$s_{i/k} = s_{i/j} - s_{k/j}.$$
(9.6)

From Equation 9.6, the following relationships would hold: (1) if $s_{i/j}$ and $s_{k/j}$ are both stationary, then $s_{i/k}$ will also be stationary; (2) if $s_{i/j}$ and $s_{k/j}$ both have a unit root, then it will generally be the case that $s_{i/k}$ will also have a unit root, *unless* $s_{i/j}$ and $s_{k/j}$ are co-integrated, in which case $s_{i/k}$ will be stationary; and (3) if either $s_{i/j}$ and $s_{k/j}$ has a unit root and the other is stationary, then $s_{i/k}$ will have a unit root because the exchange rate with the unit root will dominate. The relationships (1)–(3) can be expected to hold for the entire sample and for regimes which are identical, but not necessarily for regimes which may overlap and clearly not for regimes which differ. We should, therefore, anticipate a certain degree of consistency in the unit-root tests for the other cross-exchange rates.

In Table 9.2 (and tables 4–6 in Anthony and MacDonald, 1998), our findings for the French franc, Belgium-Luxembourg franc and Netherlands guilder are presented (excluding, of course, DM/FF, DM/BF and DM/NG because these are merely the reciprocals of the DM rates discussed in the previous section).

Looking first at the cross-exchange rates among the "inner core" currencies (that is, BF/FF, NG/FF and NG/BF exchange rates), we once more find no evidence of mean reversion: We cannot refute the unit-root hypothesis for any of the regimes of these bilateral rates.

The picture is quite similar across the bilateral rates between these "inner core" currencies and the remaining ("peripheral") currencies in the ERM. The results from these unit-root tests are unanimous in their rejection of mean reversion. Apart from two exceptions – regime 1 (79:03:13–79:09:23) for BF/IP and regime 3 (79:11:30–82:02:21) for DK/BF – we cannot reject the unit-root hypothesis for these bilateral exchange rates.

"Peripheral" exchange rates. The time-series properties of the "peripheral" exchange rates (i.e. IP/IL, DK/IL, and IP/DK exchange rates), reported in Table 9.3, resemble the other bilateral rates discussed previously. In common with the other bilateral rates, these exchange rates also depict clear evidence of being generally non-stationary. In all regimes for these three cross-exchange rates we fail to reject the unit-root hypothesis.

The main conclusion to be drawn from these unit-root results is that, in general terms, the ERM bilateral rates do not behave like typical target zone rates in that they do not demonstrate a consistent tendency towards mean

Table 9.2. *Dickey-Fuller (τ_μ) test for unit roots*

Period	FF-based exchange rates				
	BFFF	DKFF	ILFF	IPFF	NGFF
1	−2.02 (17)	−1.91 (14)	−1.12 (18)	−2.56 (16)	−0.62 (17)
2	−1.50 (11)	−1.16 (14)	−1.22 (15)	−0.55 (16)	1.76 (17)
3	−0.23 (18)	−2.36 (12)	−1.37 (19)	−1.07 (16)	0.57 (8)
4	−0.63 (19)	−2.39 (12)	−1.08 (19)	−1.04 (16)	−0.26 (16)
5	−0.27 (19)	−2.48 (12)	−1.60 (19)	−1.70 (2)	0.17 (8)
6	0.34 (19)	−2.17 (12)	−1.65 (19)	−2.44 (16)	−0.87 (5)
7	0.71 (19)	−0.98 (12)			
8		−0.62 (15)			
9		−0.19 (15)			

Notes: See Table 9.1.

Table 9.3. *Dickey-Fuller (τ_μ) test for unit roots*

Period	Peripheral exchange rates					
	DKNG	ILNG	IPNG	DKIL	IPIL	IPDK
1	−1.71 (19)	−0.79 (18)	−1.48 (4)	−1.78 (18)	−0.87 (8)	−1.21 (19)
2	−0.78 (16)	0.40 (1)	0.17 (10)	−2.61 (9)	−0.22 (8)	−0.95 (19)
3	−2.10 (17)	0.39 (18)	1.42 (7)	−2.86 (12)	−0.09 (8)	−1.85 (17)
4	−0.82 (17)	0.36 (18)	0.08 (10)	−1.67 (5)	−0.65 (1)	−1.92 (19)
5	−1.40 (19)	−0.18 (18)	0.58 (10)	−1.76 (9)	−0.31 (1)	−1.81 (19)
6	0.18 (15)	−0.48 (18)	1.24 (7)	1.35 (9)	−1.18 (1)	−1.72 (19)
7	−0.84 (15)	−0.78 (18)	−1.70 (10)	−1.35 (12)	−1.45 (1)	−0.49 (8)
8	−0.65 (15)	−1.03 (12)		0.20 (12)	−1.55 (1)	
9	−2.02 (17)	−1.76 (18)		−0.17(12)		
10				−0.19 (12)		
11				−0.28 (12)		

Notes: See Table 9.1.

reversion. The strike record is that in only 8 instances out of a potential 159 is there any evidence of mean reversion. A total of eight is only marginally greater than the number that would be expected by chance at the 5 per cent level. However, this may, in fact, be a reflection of the nature of the test used rather than an inherent lack of mean reversion in the data.

Variance Ratio Results

We have constructed our variance ratio tests for lags 2 to 24, because we believe that with daily data, any evidence of mean reversion should have revealed itself after approximately one month's trading. Before presenting a blow-by-blow account of our variance ratio statistics, it is worth giving an overall impression of the results because they portray a quite different picture from the ADF statistics considered in the previous section. In particular, out of a potential of 1,272 instances (159 exchange rate regimes multiplied by the 8 different lags reported in each table), there are 707 rejections of the random-walk hypothesis (based on the $z_2(k)$ statistic at 10 per cent level of significance).[10] These rejections can be split into two groups. The first group (191 instances) consists of variance ratios significantly above unity and the second (516 instances) comprises variance ratios significantly below one. Given that it is the latter set of results which are of interest in the current context, we comment only on these variance ratios which arc below unity; the variance ratios above one are regarded as non-stationary. We present an elaboration of the non-stationary result in the concluding section.

For comparative purposes, we scrutinise more closely our results at a relatively short lag – in this case lag 12 – and at a longer lag – the 24th lag. There are 106 instances out of a potential 159 in which the variance ratio is below one after 12 lags and 88 (again out of 159) when it is below one at 24 lags. Using the z_2 statistic as the metric of significance, there are 62 variance ratios significantly below one (using a 10 per cent significance level) at lag 12 and 58 at lag 24. This picture contrasts quite sharply with the overall impression gleaned from the univariate ADF results.

To conserve space, we do not list all of the variance ratio tables, although we do refer to results contained in the discussion paper version (see Anthony and MacDonald, 1998). We turn now to a more specific examination of these results.

German Mark Bilateral Rates

In Tables 9.4–9.7 (see tables 7–12 in Anthony and MacDonald, 1998), we present our variance ratio results for the German mark bilateral rates. Although for a number of currency/time periods, the pattern is similar to that unearthed by the Dickey-Fuller tests, there is now much more evidence of mean reversion. There are 205 instances (out of a total of 360) in which the estimated variance ratio is below unity. Of these 205 cases, 89 were statistically significant.

Consider the variance ratios for the key German mark-Belgium franc rate, BF/DM, reported in Table 9.4. Four of the periods display estimated

---

[10] Throughout our discussion of these variance ratio results we emphasise the $z_2(k)$ statistic rather than $z_1(k)$ because the former is the more appropriate of the two test statistics in the present context, as was explained in the second section.

Table 9.4. *Variance ratio statistics and significance levels. Exchange rate: BF/DM*

		2	4	6	8	12	16	20	24
1	V	0.91	0.62	0.71	0.74	0.96	1.23	1.52	1.77
	Z1	(0.30)	(0.02)	(0.19)	(0.33)	(0.90)	(0.57)	(0.29)	(0.12)
	Z2	(0.48)	(0.02)	(0.10)	(0.16)	(0.82)	(0.26)	(0.01)	(0.00)
2	V	0.89	0.86	0.89	0.92	0.93	0.91	0.90	0.91
	Z1	(0.02)	(0.10)	(0.32)	(0.53)	(0.68)	(0.64)	(0.67)	(0.71)
	Z2	(0.06)	(0.54)	(0.16)	(0.32)	(0.44)	(0.32)	(0.32)	(0.35)
3	V	0.92	0.65	0.64	0.60	0.45	0.32	0.27	0.33
	Z1	(0.47)	(0.09)	(0.17)	(0.22)	(0.18)	(0.18)	(0.21)	(0.35)
	Z2	(0.80)	(0.33)	(0.34)	(0.31)	(0.18)	(0.10)	(0.08)	(0.12)
4	V	1.00	1.37	1.80	2.19	2.94	3.93	4.59	4.78
	Z1	(0.97)	(0.12)	(0.01)	(0.00)	(0.00)	(0.00)	(0.00)	(0.00)
	Z2	(0.98)	(0.11)	(0.00)	(0.00)	(0.00)	(0.00)	(0.00)	(0.00)
5	V	1.01	1.04	1.00	0.96	0.98	1.06	1.05	1.06
	Z1	(0.90)	(0.77)	(0.99)	(0.85)	(0.95)	(0.85)	(0.90)	(0.89)
	Z2	(0.88)	(0.62)	(0.98)	(0.66)	(0.88)	(0.59)	(0.68)	(0.64)
6	V	0.82	0.77	0.81	0.81	0.86	0.87	0.89	0.90
	Z1	(0.00)	(0.00)	(0.03)	(0.08)	(0.30)	(0.43)	(0.55)	(0.60)
	Z2	(0.01)	(0.01)	(0.03)	(0.04)	(0.14)	(0.20)	(0.27)	(0.31)
7	V	1.33	1.55	1.60	1.57	1.73	2.08	2.45	2.83
	Z1	(0.00)	(0.00)	(0.00)	(0.01)	(0.01)	(0.00)	(0.00)	(0.00)
	Z2	(0.01)	(0.00)	(0.00)	(0.00)	(0.00)	(0.00)	(0.00)	(0.00)
8	V	1.02	0.88	0.85	0.84	0.85	0.83	0.83	0.86
	Z1	(0.40)	(0.02)	(0.03)	(0.05)	(0.13)	(0.17)	(0.22)	(0.34)
	Z2	(0.67)	(0.07)	(0.04)	(0.04)	(0.05)	(0.04)	(0.05)	(0.10)

Notes: The numbers in column 1 denote the sub-sample period (regime) used to construct the variance ratio statistic (V), and its associated significance levels – Z1 and Z2. The numbers at the head of each column denote the lag length (K) used to construct the variance ratio statistic. The numbers not in parenthesis in each column are the estimated variance ratios, whereas the numbers in parenthesis are the marginal significance levels of the Z1 and Z2 statistic.

variance ratios which are numerically below unity (38 instances). A number of these (16 instances) are statistically less than one, but the most noticeable depiction of mean reversion is perhaps in period 8, categorised by a large number of observations and one which is generally seen as one of the most tranquil of the ERM experience. A V-shaped pattern exists for period 1: the value for V_k falls below one to lag 4 and then rises until it becomes significantly greater than one at lag 24. The unusual pattern for period 1 may simply reflect the time taken for investors to gain experience and confidence in the operation of the ERM system. It is unlikely, however, that one can appeal to the newness of the system to explain the rather puzzling results

Table 9.5. *Variance ratio statistics and significance levels. Exchange rate: FF/DM*

		2	4	6	8	12	16	20	24
1	V	0.78	0.76	0.83	0.83	0.85	0.92	0.96	1.00
	Z1	(0.02)	(0.16)	(0.44)	(0.52)	(0.68)	(0.84)	(0.93)	(0.97)
	Z2	(0.03)	(0.04)	(0.18)	(0.21)	(0.33)	(0.60)	(0.80)	(0.99)
2	V	0.95	0.82	0.82	0.86	0.85	0.82	0.73	0.69
	ZI	(0.27)	(0.04)	(0.11)	(0.28)	(0.39)	(0.36)	(0.23)	(0.21)
	Z2	(0.56)	(0.08)	(0.11)	(0.21)	(0.23)	(0.16)	(0.04)	(0.02)
3	V	1.14	1.11	1.22	1.21	1.21	1.35	1.48	1.65
	Z1	(0.07)	(0.45)	(0.27)	(0.39)	(0.48)	(0.32)	(0.24)	(0.15)
	Z2	(0.23)	(0.46)	(0.18)	(0.23)	(0.25)	(0.08)	(0.02)	(0.00)
4	V	0.93	0.64	0.74	0.74	0.82	0.98	1.07	1.19
	Z1	(0.31)	(0.01)	(0.16)	(0.24)	(0.52)	(0.94)	(0.85)	(0.64)
	Z2	(0.54)	(0.02)	(0.12)	(0.15)	(0.36)	(0.91)	(0.73)	(0.37)
5	V	0.94	0.90	0.89	0.90	0.98	0.97	0.97	0.95
	Z1	(0.08)	(0.16)	(0.22)	(0.36)	(0.86)	(0.87)	(0.87)	(0.81)
	Z2	(0.41)	(0.29)	(0.25)	(0.32)	(0.81)	(0.81)	(0.78)	(0.67)
6	V	1.09	1.29	1.47	1.62	2.01	2.36	2.86	3.36
	Z1	(0.21)	(0.03)	(0.01)	(0.01)	(0.00)	(0.00)	(0.00)	(0.00)
	Z2	(0.29)	(0.00)	(0.00)	(0.00)	(0.00)	(0.00)	(0.00)	(0.00)
7	V	0.94	0.90	0.90	0.90	0.93	0.94	0.96	1.00
	Z1	(0.02)	(0.05)	(0.14)	(0.22)	(0.49)	(0.62)	(0.79)	(0.98)
	Z2	(0.33)	(0.21)	(0.25)	(0.27)	(0.46)	(0.55)	(0.72)	(0.97)

Notes: See Table 9.4.

for period 7. Are there then any other explanations for these results? We consider some in the concluding section.

Three other DM bilateral exchange rates – DK/DM, FF/DM and IL/DM – exhibit a similar kind of behaviour as the BF/DM rate, in the sense that there are several instances in which the variance ratio is less than unity and some significantly so. For example, the Italian lira–German mark rate (Table 9.6) displays an almost identical mix of mean-reverting and non-stationary behaviour as does the BF/DM. There are fifty-one instances in which the variance ratio lies below unity, half of which are statistically significant. Regimes 2 and 8, respectively, display clear evidence of mean reversion.

The DK/DM and the FF/DM rates (see table 8 in Anthony and MacDonald, 1998 for the former and table 5 for the latter) have thirty-eight and thirty-six instances, respectively, in which the estimated variance ratio is less than one. However, they both have relatively fewer significant

Table 9.6. *Variance ratio statistics and significance levels. Exchange rate: IL/DM*

		2	4	6	8	12	16	20	24
1	V	0.90	0.99	1.09	1.15	1.19	1.19	1.19	1.02
	Z1	(0:26)	(0.95)	(0.69)	(0.56)	(0.60)	(0.64)	(0.71)	(0.96)
	Z2	(0.38)	(0.94)	(0.56)	(0.33)	(0.27)	(0.29)	(0.31)	(0.90)
2	V	0.76	0.75	0.81	0.85	0.86	0.78	0.73	0.68
	Z1	(0.00)	(0.01)	(0.13)	(0.32)	(0.48)	(0.35)	(0.31)	(0.27)
	Z2	(0.01)	(0.02)	(0.10)	(0.21)	(0.28)	(0.10)	(0.04)	(0.02)
3	V	0.81	0.64	0.55	0.56	0.48	0.46	0.47	0.46
	Z1	(0.03)	(0.05)	(0.05)	(0.10)	(0.14)	(0.19)	(0.24)	(0.28)
	Z2	(0.04)	(0.00)	(0.00)	(0.00)	(0.00)	(0.00)	(0.00)	(0.00)
4	V	0.90	0.90	1.00	0.99	1.09	1.16	1.30	1.51
	Z1	(0.21)	(0.52)	(0.99)	(0.98)	(0.76)	(0.64)	(0.46)	(0.26)
	Z2	(0.43)	(0.51)	(0.99)	(0.97)	(0.59)	(0.35)	(0.09)	(0.01)
5	V	0.93	0.93	0.91	0.95	1.01	1.04	1.10	1.18
	Z1	(0.36)	(0.63)	(0.64)	(0.81)	(0.97)	(0.90)	(0.78)	(0.65)
	Z2	(0.45)	(0.55)	(0.48)	(0.68)	(0.94)	(0.76)	(0.48)	(0.22)
6	V	0.85	0.88	0.92	0.97	1.06	1.11	1.17	1.27
	Z1	(0.00)	(0.14)	(0.41)	(0.79)	(0.71)	(0.54)	(0.42)	(0.25)
	Z2	(0.01)	(0.10)	(0.27)	(0.68)	(0.49)	(0.20)	(0.07)	(0.00)
7	V	0.96	0.99	0.96	0.95	0.94	0.89	0.80	0.76
	Z1	(0.63)	(0.93)	(0.84)	(0.82)	(0.84)	(0.76)	(0.63)	(0.60)
	Z2	(0.59)	(0.88)	(0.70)	(0.62)	(0.61)	(0.39)	(0.14)	(0.09)
8	V	0.66	0.51	0.47	0.46	0.41	0.44	0.46	0.45
	Z1	(0.00)	(0.00)	(0.00)	(0.02)	(0.04)	(0.09)	(0.15)	(0.17)
	Z2	(0.00)	(0.00)	(0.00)	(0.00)	(0.00)	(0.00)	(0.00)	(0.00)
9	V	0.94	1.00	1.02	1.03	1.02	1.03	1.05	1.09
	Z1	(0.09)	(0.94)	(0.83)	(0.82)	(0.90)	(0.84)	(0.77)	(0.64)
	Z2	(0.32)	(0.95)	(0.80)	(0.76)	(0.84)	(0.72)	(0.57)	(0.31)
10	V	1.07	1.03	0.96	0.92	0.94	0.97	0.99	1.04
	Z1	(0.08)	(0.69)	(0.67)	(0.49)	(0.71)	(0.89)	(0.97)	(0.87)
	Z2	(0.22)	(0.68)	(0.61)	(0.35)	(0.54)	(0.80)	(0.93)	(0.72)

Notes: See Table 9.4.

variance ratios below unity than we find for both the BF/DM and IL/DM exchange rate. More importantly, these significant variance ratios are much more dispersed across several regimes and juxtaposed with either other insignificant variance ratios and/or variance ratios which are bigger than one. Thus, the evidence for mean reversion for these two rates is much less obvious than we find for the BF/DM and IL/DM rates.

Interestingly, the Irish punt–German mark rate (see table 11 in Anthony and MacDonald, 1998) exhibits rather different time-series properties relative to the other currencies. Thus, in the initial two sub-sample periods

Table 9.7. *Variance ratio statistics and significance levels. Exchange rate: NG/DM*

		2	4	6	8	12	16	20	24
1	V	1.06	1.08	1.15	1.21	1.32	1.60	2.03	2.38
	ZI	(0.54)	(0.66)	(0.51)	(0.44)	(0.36)	(0.14)	(0.04)	(0.01)
	Z2	(0.60)	(0.55)	(0.28)	(0.14)	(0.03)	(0.00)	(0.00)	(0.00)
2	V	0.91	0.87	0.94	1.01	1.05	1.05	1.05	1.05
	ZI	(0.01)	(0.05)	(0.51)	(0.94)	(0.67)	(0.74)	(0.76)	(0.79)
	Z2	(0.08)	(0.03)	(0.40)	(0.91)	(0.47)	(0.52)	(0.52)	(0.55)
3	V	0.90	0.85	0.78	0.73	0.68	0.64	0.61	0.59
	ZI	(0.00)	(0.00)	(0.00)	(0.00)	(0.00)	(0.00)	(0.00)	(0.00)
	Z2	(0.00)	(0.00)	(0.00)	(0.00)	(0.00)	(0.00)	(0.00)	(0.00)

Notes: See Table 9.4.

and in the last, there is considerable evidence of mean reversion (both numerically and statistically); in all other sub-periods, there is clear evidence of non-stationary behaviour. The strong mean reversion evidenced at the start of the overall sample perhaps reflects the significant initial gains in credibility the punt obtained by participating in the ERM, whilst the mean reversion in the last period reflects the relative tranquillity of this period. The pattern for the NG/DM rate is in concordance with the Dickey-Fuller results: Strong evidence of mean reversion is indicated for the long and tranquil period 3, a period in which the system was at perhaps its most credible.

Non-German-Mark Exchange Rates

"Inner core" exchange rates. The variance ratio results for the cross-rates of the French franc, Belgian franc and Dutch guilder are reported in tables 13–24 in Anthony and MacDonald (1998). Because the sub-sample periods may differ for these cross currencies, relative to those concerning the DM rates, the sub-samples in this sub-section are not strictly comparable with those in the previous section, and therefore caution should be exercised in any exact comparison. Although the general tenor of these results is similar to the DM rates, there are, nevertheless, some important differences.

Consider first the French franc cross-rates. One general impression to be gleaned from these results is that there is slightly more evidence in favour of mean reversion for the French franc-based cross-rates than those based on the mark. About one-quarter (89 instances out of 360) of the reported mark-based variance ratios are significantly less than unity, whereas slightly more than one-half (141 instances out of 272) of the reported French-franc based variance ratios are significantly smaller than one.

Table 9.8. *Variance ratio statistics and significance levels. Exchange rate BF/FF*

		2	4	6	8	12	16	20	24
1	V	0.92	0.78	0.71	0.68	0.64	0.62	0.54	0.54
	Z1	(0.05)	(0.00)	(0.00)	(0.01)	(0.02)	(0.03)	(0.02)	(0.04)
	Z2	(0.27)	(0.01)	(0.00)	(0.00)	(0.00)	(0.00)	(0.00)	(0.00)
2	V	0.87	0.67	0.65	0.62	0.46	0.31	0.23	0.24
	Z1	(0.22)	(0.11)	(0.19)	(0.25)	(0.18)	(0.17)	(0.18)	(0.28)
	Z2	(0.68)	(0.36)	(0.36)	(0.33)	(0.18)	(0.10)	(0.07)	(0.07)
3	V	0.80	0.51	0.53	0.51	0.45	0.43	0.44	0.49
	Z1	(0.11)	(0.04)	(0.14)	(0.19)	(0.27)	(0.33)	(0.43)	(0.47)
	Z2	(0.22)	(0.02)	(0.04)	(0.04)	(0.03)	(0.04)	(0.04)	(0.07)
4	V	0.98	0.89	0.86	0.83	0.78	0.76	0.66	0.60
	Z1	(0.80)	(0.42)	(0.45)	(0.43)	(0.42)	(0.47)	(0.37)	(0.32)
	Z2	(0.78)	(0.17)	(0.12)	(0.07)	(0.04)	(0.03)	(0.00)	(0.00)
5	V	0.76	0.62	0.61	0.61	0.58	0.54	0.47	0.43
	Z1	(0.00)	(0.00)	(0.00)	(0.00)	(0.00)	(0.00)	(0.00)	(0.00)
	Z2	(0.00)	(0.00)	(0.00)	(0.00)	(0.00)	(0.00)	(0.00)	(0.00)
6	V	1.08	1.03	0.96	0.90	1.00	1.06	1.17	1.27
	Z1	(0.29)	(0.84)	(0.82)	(0.64)	(0.97)	(0.86)	(0.66)	(0.50)
	Z2	(0.40)	(0.80)	(0.72)	(0.42)	(0.99)	(0.68)	(0.25)	(0.07)
7	V	0.90	0.79	0.74	0.73	0.75	0.76	0.78	0.81
	Z1	(0.00)	(0.00)	(0.00)	(0.00)	(0.01)	(0.04)	(0.10)	(0.21)
	Z2	(0.07)	(0.00)	(0.00)	(0.00)	(0.00)	(0.00)	(0.01)	(0.04)

Notes: See Table 9.4.

For example, for the BE/EF rate (presented in Table 9.8), all of the periods apart from period 6 produce evidence of mean reversion and this is strongly significant in many instances. This pattern contrasts quite markedly with the experience for the BF/DM rate, discussed earlier. For other French franc cross-rates a similar story can be told, even when the peripheral currencies are considered. For example, for the IL/DM, around a third (twenty-seven out of eighty-eight) of the variance ratios are above unity whereas only one-fifth (ten out of forty-eight) of the IL/FF entries (contained in Table 9.9) are above unity (and of those that are below unity, many are significantly so).

In the majority of instances, the patterns for the Belgian franc are similar to the French franc cross-rates; there is more evidence of mean reversion (slightly more than one-half [122 out of 232] of the estimated variance ratios are significantly smaller than unity) for these rates than the comparable German mark rates. However, the pattern of mean reversion is less marked for the Dutch guilder cross-rates and these are much more similar

Table 9.9. *Variance ratio statistics and significance levels. Exchange rate: IL/FF*

		2	4	6	8	12	16	20	24
1	V	0.77	0.73	0.75	0.80	0.88	0.94	1.01	1.03
		(0.00)	(0.00)	(0.02)	(0.13)	(0.46)	(0.76)	(0.97)	(0.92)
		(0.01)	(0.01)	(0.02)	(0.07)	(0.29)	(0.62)	(0.95)	(0.83)
2	V	0.92	0.77	0.71	0.65	0.60	0.55	0.46	0.46
	Z1	(0.17)	(0.03)	(0.04)	(0.05)	(0.07)	(0.08)	(0.06)	(0.11)
	Z2	(0.31)	(0.01)	(0.01)	(0.00)	(0.00)	(0.00)	(0.00)	(0.00)
3	V	0.98	0.95	0.95	0.96	0.93	0.86	0.83	0.84
	Z1	(0.64)	(0.41)	(0.54)	(0.73)	(0.59)	(0.39)	(0.35)	(0.43)
	Z2	(0.83)	(0.56)	(0.61)	(0.75)	(0.56)	(0.30)	(0.23)	(0.26)
4	V	0.90	0.90	0.91	0.93	0.90	0.81	0.72	0.70
	Z1	(0.20)	(0.48)	(0.62)	(0.77)	(0.73)	(0.49)	(0.49)	(0.50)
	Z2	(0.20)	(0.29)	(0.37)	(0.55)	(0.41)	(0.16)	(0.05)	(0.04)
5	V	0.86	0.84	0.83	0.82	0.81	0.84	0.88	0.91·
	Z1	(0.00)	(0.01)	(0.04)	(0.06)	(0.12)	(0.26)	(0.44)	(0.62)
	Z2	(0.00)	(0.01)	(0.01)	(0.01)	(0.01)	(0.03)	(0.11)	(0.26)
6	V	1.12	1.08	1.06	1.06	1.20	1.35	1.46	1.54
	Z1	(0.01)	(0.31)	(0.56)	(0.63)	(0.20)	(0.06)	(0.03)	(0.02)
	Z2	(0.14)	(0.42)	(0.57)	(0.59)	(0.09)	(0.01)	(0.00)	(0.00)

Notes: See Table 9.4.

to the German mark rates – a finding reflecting the previously noted close links between the guilder and mark throughout the ERM period.

"Peripheral" exchange rates. Most of the peripheral rates have already been addressed in the previous two sub-sections. Those that have not are contained in Tables 9.10 and 9.11 (tables 25–27 in Anthony and MacDonald, 1998). The pattern here is in general agreement with the German mark rates, although it is worth highlighting the Irish punt-Danish krone, which produces variance ratios which are below unity in every instance bar one.

PANEL UNIT-ROOT TESTS

One potential problem with the unit-root tests conducted in the previous section is that they may have low power to reject the null hypothesis of a unit root when it is, in fact, false (i.e. a type II error – see Campbell and Perron for a discussion). This is an issue which has been addressed in other related areas by expanding the span of the data (see, for example, the recent literature on PPP, surveyed in Froot and Rogoff, 1995; MacDonald,

Table 9.10. *Variance ratio statistics and significance levels. Exchange rate: DK/IL*

		2	4	6	8	12	16	20	24
1	V	1.09	1.37	1.66	1.99	2.40	2.65	2.91	3.11
	Z1	(0.31)	(0.03)	(0.00)	(0.00)	(0.00)	(0.00)	(0.00)	(0.00)
	Z2	(0.28)	(0.00)	(0.00)	(0.00)	(0.00)	(0.00)	(0.00)	(0.00)
2	V	0.87	0.62	0.79	0.98	1.19	1.23	1.07	0.81
	Z1	(0.43)	(0.23)	(0.60)	(0.97)	(0.79)	(0.82)	(0.94)	(0.85)
	Z2	(0.40)	(0.03)	(0.27)	(0.92)	(0.39)	(0.32)	(0.77)	(0.43)
3	V	0.78	0.69	0.66	0.64	0.63	0.66	0.70	0.72
	Z1	(0.00)	(0.00)	(0.02)	(0.03)	(0.08)	(0.18)	(0.30)	(0.37)
	Z2	(0.10)	(0.04)	(0.04)	(0.03)	(0.03)	(0.06)	(0.10)	(0.13)
4	V	0.82	0.67	0.68	0.79	0.83	0.85	0.85	0.78
	Z1	(0.04)	(0.05)	(0.15)	(0.43)	(0.64)	(0.71)	(0.74)	(0.66)
	Z2	(0.02)	(0.00)	(0.00)	(0.09)	(0.23)	(0.31)	(0.33)	(0.17)
5	V	0.76	0.51	0.60	0.56	0.61	0.60	0.68	0.76
	Z1	(0.02)	(0.02)	(0.14)	(0.19)	(0.34)	(0.43)	(0.58)	(0.73)
	Z2	(0.06)	(0.00)	(0.02)	(0.02)	(0.05)	(0.06)	(0.14)	(0.28)
6	V	0.87	0.81	0.96	1.01	1.15	1.25	1.43	1.69
	Z1	(0.28)	(0.43)	(0.90)	(0.97)	(0.76)	(0.66)	(0.55)	(0.33)
	Z2	(0.32)	(0.25)	(0.83)	(0.95)	(0.44)	(0.23)	(0.05)	(0.00)
7	V	0.96	0.82	0.81	0.79	0.81	0.79	0.74	0.80
	Z1	(0.55)	(0.18)	(0.29)	(0.33)	(0.51)	(0.52)	(0.49)	(0.62)
	Z2	(0.71)	(0.18)	(0.19)	(0.17)	(0.26)	(0.22)	(0.14)	(0.26)
8	V	0.86	0.84	0.82	0.84	0.90	0.93	0.98	1.04
	Z1	(0.00)	(0.04)	(0.08)	(0.20)	(0.51)	(0.70)	(0.91)	(0.87)
	Z2	(0.00)	(0.01)	(0.01)	(0.04)	(0.20)	(0.40)	(0.79)	(0.66)
9	V	0.91	0.89	0.87	0.89	0.95	1.06	1.21	1.28
	Z1	(0.23)	(0.43)	(0.48)	(0.63)	(0.86)	(0.86)	(0.61)	(0.53)
	Z2	(0.35)	(0.33)	(0.29)	(0.40)	(0.71)	(0.66)	(0.17)	(0.07)
10	V	0.93	0.94	0.99	1.06	1.11	1.17	1.25	1.31
	Z1	(0.04)	(0.30)	(0.93)	(0.55)	(0.38)	(0.23)	(0.13)	(0.09)
	Z2	(0.22)	(0.32)	(0.91)	(0.41)	(0.15)	(0.02)	(0.00)	(0.00)
11	V	1.05	0.96	0.90	0.89	0.93	0.96	0.98	1.01
	Z1	(0.25)	(0.61)	(0.33)	(0.36)	(0.68)	(0.84)	(0.91)	(0.96)
	Z2	(0.39)	(0.55)	(0.17)	(0.14)	(0.43)	(0.66)	(0.79)	(0.89)

Notes: See Table 9.4.

1995). In principle, there are two ways to expand the span of the data. One involves extending the historical span by increasing the number of years covered by the data set. In the literature on testing whether real exchange rates contain stochastic unit roots, such an extension has been demonstrated to have a dramatic effect on the ability of a researcher to reject the null of non-stationarity (see Froot and Rogoff, 1995; MacDonald, 1995).

Table 9.11. *Variance ratio statistics and significance levels. Exchange rate: IP/DK*

		2	4	6	8	12	16	20	24
1	V	0.75	0.72	0.68	0.74	0.76	0.75	0.81	0.85
	Z1	(0.01)	(0.10)	(0.15)	(0.33)	(0.51)	(0.54)	(0.70)	(0.77)
	Z2	(0.01)	(0.02)	(0.02)	(0.07)	(0.12)	(0.12)	(0.24)	(0.38)
2	V	0.74	0.58	0.47	0.46	0.49	0.43	0.45	0.46
	Z1	(0.11)	(0.19)	(0.19)	(0.28)	(0.47)	(0.57)	(0.58)	(0.59)
	Z2	(0.16)	(0.06)	(0.02)	(0.03)	(0.06)	(0.04)	(0.05)	(0.06)
3	V	0.76	0.60	0.57	0.50	0.46	0.45	0.43	0.40
	Z1	(0.00)	(0.00)	(0.00)	(0.00)	(0.00)	(0.00)	(0.01)	(0.01)
	Z2	(0.00)	(0.00)	(0.00)	(0.00)	(0.00)	(0.00)	(0.00)	(0.00)
4	V	0.89	0.73	0.76	0.72	0.70	0.72	0.71	0.74
	Z1	(0.08)	(0.02)	(0.11)	(0.13)	(0.20)	(0.31)	(0.36)	(0,46)
	Z2	(0.12)	(0.00)	(0.01)	(0.01)	(0.01)	(0.02)	(0.03)	(0.05)
5	V	0.94	0.84	0.76	0.73	0.67	0.61	0.57	0.56
	Z1	(0.08)	(0.02)	(0.01)	(0.01)	(0.02)	(0.02)	(0.02)	(0.03)
	Z2	(0.23)	(0.01)	(0.00)	(0.00)	(0.00)	(0.00)	(0.00)	(0.00)
6	V	1.04	0.99	0.86	0.70	0.65	0.69	0.66	0.55
	Z1	(0.72)	(0.95)	(0.63)	(0.40)	(0.44)	(0.59)	(0.63)	(0.53)
	Z2	(0.71)	(0.91)	(0.34)	(0.06)	(0.05)	(0.09)	(0.07)	(0.02)
7	V	0.99	0.88	0.87	0.89	0.89	0.90	0.89	0.90
	Z1	(0.57)	(0.02)	(0.05)	(0.14)	(0.25)	(0.37)	(0.40)	(0.48)
	Z2	(0.80)	(0.08)	(0.07)	(0.13)	(0.15)	(0.20)	(0.18)	(0.23)

Notes: See Table 9.4.

In the current application, such an extension is, unfortunately, not an option. However, the recent literature on PPP demonstrates that precisely the same result as is obtained from a long-run of annual data may also be obtained by expanding the panel dimensions of the data set.[11] In this section, therefore, we propose expanding the span of the data by pooling across the currencies participating in the ERM and testing for a unit root across the panel. Panel unit-root tests may be motivated using the following equation:

$$\Delta s_{it} = \alpha + \delta s_{it-1} + \left\{ \sum_i \gamma_i D_i \right\} + \left\{ \sum_t \gamma_t D_t \right\} + \left\{ \sum_i \beta_i t_i \right\} + v_{it}, \qquad (9.7)$$

[11] In particular, Frenkel and Rose (1995) and MacDonald (1995) have demonstrated that with long runs of historical data, the proposition that real exchange rates contain a unit root may be rejected in favour of the alternative hypothesis that they are mean-reverting with a half-life of around four years. Exactly the same result may be obtained by expanding the cross-sectional dimensions of a given time-series data set.

where i denotes a currency, D_i and D_t denote, respectively, country-specific and time-specific fixed-effects dummy variables, a t_i denotes a country-specific time trend. Equation 9.7 is essentially the panel analogue to Equation 9.3 and of interest is the magnitude of δ, which will indicate the speed of mean reversion, and its significance as judged by the estimated t-ratio. As Levin and Lin (1992, 1993) have demonstrated, the critical values for the latter statistic are affected by the particular deterministic specification used.

In circumstances where all of the deterministic elements in Equation 9.7 are excluded apart from the single constant term, α, Levin and Lin (1992) demonstrate that the t-statistic on β converges to a standard normal distribution. Including individual specific effects (either $\left\{\sum_i \gamma_i D_i\right\}$ or $\left\{\sum_i \beta_i t_i\right\}$ or both) but excluding time-specific intercepts, Levin and Lin (1992) demonstrate that the t-ratio converges to a non-central normal distribution, with substantial impact on the size of the unit-root test (and they tabulate critical values). However, Levin and Lin (1993) argue that unless there are very strong grounds for exclusion, time-specific intercepts should always be included in these kinds of panel tests. The reason for this is that the inclusion of such dummies is equivalent to subtracting the cross-section average in each period. This subtraction may be dispensed within cases where the units in the panel are independent of each other; however, in cases where this is not the case, such a subtraction is vital to ensure independence across units.

In addition to facilitating the removal of time means, the panel methods of Levin and Lin (1993) have a number of other advantages such as allowing the residual term to be heterogeneously distributed across individuals (in terms of both non-constant variance and auto-correlation) rather than a white noise process. Given that, as we have argued previously, such heterogeneity is a feature of daily exchange rate data, the Levin-Lin method has clear advantages in the current context.

The testing method has the null hypothesis that each individual time series in the panel has a unit root, against the alternative that all individual units taken as a panel are stationary. The procedure consists of four steps which we now briefly note (these steps do not correspond exactly to the steps in Levin and Lin).

The first step involves subtracting the cross-section mean from the observed exchange rate series. Thus, we now have s_{it} where i runs from 1 to N, where N denotes the total number of currencies in the ERM, and we construct $\bar{s}_t = (1/N)\sum_{i=1}^{N} s_{it}$. In the following steps, the term s_{it} is interpreted as having been adjusted by $\bar{s}_t$.

Step 2 involves performing the following two regressions:

$$\Delta s_{it} = \sum_{L=1}^{p_i} \hat{\pi}_{iL} \, \Delta s_{it-L} + \hat{\alpha}_{mi} \, d_{mt} + \hat{\varepsilon}_{it} \qquad (9.8a)$$

$$s_{it-1} = \sum_{L=1}^{p_i} \hat{\phi}_{iL} \, \Delta s_{it-L} + \hat{\alpha}_{mi} \, d_{mt} + \hat{v}_{it-1} \qquad (9.8b)$$

where a $\wedge$ denotes a fitted value, ε_{it} and v_{it-1} denote estimated residuals and d_{mt} denotes appropriate deterministic variables defined for three different models, $m = 1, 2, 3$. Model 1 contains no exchange rate specific deterministic elements, Model 2 contains a (country-specific) constant term and Model 3 contains a (country-specific) constant and a deterministic trend. Having estimated Equation 9.8b, the following regression is run:

$$\hat{\varepsilon}_{it} = \delta_i \, \hat{v}_{it-1} + e_{it} \qquad (9.9)$$

The t-ratio calculated on the basis of $\hat{\delta}_i$ is the panel equivalent to an ADF calculated on the basis of Equation 9.3. In order to control for heterogeneity across individuals, both ε_{it} and v_{it-1} are deflated by the regression standard error from Equation 9.9; these adjusted errors are labelled $\tilde{\varepsilon}_{it}$ and $\overline{v}_{it-1}$. Under the null hypothesis, these normalised innovations should be independent of each other, and this may be tested by running the following regression:

$$\tilde{\varepsilon}_{it} = \delta_i \tilde{v}_{it-1} + \tilde{e}_{it}. \qquad (9.10)$$

Under the null hypothesis that $\delta_i = 0$ for all $i = 1, \dots N$, the asymptotic theory in the fourth section of Levin and Lin indicates that the regression t-statistic t_δ has a standard normal distribution for model 1, but diverges to negative infinity for models 2 and 3. However, Levin and Lin demonstrate that the following adjusted t-ratio has an N(O,1) distribution, and the critical values of the standard normal distribution can be used to test the null hypothesis that $\delta_i = 0$ for all $i = 1, \dots, N$:

$$t_\delta^* = \frac{t_\delta - N\tilde{T} \, \hat{S}_{NT} \, \hat{\sigma}_e^{-2} \, RSE(\hat{\delta}) \mu_{m\tilde{T}}^*}{\sigma_{m\tilde{T}}^*}. \qquad (9.11)$$

The terms in Equation 9.11 other than t_δ are calculated under step 4. In particular, $\hat{S} = (1/N) \sum_{i=1}^{n} \hat{s}, \hat{s}_i = \hat{\sigma}_{si} / \hat{\sigma}_{ei}, \hat{\sigma}_{ei}$ residual standard error from Equation 9.9 and $\hat{\sigma}_{si}$ is an estimate of the long-run standard deviation, RSE($\hat{\delta}$) is an estimate of the reported standard error of $\hat{\delta}$ (the latter being a least-squares estimate), $\hat{\sigma}_\varepsilon$ is the estimated standard error of regression in Equation 9.10, $\tilde{T} \equiv (T - \bar{p} - 1)$ is the average number of observations per individual in the panel and $\bar{p} = (1/N)\sum_{i=1}^{N} p_i$ is the average lag order for the individual ADF statistics. $\sigma_{m\tilde{T}}^*$ and $\mu_{m\tilde{T}}^*$ represent the mean and standard deviation adjustments, respectively, and are tabulated in table 1 of Levin and Lin for different deterministic specifications $(m = 1, 2, 3)$.

In implementing the Levin and Lin (1993) test, we combined our data to form panels in the following way. We examined each realignment period, and for those which contained five or six overlapping currencies, a panel was then formed. From the full-sample period, this generated five separate panel data sets: 79:03:13–79:09:23, 86:04:07–86:08:03, 86:08:04–87:01:11, 87:01:12–90:01:08 and 90:01:08–92:04:09. Given that country-specific fixed-effects dummy variables were significantly different across currencies, we did not compute a panel ADF test across the panel. Rather, we constructed the Levin and Lin (1993) t-ratios which allow for differing fixed-effects dummies across countries; that is, for each of the data periods we constructed an unadjusted panel unit-root t-test, t_δ, and the adjusted t-ratio given by Equation 9.11.

Our panel results are reported in Table 9.12. We note that the unadjusted t-ratio, t_δ, is negative and, in all cases apart from panel 4, is less than the standard Dickey-Fuller 5 per cent critical value of −2.97. However, these statistics are not valid for reasons we have just noted. The adjusted t-ratios, the t_δ^*'s, portray a rather different story in that only two of the statistics are negative and none of these are significant at the 5 per cent level. However, there is some evidence of rejection of the joint null in the case of panel 3, where the t_δ^* is significant on the basis of a one tail test at the 8 per cent level.

We attribute the failure to reject the null of non-stationarity in the panel setting to two factors. First, our variance ratio tests demonstrate that within a particular realignment period, some currencies do exhibit mean reversion whereas others do not. If the failure to reject the null for some currencies is due to a lack of credibility, then this may simply confound the rejection signal from other currencies when all of the currencies are stacked into a panel format. Second, it is well known that panel-testing methods work best when the dimensions of the panel are approximately square (i.e. the time-series dimension is approximately equal to the cross-sectional dimension). Unfortunately, the nature of our database makes it impossible to construct square panel data sets, so our failure to reject the null in a panel context

Table 9.12. *Panel unit-root tests*

	Panel 1	Panel 2	Panel 3	Panel 4	Panel 5
t_δ	−3.96	−5.56	−6.04	−2.34	−3.81
t_δ^*	−0.58	0.11	−1.43	2.77	0.65

Notes: t_δ and t_δ^* are, respectively, the unadjusted and adjusted panel unit-root t-ratios, defined in the text. The t_δ^* statistic has a standard normal distribution and none are significant at conventional significance levels. The five panel data sets used to construct these statistics are defined in the text.

could simply be a reflection of the relatively low power of the test (relative to a square panel).

CONCLUDING COMMENTS

In this chapter we have implemented a battery of tests concerning the mean-reverting properties of currencies participating in the ERM up to 1992. Although the mean-reverting properties of such currencies are a central prediction of the target zone literature, little research effort has been devoted to verifying it (indeed, as we demonstrated, the tests undertaken to date have been flawed). The main conclusion stemming from our work is that in the majority of instances, ERM exchange rates appear to be non-stationary. Although we have emphasised the relatively low power that our univariate tests have to reject the null hypothesis of a random walk, we nevertheless find that there are important and significant exceptions to our failure to reject the null hypothesis of a unit root.

The exceptions we find to the unit-root null are perhaps explicable in terms of the kinds of policies that have to be pursued by national governments if they are to be truly committed to an ERM-style arrangement. For example, Netherlands guilder–German mark exchange rate exhibited strong mean reversion. Given that a de facto monetary union existed between these two currencies for our sample periods, this perhaps indicates the kind of monetary policy a country needs to adopt to effectively participate in an exchange rate mechanism like the ERM. An interesting sub-plot in our story, which we do not wish to emphasise too much, is the finding that of the instances where mean reversion does occur (based on the evidence from our variance ratio results), it seems to be more prevalent for French franc and Belgian franc bilateral rates than for German mark bilaterals. The fact that these rates exhibit more of the characteristics of a target zone perhaps indicates that the rejections we observe for the DM-based rates cannot be wholly attributable to a power problem; they are, perhaps, evidence of a lack of credibility.

To a large extent, the lack of support for a mean-reverting tendency among the ERM bilateral rates for the period prior to January 1987 is not totally unexpected. First, there was the period from February 1985 to December 1987 in which the dramatic depreciation of the U.S. dollar resulted in speculation against the dollar towards other currencies, including participants in the ERM. This period was therefore seen as exceptional and led to the dramatic realignment in January 1987 and the Basle-Nyborg agreement of 1987.[12] Thus, even considering within-realignment data may not ensure mean-reverting exchange rate behaviour.

Secondly, from its commencement in March 1979 to January 1987, there were eleven realignments in the ERM – a clear indication of the relative instability of this early phase in the operation of the system. The frequency of realignments in this period depicted the persistence of inflation differentials across the EMS currencies. As was pointed out by De Grauwe (1989b), the volatility of inflation rates across the EMS countries rose between 1979 and 1983 and remained substantial until 1986. Similar (but weaker) conclusions were made by Robertson and Symons (1990). Looking for mean reversion using within-realignment data may have been expected to overcome this problem. However, the fact that prices were trended for the whole period means that such trending behaviour would also manifest itself in the behaviour of ERM exchange rates in the sub-sample constituents of the full sample, and this, in turn, could generate non-mean-reverting behaviour, which is indeed what we find.

Although there was undeniably some improvement in convergence in prices (and policy objectives) after January 1987, there was still lingering divergences which meant that "*neither the necessary (convergence of costs and prices) nor the necessary and sufficient conditions (convergence of costs, prices, and policies) for irrevocably fixed exchange rates among all ERM participants have been fulfilled*" (Ungerer et al., 1990) (emphasis added). Despite this, policy makers pursued a no-realignment strategy, in the process creating a de facto pegged exchange rate system.[13]

This post-1987 period also witnessed two important developments which (as the September 1992 events would subsequently confirm) had deleterious implications for the EMS. First, commencing in 1990, the German economic

---

[12] This was an agreement designed to strengthen foreign intervention against speculative attacks and encourage policy coordination (see Eichengreen and Wyplosz, 1993).

[13] The Italian lira was devalued on January 8, 1990 by placing it in the narrow 2.25 band.

and monetary unification (GEMU) imposed a massive asymmetric shock on the EMS, which implied a (long-run) depreciation of the German mark. Second, 1990 also saw the removal of existing capital controls in some EMS countries as part of the 1992 Single Market Programme. But the removal of controls on capital flows substantially reduced the monetary authorities' ability to withstand speculative attacks – a necessary precondition for the viability of any fixed exchange rate system,

Although an analysis of the September 1992 crisis in the ERM is beyond the purview of this chapter,[14] with hindsight, it is apparent that the absence of realignments in the post-1987 period temporarily masked the intrinsic pressures which were already built up in the ERM. Our findings of a general absence of a mean-reverting tendency after 1987 would therefore be consistent with such a view. The nominal exchange rates in the ERM were not as stable as the absence of realignments superficially suggested. But the instances in which we do observe mean reversion are suggestive of the kinds of policies that have to be pursued if an ERM arrangement is to be successful.

Acknowledgements

Reprinted from the *European Economic Review*, 42 (8), Myrvin Anthony and Ronald MacDonald, "On the Mean-Reverting Properties of Target Zone Exchange Rates: Some Evidence from the ERM," pp. 1493–1523, Copyright (1998); *Journal of International Money and Finance*, 18 (3), Myrvin Anthony and Ronald MacDonald, "The Width of the Band and Exchange Rate Mean-Reversion: Some Further ERM-Based Results," pp. 411–428, Copyright (1999), with permission from Elsevier. We are grateful to Francesco Giavazzi and to two anonymous referees for their helpful comments on an earlier draft of this paper. We would also like to thank John McConnell, Alison Wright, and Andrew Deykin for their efficient research assistance. MacDonald acknowledges financial support from the ESRC (L120251 023) and the Leverhulme foundation.

---

[14] See Eichengreen and Wyplosz (1993) for an excellent analysis of the causes of the September 1992 crisis in the ERM.

TEN

Credibility and Interest Rate
Discretion in the ERM

Hali Edison and Ronald MacDonald

INTRODUCTION

The aim of this chapter is to analyze interest rate linkages for a number of countries participating in the exchange rate mechanism (ERM) of the European monetary system (EMS). Although others have examined such linkages, the focus of previous work differs to that considered here.[1] In particular, we seek to evaluate how much short-run interest rate discretion (SRID) participation in the ERM conferred on a country, rather than focussing on the symmetric/asymmetric properties of an EMS participant's interest rate policies. By SRID we simply mean the ability of the interest rate of a country to deviate, in the short run, from a long-run variant of uncovered interest parity. For example, Svensson (1994) has demonstrated that if a target zone system, such as the ERM, is credible, it will facilitate some SRID, particularly at the short end of the maturity spectrum. Most, if not all, fixed exchange rate systems may be modeled as a target zone mechanism. Officer (1997) and Hallwood, MacDonald, and Marsh (1995), for example, have demonstrated that the classical gold standard represented a highly credible target zone system, and Bordo and MacDonald (1997) (see Chapter 3 in this volume) have established that this conferred SRID of up to one year on countries participating in the gold standard mechanism. Although a number of works have examined the credibility of the ERM experience (see, for example, Rose and Svensson, 1994) none, to our knowledge, has examined its implications for SRID during the ERM period.

---

[1] For example, previous research on interest rate interactions within the ERM has focused on issues relating to the symmetric or asymmetric operation of the system; see, *inter alia*, De Grauwe (1989a), Edison and Kole (1995), Von Hagen and Fratianni (1990), and Weber (1990).

It is now widely accepted that for much of its operation, the ERM did not represent a credible target zone. However, for particular time periods, some countries' monetary policy did appear to be highly credible (e.g., the Netherlands toward the end of the original ERM experiment) and also countries that lacked full credibility could still be distinguished in terms of differing degrees of non-credibility. How then did the general lack of absolute credibility and, more specifically, the differing degrees of relative credibility show up in interest rate policy? Did it give some countries more SRID than others, or were all countries equally plagued by the general lack of (absolute) credibility? In this chapter we examine these kinds of questions using daily interest rate data, for the period from March 1979 to May 1996, for six ERM countries against Germany and the United States. Additionally, two control countries – Canada and Japan – are used to check the sensitivity of our results. Of course, the existence of a full-blown monetary union in Europe since 1999 means that there is now only a single interest rate policy across Europe. However, we believe it is still of interest to examine the precursor to this single interest rate policy in order to see how the rules of the game have changed over time. This is of special interest given that proposals for greater fixity for the tripolar grouping of the dollar, euro and yen seem to be back on the policy agenda again.

Clearly, although the ERM shares with the classical gold standard (and the Bretton Woods system) the basic structure of a bilateral par value embedded within a band of permissible fluctuations, the rules of the game differed. In particular, the EMS was by far the most cooperative historical fixed rate systems in the use of common funds for interventions and in the frequency of realignments. This means, of course, that we cannot generalize the experience of the ERM to other systems of fixed but adjustable exchange rate systems. However, Bordo and MacDonald (1997 and Chapter 3 in this volume) have assessed the SRID conferred on countries participating in the classical gold standard, and we refer the reader to their work for comparable empirical evidence drawn from a different historical setting.

The outline of the remainder of this chapter is as follows. In the next section, we present a brief motivational framework for our econometric modeling. Our data sources are discussed in the third section and the econometric results are contained in the fourth section 4. The final section contains our conclusions.

MOTIVATION

A number of empirical studies on the time-series behavior of ERM exchange rates have used a target zone framework (see, for example, Rose and Svensson, 1994 and Anthony and MacDonald, 1998, Chapter 9 in this volume). A key assumption in this framework is the condition of uncovered interest rate parity (UIP), which is defined as:

$$i_t = i_t^* + E_t \Delta s_{t+k} \tag{10.1}$$

where i_t denotes the domestic interest rate, i_t^* denotes the foreign rate, s_t is the spot exchange rate, E_t is the conditional expectations operator, and s_t is transformed logarithmically. It is this relationship that is the focus of our study. In a credible target zone, the term $E_t \Delta s_{t+k}$ should equal zero and there will be a long-run lock between the two interest rates. However, Svensson (1994) has argued that even in a credible target zone, there should be some "short-run" scope for the home short interest rate to deviate from the comparable foreign rate, although in the longer term, such independence vanishes (see Chapter 3 in this volume). By examining interest rate relationships for the ERM countries, we hope to capture this feature of the Svensson model. We follow the methodology of Bordo and MacDonald (1995 and Chapter 3 in this volume) and in particular their system 1, as described in Chapter 3. That is, we focus on interest rate co-integrating relationships between interest rate pairs, as described in Equation 3.6 and the surrounding discussion, and in the presence of co-integration we generate dynamic error correction equations of the form given by Equations 3.7 and 3.7′.

It is important to emphasize that what we are testing in this chapter is not the degree of monetary independence afforded to a country by participating in a credible target zone, but simply the degree of short-run interest rate discretion. Such discretion could not, for example, be used to pursue an independent monetary policy that tried to reduce unemployment below the natural rate, because such a policy would be inconsistent with the credibility of the central parity rate. Rather, the term "discretion" indicates that interest rates could be used or allowed to absorb transitory shocks to, say, velocity, or perhaps to smooth volatility in interest rates (Svensson, 1994).

Given that the main focus of our study is the behavior of the interest rates of countries participating in the ERM, it seems natural to take the German-based rate as the "foreign" interest rate. However, previous studies (see, for example, Edison and Kole, 1995) have demonstrated the need to additionally include a comparable U.S. interest rate into such a system because of the pivotal role of U.S. monetary policy for international interest rate linkages. Whether the U.S. interest rate appears explicitly in the long-run relationships or simply in the short-run dynamics is something we actually test in the next section. However, assuming for the time being that it appears in the long-run relationship, we have a system made up of the home short interest rate, i_t, a comparable short German rate, i_t^{GY}, and the U.S. rate, i_t^{US}. With two "foreign" rates, the dynamic error correction representation for the home country becomes:

$$\Delta i_t = -\alpha_0 (i - i^{GY} - i^{US})_{t-1} + \sum_{i=1}^{p} \kappa_i \Delta i_{t-i} + \sum_{i=1}^{p} \gamma_i \Delta i_{t-i}^{GY} + \sum_{i=1}^{p} \mu_i \Delta i_{t-i}^{US} \quad (10.2)$$

where ecm^2 is the error correction term from this more general system. Of course associated with Equation 10.2 will be two additional dynamic equations, one for the change in the U.S. rate and the other for the change in German short rates. Again, as in the bivariate model, the α_0 coefficient will be informative about the extent of any policy independence.

DATA SOURCES

The interest rates analyzed in this chapter all have a three-month maturity and were obtained from the Bank of International Settlements. We examine the rates for seven European countries – Belgium (BM), Denmark (DK), France (FE), Germany (GY), Italy (IY), the Netherlands (ND), and the United Kingdom (UK) – and three control rates – the United States (US), Canada (CA), and Japan (JA). The sample period runs from January 1979 to May 1996, and the observational frequency is daily. In Figure 10.1 we plot the co-movements of each of the ERM interest rates with both German and U.S. rates, and the co-movements of the Canadian and Japanese rates are plotted relative to the U.S. rates. For the ERM rates we note a number of general properties. First, there is considerable turbulence in the three rate combinations around the inception of the ERM, although turbulence in the "own" rate is usually the most pronounced. This turbulence may be a reflection of the start-up of the ERM or the change in the operation of U.S. monetary policy during this period. The rates then go through a period of relative tranquility until the demise of the ERM in the early 1990s, when there is again marked turbulence, although not of the same magnitude as at the start of the sample. Interestingly, the United Kingdom, which was only a member of the ERM only for part of the sample, appears to have suffered higher own rate volatility throughout the sample than other European interest rates that were full participants in the ERM. As expected, perhaps, the correlation between Canadian and U.S. interest rates is very close throughout the sample and, interestingly, the same volatility we observe in ERM rates in the late 1970s–early 1980s is also evident here. This would seem to suggest that the volatility

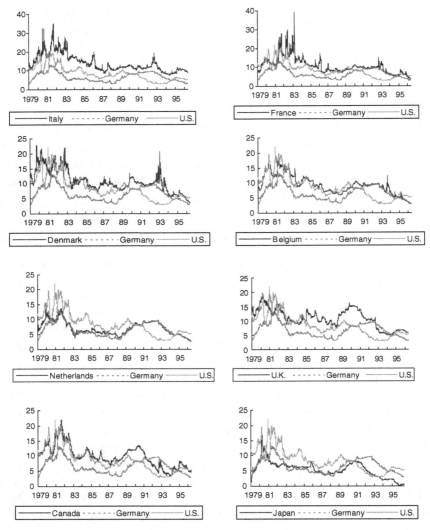

Figure 10.1. Co-movements of interest rates.

in European rates for this period, noted earlier, may be driven by changes in U.S. monetary policy rather than turbulence associated with the ERM. The Japanese three-month rate also has some of this early volatility, although it is less pronounced than for any of the other interest rates and, in general, the Japanese rate exhibits much less volatility for the full sample.

ECONOMETRIC RESULTS

This section presents our econometric results. Our testing strategy may be summarized in the following way. First, we test for the existence of co-integration among our interest rate groupings. This is taken to be our baseline test for the existence of a long-run relationship between an interest rate pairing. Of course, the existence of co-integration between interest rates is a necessary, although not sufficient, condition for long-run UIP in the presence of non-stationary (particularly I[1]) interest rates. A necessary and sufficient condition is that the interest rates should co-integrate and that the slope on the foreign interest rate should equal unity. We also test this hypothesis as deviations of the slope coefficient from unity will give insight into the credibility of a particular interest rate pairing. Second, in addition to testing these hypotheses, we also test if a representative U.S. interest rate is needed in the long-run co-integrating relationship as originally suggested by Edison and Kole (1995). Third, we then examine the hypothesis concerning the adjustment of interest rates to the long-run UIP relationships. In particular, given that we find that U.S. interest rates are important for the long run, we test if they are weakly exogenous; that is, whether the U.S. rates "push" the ERM-based systems to equilibrium or play a role in the adjustment to equilibrium. Fourth, we then examine the adjustment of the own "home" rate and compute the implied half-life. The latter gives the degree of SRID. Finally, as a check on the robustness of our results, we test how sensitive some of the results are to a change in the sample period and also how interest rates unconnected to the ERM behaved over the full sample period.

Co-integration Results

Our initial results from estimating bivariate interest rate systems for each of the European interest rates against Germany proved problematic, irrespective of including exchange rate realignment dummies or not.[2] In particular, the evidence for co-integration was weak and the residuals were not well behaved and exhibited clear evidence of autocorrelation and heteroscedasticity. Consequently, these results are not reported here. However, consistent with Edison and Kole (1995), we found that introducing the

---

[2] We experimented with a whole range of different dummies, including step dummies, corresponding to the time of an exchange rate realignment, and various "moving window" dummies that were designed to capture turbulence both before and after a realignment.

Table 10.1. *Multivariate unit-root tests*

	Interest Rate System (conditional on a rank of one co-integrating vector)					
	BM3	DK3	FE3	IY3	ND3	UK3
Home	8.42	6.71	31.54	31.20	33.13	5.99
GY3	5.99	4.70	6.76	7.05	33.52	8.21
US3	9.68	4.35	29.69	30.75	0.13	3.63

U.S. rate into the bivariate pairings produced systems with clear evidence of co-integration and which contained non-autocorrelated residuals. We therefore focus on these trivariate systems here. The justification for including the U.S. rate in these systems is that despite the deliberate attempts by countries participating in the ERM to converge on German monetary policy during this period, U.S. monetary policy still provided the central axis in terms of interest rate policy.

Before testing for co-integration in the trivariate system, we tested each country system to determine the order of the VAR, using the Schwartz criterion. We also tested for unit roots using a multivariate test. Table 10.1 contains the results of the multivariate unit-root tests, which are conditional on the rank of the VAR, discussed later in the chapter. The null hypothesis is that the series in question is stationary and the test statistic has a χ^2 distribution with one degree of freedom (see Johansen, 1995). The columns describe the interest rate systems. So, for example, BM3 describes the interest rate system for the Belgian interest rate (home) on the German three-month rate (GY3) and the U.S. three-month rate (US3). The numbers in each cell are the estimated χ^2 statistics for the stationarity of the home, GY3, and US3 rates in each system.

Since the 5 percent critical value for the statistics reported in Table 10.1 is 3.84, the null hypothesis of stationarity is clearly rejected in all cases except one. The exception is the US3 rate, which appears stationary in the ND3 equation. Because this variable is non-stationary in all other systems, it is likely that it is also non-stationary in the Netherlands system, despite the value of the test statistic (however, because it is legitimate to mix both I[1] and I[0] variables in the multivariate methods of Johansen, this issue is not critical).

Table 10.2 reports tests for the numbers of co-integrating relationships in the trivariate ERM systems, using the Trace test statistic where r in this table denotes the number of co-integrating vectors.[3] All of the systems

[3]   Cheung and Lai (1993) have shown that the Johansen Trace test is robust to non-normality in the residuals, and given that, as we have seen, each of our systems does exhibit some

Table 10.2. *Numbers of co-integrating relationships in the trivariate ERM systems*

Trace	BM3	DK3	FE3	IY3	ND3	UK3	95%
r = 0	34.47	33.36	32.76	53.08	55.27	57.74	31.53
r ≤ 1	13.10	14.99	14.16	11.70	11.30	13.08	17.95
r ≤ 2	3.69	4.10	3.49	4.30	3.86	3.96	8.17

indicate that there is a single co-integrating vector (i.e., the null hypothesis, $r = 0$, is rejected in favor of the alternative $r \leq 1$), using a 95 percent critical value. This confirms the point made earlier: The existence of the U.S. interest rate in the data-generating process is crucial to producing a co-integration result. In what follows we implement some hypothesis tests on these relationships to determine if any of the interest rates can be excluded from the long-run co-integrating space, and also if any of the rates are weakly exogenous to the system and therefore may be driving (but not reacting to) the other rates.

Table 10.3 shows the estimated values of the unrestricted co-integrating vectors (normalized on the "home" or "own" interest rate) and the associated alpha vectors (and the corresponding t-ratios). This table should be read in the following way. The row headings relate to the interest rate systems. So, for example, BM3 is the system comprising the Belgian, German, and U.S. rates. The columns below "β vector" contain the estimates of the co-integrating coefficients (normalized on the "home" country), whereas the columns below "α vector" contain estimates of the adjustment speeds.

The general tenor of the results contained in Table 10.3 may be summarized in the following way. Starting with the betas, we see that for all of the European countries, there is a positive relationship between the home country interest rate and that for Germany, with the Netherlands having the highest point estimate and Italy the lowest. For all countries, apart from the United Kingdom, there is also a positive association between the home rate and the U.S. rate, and it is interesting to note that for France and Italy, this dominates the DM coefficient, whereas for Belgium, Denmark, and the Netherlands, the DM coefficient dominates. It would seem, therefore, that even for a group of countries committed to European integration some of the countries have closer ties with the United States than with Germany. It is

non-normality, we prefer to use this statistic rather than the λMax statistic, which is known to be biased in the presence of non-normality.

Table 10.3. *Estimates of the unrestricted β and α vectors*

	β Vector				α Vector		
	Home	GY3	US3	Constant	Home	GY3	US3
BM3	1	−0.823	−0.710	0.819	−0.003	−0.001	0.001
					(3.99)	(1.77)	(1.19)
DK3	1	−0.781	−0.491	0.146	−0.006	−0.000	0.001
					(3.79)	(0.24)	(1.61)
FE3	1	−0.417	−0.664	−0.172	−0.008	−0.003	0.000
					(4.67)	(4.58)	(0.19)
IY3	1	−0.324	−0.583	−0.800	−0.008	−0.004	0.001
					(4.41)	(4.46)	(1.06)
ND3	1	−0.953	−0.019	−0.093	−0.005	0.006	0.001
					(3.59)	(4.42)	(0.42)
UK3	1	−0.524	0.072	−1.494	0.000	0.002	−0.000
					(0.03)	(3.94)	(0.61)
CA3	1	−	−0.800	−0.564	−0.009	−	−0.004
					(5.00)		(2.92)
JA3	1	−	−0.792	−0.092	−0.007	−	−0.001
					(7.05)		(1.04)

perhaps surprising that the United Kingdom, which only had a half-hearted relationship with Europe during this period, appears to have a much stronger linkage with Germany than with the United States. For the two control countries – Canada and Japan – the β coefficients on the U.S. rate is larger than for any of the European countries. Note also that for the majority of interest rate combinations in Table 10.3, there is a constant positive wedge separating the domestic rate from the linear combination of the German and U.S. rates. We interpret this as a (constant) risk premium. Notice, however, that for two of the interest rate systems – Belgium and Denmark – this risk premium is actually negative, suggesting that their rates could, on average, have been lower than the sum of the German and U.S. rates. This finding perhaps reflects the greater credibility with which these countries participated in the ERM. We explore the significance of these constant wedges later in the chapter.

In terms of the adjustment coefficients in Table 10.3 (the α vector), we note that there is "own" adjustment to the significant co-integrating vector in all of the systems, with the exception of the United Kingdom, where it appears that the DM rate is adjusting. The latter result perhaps reflects the importance of the United Kingdom as an independent financial center. Significant negative adjustment occurs in the home rate for the two

Table 10.4. *Hypothesis tests on β and α,*
where $x=[i^{own},i^{gy3},i^{us3},con]'$

H1: $\beta_1 = 0$	H5: $\alpha_3 = 0$
H2: $\beta_2 = 0$	H6: $\beta_4 = 0$, $\alpha_3 = 0$
H3: $\beta_3 = 0$	H7: $[1,-1,0,0] \in Sp(\beta)$, $\alpha_3 = 0$
H4: $\beta_4 = 0$	H8: $[1,-1,0,*] \in Sp(\beta)$, $\alpha_3 = 0$

control equations. We discuss the implications of these adjustment speeds for SRID later in the chapter.[4]

Hypothesis Tests

We now attempt to push our interpretation of the results contained in Table 10.3 further by explicitly testing various hypotheses on the β and α vectors. These tests are designed to capture the form of "long-run" UIP that holds for each of the currency pairings, in terms of the magnitude of the estimated coefficients, and also which rates – home or foreign – adjust to the long-run equilibrium. The different hypothesis tests implemented are summarized in Table 10.4.

The hypotheses tests summarized in Table 10.4 involve sequentially test-ing zero restrictions in the long-run co-integrating relationships (H1–H4), testing for weak exogeneity of the U.S. interest rate (H5–H6) and, finally, testing whether the coefficients on the home and German interest rate can be restricted to a spread (H7–H8). The objective here is to discover what kind of interest parity relationship holds for the different pairings. Is it a "pure form" of interest parity, in which only the home and German inter-est rates enter as a spread, or is there a wedge between these two rates? And what role does the U.S. interest rate play (does it explicitly enter the long-run relationship, or simply feature in the underlying dynamics)? In particular, we test eight hypotheses on each system, and the hypothesis on β may be most easily understood by referring to the following equation, which represents one of the normalized co-integrating vectors contained in Table 10.3:

$$\beta_1 i_t - \beta_2 i_t^{gy} - \beta_3 i_t^{us} - \beta_4 = 0 \qquad (10.3)$$

---

[4] The finding that for four of the systems (BM3, FE3, IY3, and ND3), adjustment to shocks was shared between the "home" country and Germany confirms the earlier work of von Hagen and Fratianni (1990) that German monetary policy was not dominating the ERM.

where β_1 is the coefficient on the own interest rate, β_2 is the coefficient on the German rate, β_3 is the coefficient on the U.S. rate, and β_4 is the constant. The subscripts on the α terms in Table 10.3 have the same assignments as those on the β coefficients.

Hypotheses H_1 to H_4 are tests for the long-run exclusion of the interest rates and the constant term from the co-integration space. More specifically, H_1 tests for long-run exclusion of the "home" or "own" interest rate, H_2 tests for the long-run exclusion of GY3, and H_3 tests for the long-run exclusion of US3. H_4 assesses if a constant is needed in the co-integration space. Clearly, if the constant term is significant in the long-run relationship, this implies that we do not have a pure form of interest rate parity; the constant may be interpreted as a risk premium.

Hypothesis H_5 tests for the weak exogeneity of the U.S. interest rate (and therefore does not place any restrictions on the β vector). If H_5 is not rejected, then it is possible to treat US3 as weakly exogeneous, and the U.S. rate may be interpreted as the exogenous variable driving the system. H_6 tests for weak exogeneity of the U.S. rate together with a zero restriction on the constant. Hypothesis 7, H_7, tests for the weak exogeneity of US3 together with the coefficient restriction that the co-integration vector is given by $(1, -1, *)$ (the asterisk indicates that no restriction is placed on the constant term). So H_7 tests if US3 is a weakly exogenous variable driving a constant spread between bivariate ERM and GY interest rates. Hypothesis H_8 is the most restrictive test and, relative to H_7, places a zero restriction on the constant $(1, -1, 0)$. If this hypothesis is not rejected, the interpretation is that US3 is a weakly exogenous driving force behind the spread between ERM interest rates.

The estimated values of H_1 to H_4 are reported in Table 10.5a, while those of H_5 to H_8 are reported in Table 10.5b. The tests are linear Wald statistics, with an approximate chi-squared distribution indicated in brackets. The estimated p-value is recorded below the Wald test, and numbers in bold type indicate that the null hypothesis is not rejected at the 5 percent level; numbers not in bold type indicate that the null is rejected. A test of weak exogeneity in the bivariate system consisting of CA3 and JP3 is rejected ($\chi^2(1) = 7.28$, p = 0.01).

Results for the ERM Countries

Consider the results for the Belgian system, which are illustrative of the general testing procedure. We note that on the basis of H1 to H3, we

Table 10.5a. *Estimated values of H1 to H4*

	H1	H2	H3	H4
	Trivariate Systems			
BM3	$\chi^2(1) = 8.42$ $p = 0.0$	$\chi^2(1) = 5.99$ $p = 0.01$	$\chi^2(1) = 9.68$ $p = 0.0$	$\chi^2(1) = 4.24$ $p = 0.04$
DK3	$\chi^2(1) = 7.51$ $p = 0.01$	$\chi^2(1) = 5.82$ $p = 0.02$	$\chi^2(1) = 3.94$ $p = 0.05$	$\chi^2(1) = 0.09$ $p = 0.76$
FE3	$\chi^2(1) = 30.56$ $p = 0.0$	$\chi^2(1) = 7.17$ $p = 0.01$	$\chi^2(1) = 28.5$ $p = 0$	$\chi^2(1) = 0.36$ $p = 0.55$
IY3	$\chi^2(1) = 31.04$ $p = 0.0$	$\chi^2(1) = 6.28$ $p = 0.01$	$\chi^2(1) = 31.72$ $p = 0.0$	$\chi^2(1) = 8.20$ $p = 0.0$
ND3	$\chi^2(1) = 33.13$ $p = 0.0$	$\chi^2(1) = 33.52$ $p = 0.0$	$\chi^2(1) = 0.13$ $p = 0.73$	$\chi^2(1) = 0.42$ $p = 0.52$
UK3	$\chi^2(1) = 3.77$ $p = 0.05$	$\chi^2(1) = 3.06$ $p = 0.08$	$\chi^2(1) = 0.05$ $p = 0.82$	$\chi^2(1) = 3.93$ $p = 0.05$
	Bivariate Systems			
CA3	$\chi^2(1) = 22.77$ $p = 0.0$		$\chi^2(1) = 21.56$ $p = 0.0$	$\chi^2(1) = 7.74$ $p = 0.01$
JA3	$\chi^2(1) = 41.02$ $p = 0.0$		$\chi^2(1) = 39.74$ $p = 0.0$	$\chi^2(1) = 0.20$ $p = 0.66$

Table 10.5b. *Estimated values of H5 to H8*

	BM3	DK3	FE3	IY3	ND3	UK3
H5	$\chi^2(1) = 1.13$ $p = 0.29$	$\chi^2(1) = 2.09$ $p = 0.15$	$\chi^2(1) = 0.03$ $p = 0.85$	$\chi^2(1) = 1.16$ $p = 0.28$	$\chi^2(1) = 0.14$ $p = 0.75$	$\chi^2(1) = 0.24$ $p = 0.62$
H6	$\chi^2(2) = 4.29$ $p = 0.12$	$\chi^2(2) = 2.13$ $p = 0.34$	$\chi^2(2) = 0.51$ $p = 0.78$	$\chi^2(2) = 11.0$ $p = 0.0$	$\chi^2(2) = 0.79$ $p = 0.67$	$\chi^2(2) = 4.63$ $p = 0.10$
H7	$\chi^2(2) = 2.65$ $p = 0.27$	$\chi^2(2) = 3.75$ $p = 0.15$	$\chi^2(2) = 14.2$ $p = 0.0$	$\chi^2(2) = 16.8$ $p = 0.0$	$\chi^2(2) = 1.36$ $p = 0.51$	$\chi^2(2) = 0.88$ $p = 0.64$
H8	$\chi^2(3) = 10.7$ $p = 0.01$	$\chi^2(3) = 4.96$ $p = 0.17$	$\chi^2(3) = 21.3$ $p = 0.0$	$\chi^2(3) = 27.2$ $p = 0.0$	$\chi^2(3) = 0.77$ $p = 0.86$	$\chi^2(3) = 7.84$ $p = 0.05$

cannot exclude any of the interest rates from the long-run relationship. The exclusion of the constant term from the co-integrating space is marginal (H4), although when this is combined with the weak exogeneity of the U.S. interest rate (H6), the joint hypothesis cannot be rejected. Of more interest, perhaps, are the last two hypotheses in which we restrict the own-German interest rates to enter as a spread: H7 is clearly acceptable at the 5 percent level, whereas H8 is rejected. This means

Table 10.6. *Implied half-lives (in days)*

	BM3	DK3	FE3	IY3	ND3	UK3	CA3	JA3
Half-Life	231	116	87	87	139	–	77	99

that we can restrict the long-run relationship for Belgium to have the following form:

$$i_t^{BF} = i_t^{GY} + \underset{(0.15)}{0.697}\, i_t^{US} - \underset{(0.31)}{1.146} \qquad (10.4)$$

where numbers in parenthesis are estimated standard errors. So there is a one-to-one lock between the Belgian and German interest rates, whereas the coefficient on the U.S. rate is significantly less than unity. Confirming the result in Table 10.3, we see that there is a negative constant wedge between Belgian, German, and U.S. interest rates for the full sample period and that this is statistically significant.

Referring back to Table 10.3, we note that only the Belgian rate adjusts significantly to the equilibrium error. The implied half-life for the Belgian interest rate, reported in Table 10.6, is 231 days, which indicates the extent of SRID conferred by participation in the target zone. It is interesting to note that this half-life is slightly longer than that obtained by Bordo and MacDonald (1997) for the classical gold standard period (which has been shown to be highly credible international monetary system).

How does the Belgian experience differ from countries with differing experiences in the ERM? For France, the restrictions tests reported in Table 10.5 indicate that the only two hypotheses that cannot be rejected are H4, which has only the constant restricted to zero, and H6, where the restriction on the constant and the weak exogeneity of the U.S. rate goes through. This means that the long-run French relationship has the following form:

$$i_t^{FF} = \underset{(0.09)}{0.468}\, i_t^{GY} + \underset{(0.08)}{0.700}\, i_t^{US} \qquad (10.5)$$

It is quite striking that the coefficient on the German interest rate is both significantly less than unity and also that it is almost half the magnitude of the coefficient on the U.S. rate. Of course, the fact that there is such a large wedge between the two rates may be explicable in terms of the number of currency realignments that took place during this period and the fact that we do not condition on the expected change in the exchange rate. As in the Belgian system, adjustment to equilibrium takes place both through the 'own' and German rates; here, however, both α terms are significant. The half-life for the French system is approximately half that of the Belgian system, indicating, perhaps, that the lesser commitment of the Banque de France to the ERM during much of this period gave it less policy independence (because of the lack of credibility).

The contrast between the French results and those for the Netherlands is quite striking. The Dutch central bank probably had the strongest commitment to the ERM during our sample (particularly for the latter half of the period), and this seems to be borne out by the hypothesis tests reported in Table 10.5. Not only can the co-integrating vector be restricted to $(1, -1)$ for NG3 and DM3, but the U.S. rate is weakly exogenous (H6) and indeed can also be excluded completely from the long-run space (H7). Therefore, in the case of the Dutch system, we can recover a long-run interest parity relationship of the following form[5]:

$$i_t^{NG} = i_t^{GY}. \tag{10.6}$$

The estimated value of the LR(2) test, which is a test that the restrictions imposed in Equation 10.6, is 3.77, with a p-value of 0.15. The alpha values associated with Equation 10.6 are $-0.004(3.57)$ for Δi_t^{NG} and $0.005(4.07)$ for the Δi_t^{GY} equation. Therefore, only the home rate adjusts toward equilibrium in this system, and the half-life is the same as that in the Belgian system. Thus the two countries, which had a similar commitment to the ERM, had similar degrees of freedom in their monetary policy decision making. It is interesting that this freedom is clearly greater than for partner countries (such as France and Italy), which perhaps had a lesser commitment to the system.

Summarizing the remaining long-run results contained in Tables 10.3 and 10.5, we see that the Italian system has properties similar to the French system – non-homogeneity in the long-run relationship and an adjustment speed that suggests a similar half-life. The Danish system is much closer to the Belgian and Dutch systems, with homogeneity holding and the adjustment speeds being similar as well. The results for the British system are interesting because they produce long-run interest rate homogeneity for the period, but there is no adjustment toward equilibrium for the home interest rate.

In a bid to determine if the existence of the significant constants are sample-specific, we recomputed hypothesis test H4 for Belgium, Italy,

---

[5] It is important to note that this test does not involve dropping the U.S. interest rate from the conditioning information set.

Table 10.7. *Estimated values of H1
to H4 for sub-sample 1987–1991*

	H4
BM3	$\chi^2(1) = 13.93$
	$p = 0.00$
IY3	$\chi^2(1) = 2.50$
	$p = 0.11$
UK3	$\chi^2(1) = 0.25$
	$p = 0.62$

and the United Kingdom (the three countries with significant wedges in Table 10.4), using the sample period from January 1987 to the last observation in December 1991. This sample encompasses a period in which the ERM was at its most tranquil and therefore should be the period most likely to produce a zero risk premium. The results, reported in Table 10.7, indicate that for two of the countries – Italy and the United Kingdom – the significant wedge disappears. However, for Belgium, the significance of the wedge seems to have increased for this sub-period, because the p-value has dropped from 0.04 to 0.00. The results for Italy and even the United Kingdom (which initially shadowed the mark and then was a full participant of the ERM during this period) seem intuitively plausible. The results for Belgium are perhaps more puzzling given that its central bank was closely aligned to the Bundesbank's monetary policy during this period.

Results for Canada and Japan

In this section we examine how two interest rate pairings that were not involved in the ERM experience compare, in terms of their short- and long-run responses, to the ERM-based pairings. In particular, we consider results for the two control systems, namely Canada-U.S. and Japan-U.S., over the same sample period as our ERM currencies. The bilateral exchange rate for each of these currency pairings were floating throughout the sample period. These results are reported in the bottom half of Table 10.3, in Table 10.5, and in Table 10.6. The Canada-U.S. system produces one statistically significant co-integrating relationship. However, we are unable to restrict the co-integrating space using any of the hypothesis considered for the ERM countries. The unrestricted vector has the following form:

$$i_t^{CA} = \underset{(0.06)}{0.80}\, i_t^{US} + \underset{(0.13)}{0.56}$$

which indicates that Canadian short rates are permanently higher than U.S. rates by a constant factor of 0.56. Further, there would also seem to be long-run policy independence for Canada in the sense that there is not a one-to-one lock between Canadian and U.S. interest rates. This result presumably reflects the fact that the Canadian dollar was not involved in a target zone arrangement during this sample period. We also note that both rates adjust to the disequilibrium, although the largest adjustment occurs through the Canadian rate.

The Japan-U.S. system also produces clear evidence of a single co-integrating vector and, in contrast to the Canadian system, this can be restricted so that the U.S. rate is weakly exogenous and the constant is zero. The restricted long-run relationship has the following form:

$$i_t^{JP} = \underset{(0.08)}{0.839}\, i_t^{US}.$$

As in the Canadian interest rate relationship, this equation also has the feature that there is not a proportional relationship between the Japanese and U.S. short rates, again presumably reflecting the fact that the Japanese yen was not involved in a target zone arrangement during this period. Perhaps this result is less surprising for Japan because the country is less likely to approximate a small open economy than Canada. The alpha matrix in Table 10.3 indicates that there is significant adjustment by Japanese rates to the disequilibrium between Japanese and U.S. interest rates, although this adjustment is faster than that found for the most "credible" ERM countries.

SUMMARY AND CONCLUSIONS

This chapter attempts to quantify the degree of short-run interest rate discretion (SRID) that existed for a group of countries participating in the ERM of the EMS. Our tests are motivated by Svensson (1994) who argues that the credibility of a target zone will crucially determine the extent of SRID. As a target zone experience, the ERM is known to have a lesser degree of absolute credibility than the classical gold standard period. However, although the system may have been non-credible in absolute terms, there were some important relative credibility effects both across time and also across countries. This chapter seeks to focus on the latter element, although the relative time credibility has also been touched on.

As in Bordo and MacDonald (1997 and Chapter 3 in this volume), the interest parity arbitrage condition is the basis of our analysis. In particular, if a target zone system is credible, then, on average, uncovered interest parity should hold. Given the potential non-stationarity of the variables, we test this proposition using the co-integration framework of Johansen. This framework has the added advantage that a number of hypotheses regarding both the long- and short-run behavior of the different systems may be tested. For example, we tested if the coefficient on the foreign interest rate is insignificantly different from unity, whether the constant is significantly different from zero, and which of the rates adjust to the long-run disequilibrium.

We summarize our results for the ERM-based systems in the following way. First, simply considering bivariate pairings of a domestic and German interest rate was not sufficient to produce a significant co-integrating vector for any pairing. However, when a U.S. rate with a comparable maturity was introduced into the bivariate ERM systems, this produced a unique co-integrating vector in each case. We interpret the importance of the U.S. rate as indicative that the United States still provides the central axis for the determination of international interest rate policy, despite the fact that all but one of the central banks considered here were actively trying to converge on German monetary policy for much of this period.

In terms of both our long- and short-run results, we find that there are essentially two groupings of countries. In the case of Belgium, Denmark, and the Netherlands, we are able to restrict the coefficient on the German rate to be unity; additionally, the constant may be restricted to zero in the Danish and Dutch cases. Indeed, the system for the Netherlands may be reduced to the most restrictive UIP system of all in which the U.S. rate is also excluded from the long-run co-integrating space, leaving only a tight one-to-one lock between the Dutch and German rates. The experience of France and Italy is different in the sense that there is not degree-one homogeneity between domestic and German interest rates, even when the U.S. rate is included. Also the adjustment to disequilibrium for France and Italy are much faster, producing half-lives that indicate much less scope for SRID. These rates, therefore, form a second grouping, which we interpret as a less credible grouping and one in which convergence was still taking place during our sample period. On the periphery is the United Kingdom, which exhibits properties that straddle the two groups: It has a unitary coefficient on the German interest rate, but adjustment to disequilibrium occurs through the German rate rather than the own rate, which has a coefficient of effectively zero.

The results in this chapter seem to validate the central prediction of the Svensson (1994) model. Countries that adopt credible monetary policies have some leeway in short-run discretionary movements in interest rates. Our calculation of the extent of SRID is around one and a half years for a reasonably credible country like the Netherlands. Although this, of course, does not offer countries sufficient discretion to engage in traditional demand-management policies, it does suggest that the time horizon is important when considering the "unholy trinity" of perfect capital mobility, fixed exchange rates, and an independent monetary policy.

Acknowledgments

Reprinted from the *Open Economies Review*, 14 (4), Hali Edison, "Credibility and Interest Rate Discretion in the ERM," pp. 351–368, Copyright (2003), with permission from Elsevier. The authors thank Heejoon Kang and two anonymous referees for their constructive comments on an earlier draft of this chapter. The authors also thank Norbert Fiess for excellent research assistance. This work was written at the time the first author was a senior economist in the Division of International Finance at the Board of Governors of the Federal Reserve System. The views in this work are solely those of the author and should not be interpreted as reflecting the views of the Board of Governors of the Federal Reserve System or of any other person associated with the Federal Reserve System.

References

Anthony, Myrvin and MacDonald, Ronald (1998). "On the Mean-Reverting Properties of the Target Zone Exchange Rates: Some Evidence from the ERM." *European Economic Review* 42 (8), 1493–1523.

Bale, T. (1999). "Dynamics of a non-decision: the 'failure' to devalue the pound, 1964–67." *Twentieth Century British History* 10, 192–217.

Banerjee, A., Dolado, J., Galbraith, J. W. and Hendry, D. F. (1993). *Cointegration, Error-Correction, and the Econometric Analysis of Non-Stationary Data.* Oxford: Oxford University Press.

Banerjee, A., Lumsdaine, R. L. and Stock, J. H. (1992). "Recursive and Sequential Tests of the Unit Root and Trend-Breaking Hypothesis: Theory and International Evidence." *Journal of Business and Economic Statistics* 10, 271–287.

Bank for International Settlements (1937). *Seventh Annual Report, April 1st 1936–March 31st 1937*, Basle.

Barsky, R. B. and De Long, J. B. (1989). "Forecasting Pre–World War I Inflation: The Fisher Effect and the Gold Standard," *Quarterly Journal of Economics* 106, 815–836.

Beaudry, P. and Portier, F. (2002). "The French Depression in the 1930s." *Review of Economic Dynamics* 5, 73–99.

Bernanke, B. (1986). "Alternative Explanations of the Money-Income Correlation." *Carnegie-Rochester Conference Series on Public Policy* 25, 49–100.

Bernanke, B. S. (1995). "The Macroeconomics of the Great Depression: A Comparative Approach." *Journal of Money, Credit and Banking* 27 (1), 1–28.

Bertola, G. and Svensson, L. E. O. (1993). "Stochastic Devaluation Risk and the Empirical Fit of Target-Zone Models." *Review of Economic Studies* 60, 689–712.

Blackaby, F. T. (1978). "Narrative, 1960–74." In F. T. Blackaby (ed.), *British Economic Policy 1960–1974*. Cambridge: Cambridge University Press, pp. 11–76.

Blanchard, O. and Quah, D. (1989). "The Dynamic Effects of Aggregate Supply and Demand Disturbances." *American Economic Review* 79, 655–673.

Bloomfield, Arthur I. (1959). *Monetary Policy under the International Gold Standard.* New York: Federal Reserve Bank of New York.

Board of Governors of the Federal Reserve Board (1943). *Banking and Monetary Statistics, 1914–1941.* Washington, DC: Government Printing Office.

Bohn, H. (1991). "Budget Balance through Revenue or Spending Adjustments? Some Historical Evidence for the United States." *Journal of Monetary Economics*, 333–360.

Bordo, M. D. (1993). "The Bretton Woods International Monetary System: A Historical Overview." In M. D. Bordo and B. Eichengreen (eds.), *A Retrospective on the Bretton Woods System*. Chicago: University of Chicago Press, pp. 3–108.

Bordo, M. and Eichengreen, B. (2000). "The Rise and Fall of a Barbarous Relic: The Role of Gold in the International Monetary System." In G. Calvo, R. Dornbusch, and M. Obstfeld (eds.), *Essays in Honor of Robert Mundell*. Cambridge, MA: MIT Press, 53–71.

Bordo, Michael D., Eichengreen, B. and JongWoo, Kim (1998). "Was There Really an Earlier Period of International Financial Integration Comparable to Today?" in *The Implications of Globalization of World Capital Markets*, Seoul: Bank of Korea, pp. 27–82.

Bordo, M., Eichengreen, B., Klingebiel, D. and Martinez-Peri, M. S. (2001). "Is the crisis problem growing more severe?" *Economic Policy* 16, 51–82.

Bordo, M., Helbling, T. and James, H. (2006). "Swiss Exchange Rate Policy in the 1930s. Was the Delay in Devaluation Too High a Price to Pay for Conservatism?" *National Bureau of Economic Research*, Working Paper 12491, August.

Bordo, M. D., Humpage, O. and Schwartz, A. J. (2006). "The Historical Origins of US Exchange Market Intervention Policy." *NBER Working Paper* No. 12662.

Bordo, M. and Kydland, F. (1992). "The Gold Standard as a Rule." Federal Reserve Bank of Cleveland Working Paper 9205.

Bordo, Michael D. and MacDonald, Ronald (1997). "Violations of the 'Rules of the Game' and the Credibility of the Classical Gold Standard, 1880–1914," *NBER Working Paper* No. 6115.

Bordo, M. D., and Schwartz, A. J. (1996). "Why Clashes between Internal and External Stability End in Currency Crises, 1797–1994." *Open Economies Review* 7, 437–468.

Boughton, J. M. (2001). "Northwest of Suez: The 1956 Crisis and the IMF." *IMF Staff Papers* 48, 425–446.

Brandon, H. (1966). *In the Red: the Struggle for Sterling, 1964–1966*. London: Deutsch.

Brittan, S. (1971). *Steering the Economy: The Role of the Treasury*. Harmondsworth: Penguin.

Brown, W. A. (1940). *The International Gold Standard Reinterpreted 1914–34*. New York: National Bureau of Economic Research.

Cairncross, A. K. (1985). *Years of Recovery: British Economic Policy 1945–51*. London: Methuen.

    (1996). *Managing the British Economy in the 1960s: A Treasury Perspective*. Basingstoke: Macmillan.

Cairncross, A. and Eichengreen, B. (1983). *Sterling in Decline: The Devaluations of 1931, 1949 and 1967*. Oxford: Blackwell.

Cairncross, A. K. and Eichengreen, B. (2003). *Sterling in Decline: The Devaluations of 1931, 1949 and 1967*, 2nd edition. Basingstoke: Palgrave Macmillan.

Calomiris, C. W. (1992). "Greenback Resumption and Silver Risk: The Economics and Politics of Monetary Regime Change in the United States, 1862–1900." *NBER Working Paper* 4166. Reprinted in M. Bordo and F. Capie (eds.) (1994). *Monetary Regimes in Transition*. Cambridge: Cambridge University Press.

Campbell, John and Perron, Pierre (1991). "Pitfalls and Opportunities: What Macroeconomists Should Know About Unit Roots." *NBER Macroeconomics Manual* 6, 141–220.

Campbell, John and Shiller, Robert (1987). "Cointegration and Tests of Present Value Models." *Journal of Political Economy* 95, 1062–1088.

Capie, F. and Webber, A. (1985). *A Monetary History of the United Kingdom, 1870–1982 Volume 1*. London: Allen and Unwin.

Caramazza, F. (1993). "French-German Interest Rate Differentials and Time-Varying Realignment Risk." *IMF Staff Papers* 40, 567–583.

Cassiers, I. (1995). "Managing the Franc in Belgium and France: The Economic Consequences of Exchange Rate Policies, 1925–1936." in Feinstein, *op.cit.*, 214–236.

Castillo, J., Lowell, J., Tellis, A. J., Munoz, J. and Zycher, B. (2001). *Historical Case Studies of the Alternative Hypothesis*. http://www.rand.org/pubs/monograph_reports/MR1112/MR1112.ch5.pdf

Chen, Z. and Giovannini, A. (1994). "The Determinants of Realignments Expectations under the EMS: Some Empirical Regularities." London School of Economics: *Financial Markets Group Discussion Paper* No. 184.

Cheung, Yin-Wong and Kon, Lai (1993). "Finite Sample Sizes of Johansen Likelihood Ratio Tests for Cointegration." *Oxford Bulletin of Economics and Statistics* 55: 313–328.

Clark, P. B. (1970). "Optimum International Reserves and the Speed of Adjustment." *Journal of Political Economy* 78, 356–376.

Clark, T. A. (1984). "Violations of the Gold Points, 1890–1908." *Journal of Political Economy* 92, 791–823.

Cochrane, J. H. (1988). "How Big Is the Random Walk in GNP?" *The Journal of Political Economy*, 96 (5), 893–920.

Coleman, W. (1992). "The New Deal's New Gold Policy: A Case Study in the Power of (Old) Ideas." Discussion Paper 1992–04, Dept. of Economics U. of Tasmania.

Conetta, C. (2006). *We Can See Clearly Now*. PDA Research, Monograph #12, March 2.

Cunliffe Report (1979 [1918]). *First Interim Report of the Committee on Currency and Foreign Exchanges after the War*. Cmnd 9182. Reprint. New York: Arno Press.

Davaytan, Nathan and Parke, William R. (1995). "The Operations of the Bank of England, 1890–1908: A Dynamic Probit Approach." *Journal of Money, Credit and Banking* 27 (4), 1099–1112.

Davis, W. (1968). *Three Years Hard Labour: The Road to Devaluation*. London: Deutsch.

De Grauwe, P. (1989a). "Is the European Monetary System a DM-zone?" Discussion paper No 297, Centre for Economic Policy Research, London, March.

(1989b). "The Cost of Disinflation and the European Monetary System." Discussion paper 326, Centre for Economic Policy Research, London.

(1997). *The Economics of Monetary Integration*. Oxford: Oxford University Press.

De Jong, E., Drost, E. C. and Werker, R. J. M. (1996). "Exchange Rate Target Zones: A New Approach." Department of Economics. Tilburg University, The Netherlands.

Dickey, D. and Fuller, W. A. (1979). "Distribution of the Estimators for Autoregressive Time Series with a Unit Root." *Journal of the American Statistical Association* 74, 427–431.

Dockrill, S. (2002). *Britain's Retreat from East of Suez: The Choice between Europe and the World, 1945–1968*. Basingstoke: Palgrave Macmillan.

Doornik, John and Hansen, Henrik (1994). "A Practical Test of Multivariate Normality." Unpublished paper, Nuffield College, Oxford.

Dornbusch, R. (1973). "Devaluation and Nontraded Goods." *American Economic Review* 63, 871–880.

(1976). "Expectations and Exchange Rate Dynamics." *Journal of Political Economy* 84, 1161–1176.

Dotsey, M. (1998). "The Predictive Content of the Interest Rate Term Spread for Future Economic Growth." *Economic Quarterly* 84 (3), 31–51.

Dow, J. C. R. (1964). *The Management of the British Economy, 1945–1960*. Cambridge: Cambridge University Press.

(1998). *Major Recessions: Britain and the World, 1920–1995*. Oxford: Oxford University Press.

Dutton, John (1984). "The Bank of England and the Rules of the Game under the International Gold Standard: New Evidence." In Michael D. Bordo and Anna J. Schwartz (eds.), *A Retrospective on the Classical Gold Standard, 1821–1931*. Chicago: University of Chicago Press for the NBER.

Edison, Hali and Fisher, Eric (1991). "A Long-Run View of the European Monetary System." *Journal of International Money and Finance* 10, 53–70.

Edison, Hali and Kole, Linda (1995). "European Monetary Arrangements: Implications for the Dollar, Exchange Rate and Credibility." *European Financial Management* 1, 61–86.

Edwards, S. (1984). "The Demand for International Reserves and Monetary Equilibrium: Some Evidence from Developing Countries." *Review of Economics and Statistics* 78, 495–500.

Eichengreen, B. (1986). "The Bank of France and the Sterilization of Gold, 1926–1932." *Explorations in Economic History* 23 (1), 56–84.

(1987). "Conducting the International Orchestra: Bank of England Leadership under the Classical Gold Standard." *Journal of International Money and Finance* 6, 5–29.

(1990). *Elusive Stability: Essays in the History of International Finance*. Cambridge: Cambridge University Press.

(1992). *Golden Fetters: The Gold Standard and the Great Depression, 1919–1939*. Oxford and New York: Oxford University Press.

Eichengreen, B. and Flandreau, M. (1996). "Blocs Zones, and Bands: International Monetary History in Light of Recent Theoretical Developments." *Scottish Journal of Political Economy* 43 (4), 398–414.

Eichengreen, B., Rose, A. K. and Wyplosz, C. (1996). "Speculative Attacks on Pegged Exchange Rates: An Empirical Exploration with Special Reference to the European Monetary System." In M. B. Canzoneri, W. J. Ethier and V. Grilli (eds.), *The New Trans-Atlantic Economy*. Cambridge: Cambridge University Press, pp. 191–235.

Eichengreen, B. and Temin, P. (2000). "The Gold Standard and the Great Depression." *Contemporary European History* 9 (2), 183–207.

Eichengreen, B., Watson, M. W. and Grossman, R. S. (1985). "Bank Rate Policy Under the Inter-war Gold Standard: A Dynamic Model." *Economic Journal* 95, 725–746.

Eichengreen, B. and Wyplosz, C. (1993). "The Unstable EMS." Discussion paper 817, Centre for Economic Policy Research, London.

Einzig, P. (1931). *International Gold Movements*. London: MacMillan.

(1937a). *The Theory of Forward Exchange*. London: MacMillan.

(1937b). *World Finance 1935–1937*. New York: MacMillan.

Engel, C. (1996). "The Forward Discount Anomaly and the Risk Premium." *Journal of Empirical Finance* 2, 123–191.

Engle, Robert and Granger, Clive (1982). "Cointegration and Error Correction: Representation, Estimation and Testing." *Econometrica* 55, 251–276.

Epstein, G. and Ferguson, T. (1984). "Monetary Policy, Loan Liquidation and Industrial Conflict: The Federal Reserve and the Open Market Operations of 1932." *Journal of Economic History* 44 (4), 957–983.

Eschweiler, B. and Bordo, M. D. 1994. "Rules, Discretion and Central Bank Independence: The German Experience, 1880–1989." In P. Siklos (ed.), *Varieties of Monetary Reform: Lessons and Experience on the Road to Monetary Union.* Boston: Kluwer Academic Publishers, pp. 279–321.

Federal Reserve Board (1943). *Banking and Monetary Statistics, 1914–1941.* Washington, DC: GPO.

Fisher, I. (1907). *The Rate of Interest.* New York: MacMillan.

Flood, R. P., Rose, A. K. and Mathieson, D. J. (1991). "An Empirical Exploration of Exchange Rate Target-Zones." *Carnegie-Rochester Series on Public Policy* 35, 7–66.

Frank, R. (1982). *Le Rearmement Francais, 1935–1939.* Paris: Publications de la Sorbonne.

Frenkel, J. A. (1994). "Quantifying International Capital Mobility in the 1980s." In J. A. Frenkel (ed.), *On Exchange Rates.* Cambridge, MA: MIT Press, pp. 227–260.

(1976). "A Monetary Approach to the Exchange Rate." *Scandinavian Journal of Economics* 2, 200–221.

Frenkel, J. A. and Johnson, H. G. (1976). *The Monetary Approach to the Balance of Payments.* London: Allen and Unwin.

Frenkel, J. A. and Rose, A. K. (1995). A Panel Project on Purchasing Power Parity: Mean Reversion within and between Countries, *NBER Working paper* 5006.

Friedman, M. (1990a). "The Crime of 1873." *Journal of Political Economy* 98, 1159–1194.

(1990b). "Bimetallism Revisited." *Journal of Economic Perspectives* 4, 85–104.

(1992). "A Counterfactual Exercise: Estimating the Effect of Continuing Bimetallism after 1873." In *Money Mischief: Episodes of Monetary History*, New York: Harcourt Brace and Co., pp. 80–103.

Friedman, M. and Schwartz, A. J. (1963). *A Monetary History of the United States, 1867–1960.* Princeton, NJ: NBER and Princeton University Press.

(1970). *Monetary Statistics of the United States.* New York: Columbia University Press.

(1982). *Monetary Trends in the United States and United Kingdom.* Chicago: University of Chicago Press.

Froot, K. and Rogoff, K. (1995). "Perspectives on PPP and Long-Run Real Exchange Rates." In E. Grossman and K. Rogoff (eds.), *The Handbook of International Economics.* Amsterdam: North-Holland.

Fuller, W. A. (1976). *Introduction to Statistical Time Series.* New York: Wiley.

Granger, C. W. (1986). "Developments in the Study of Cointegrated Economic Variables." *Oxford Bulletin of Economics and Statistics* 48, 213–228.

Garber, P. M. (1986). "Nominal Contracts in a Bimetallic Standard." *American Economic Review* 76, 1012–1030.

Giovannini, Alberto (1986). "Rules of the Game during the International Gold Standard: England and Germany." *Journal of International Money and Finance* 5 (December), 467–483.

(1989). "How Fixed Exchange Rate Regimes Work: Evidence from the Gold Standard, Bretton Woods and the European Monetary System." In M. Miller, B. Eichengreen and R. Portes (eds.), *Blueprints for International Monetary Reform*. Cambridge: Cambridge University Press.

(1993). "Bretton Woods and Its Precursors: Rules versus Discretion in the History of International Monetary Regimes." In M. D. Bordo and B. Eichengreen (eds.), *A Retrospective on the Bretton Woods System: Lessons for International Monetary Reform*. Chicago: Chicago University Press.

Glosten, L., Jagannathan, R. and Runkle, D. (1993). "On the Relation between the Expected Value and the Volatility of the Nominal Excess Return on Stocks." *Journal of Finance* 48, 1779–1801.

Griffiths, R. T. (ed.) (1987). *The Netherlands and the Gold Standard, 1931–36*. Amsterdam: Neha.

Grilli, V. (1990). "Managing Exchange Risk: Evidence from the 1890s." *Journal of International Money and Finance* 9, 258–275.

Grubel, H. G. (1971). "The Demand for International Reserves: A Critical Review of the Literature." *Journal of Economic Literature* 9, 1148–1165.

Hall, A. (1994). "Testing for a Unit Root in Time Series with Preset Data Based Model Selection." *Journal of Business and Economic Statistics* 12, 461–470.

(1990). "Testing for a Unit Root in Time Series with Preset Data Based Model Selection." *Mimeo*. North Carolina State University, Durham, NC.

Hallwood, C. P. and MacDonald, R. (1994). *International Money and Finance*. Oxford: Blackwell.

Hallwood, C. P., MacDonald, R. and Marsh, I. W. (1997a). "Credibility and Fundamentals: Was the Gold Standard a Well-Behaved Target Zone?" In T. Bayoumi, B. Eichengreen and M. Taylor (eds.), *Modern Perspectives on the Gold Standard*. Cambridge: Cambridge University Press.

Hallwood, C. P., MacDonald, R. and Marsh, I. W. (1997b). "Crash! Expectational Aspects of the UK's and the USA's Departures from the Inter-War Gold Standard." *Explorations in Economic History* 34 (2), 174–194.

(2000a). "An Assessment of the Causes of the Abandonment of the Gold Standard by the USA in 1933." *Southern Economic Journal* 67 (2), 448–459.

(2000b). "Realignment Expectations and the US Dollar, 1890–1897: Was There a 'Peso Problem'?" *Journal of Monetary Economics* 46 (3), 605–620.

Hamilton, A. (2008). "Beyond the Sterling Devaluation: The Gold Crisis of March 1968." *Contemporary European History* 17, 73–95.

Hautcoeur, P. (1997). "The Great Depression in France (1929–1938)." In D. Glasner, (ed.), *Business Cycles and Depressions: An Encyclopedia*. New York: Garland.

Hautcoeur, P.-C. and Sicsic, P. (1999). "Threat of a Capital Levy, Expected Devaluation and Interest Rates in France during the Interwar Period." *European Review of Economic History* 3, 25–56.

Heller, R. H. (1966). "Optimal International Reserves." *Economic Journal* 76, 296–311.

Hendry, D. and Mizon, G. (1993). "Evaluating Dynamic Econometric Models by Encompassing the VAR." In P. C. B. Phillips (ed.), *Models, Methods and Applications of Econometrics*. Oxford: Blackwell, pp. 272–300.

Hirsch, F. (1965). *The Pound Sterling: A Polemic*. London: Victor Gollancz.

Hodrick, R. J. (1987). *The Empirical Evidence on the Forward and Futures Foreign Exchange Markets*. Harwood: Chur.

Hogg, R. L. (1987). "Belgium, France, Switzerland and the End of the Gold Standard." In R. T. Griffiths, op. cit. pp., chapter 9.

Homer, S. (1963). *A History of Interest Rates*. New Brunswick, NJ: Rutgers University Press.

(1977). *A History of Interest Rates*. New Brunswick, NJ: Rutgers University Press.

Hutchison, T. W. (1977). *Knowledge and Ignorance in Economics*. Oxford: Blackwell.

Jackson, J. (1988). *The Popular Front in France: Defending Democracy, 1934–38*. Cambridge: Cambridge University Press.

James, H. (1996). *International Monetary Cooperation since Bretton Woods*. Oxford: Oxford University Press.

Jeanne, Olivier (1995). "Monetary Policy in England 1893–1914: A Structural VAR Analysis." *Explorations in Economic History* 32, 302–326.

Johansen, S. (1988). "Statistical Analysis of Cointegrating Vectors." *Journal of Economic Dynamics and Control* 2, 7–46.

(1991). "Estimation and Hypothesis Testing of Cointegration Vectors in Gaussian Vector Autoregressive Models." *Econometrica* 59 (6), 1551–1580.

Johansen, S. and Juselius, K. (1994). "Identification of the Long-Run and Short-Run Structure: an Application to the ISLM Model." *Journal of Econometrics* 63, 7–36.

Johansen, Soren (1995). *Likelihood-Based Inference in Cointegrated Vector Auto-Regressive Models*. Oxford: Oxford University Press.

Johnson, H. G. and Frenkel, J. A. (1976). *The Monetary Approach to the Balance of Payments*. London: Allen and Unwin.

Jonung, Lars (1984). "Swedish Experience under the Classical Gold Standard, 1873–1914." In Michael D. Bordo and Anna J. Schwartz (eds.), *A Retrospective on the Classical Gold Standard, 1821–1931*. Chicago: University of Chicago Press for NBER.

Kenen, P. R. (1995). *Economic and Monetary Union in Europe*. Cambridge: Cambridge University Press.

Kergoat, J. (1986). *La France du Front Populaire*. Paris: La Découverte.

Keynes, J. M. (1925). "The Economic Consequences of Mr. Churchill." In *The Collected Writings of John Maynard Keynes, Vol. IX. Essays in Persuasion*. London: Macmillan.

Kindleberger, C. P. (1986). *The World in Depression 1929–1939*. Berkeley: University of California Press.

Kirshner, J. (2007). *Appeasing Bankers: Financial Caution on the Road to War*. Princeton, NJ: Princeton University Press.

Kissinger, H. (1994), *Diplomacy*. New York: Simon and Schuster.

Klug, A. and Smith, G. W. (1999). "Suez and Sterling, 1956." *Explorations in Economic History* 36, 181–203.

Krasker, W. S. (1980). "The 'Peso Problem' in Testing the Efficiency of Forward Exchange Markets." *Journal of Monetary Economics* 6, 269–276.

Krugman, Paul R. (1979). "A model of Balance of Payments Crises." *Journal of Money, Credit and Banking* 11, 311–325.

(1991). "Target Zone and Exchange Rate Dynamics." *Quarterly Journal of Economics* 106 (3), 669–682.

Kwiatkowski, D., Phillips, P. C. B., Schmidt, P. and Shin, Y. (1992). "Testing the Null Hypothesis of Stationarity against the Alternative of a Unit Root." *Journal of Econometrics* 54, 159–178.

Lacouture, J. (1982). *Leon Blum*. Paris and New York: Holmes & Meier Publishers.

Levin, A. and Lin, C. F. (1992). "Unit Roots in Panel Data: Asymptotic and Finite Sample Properties." *Mimeo*. University of California, San Diego, CA.

(1993). "Unit Roots in Panel Data: Asymptotic and Finite Sample Properties." *Revised Mimeo*. University of California, San Diego, CA.

Lindberg, H., Soderlind, P. and Svensson, L. E. O. (1993). "Devaluation Expectations: The Swedish Krona 1985–92." *Economic Journal* 103, 1170–1179.

Lindert, Peter (1969). "Key Currencies and Gold, 1900–1913." *Princeton Studies in International Finance* 24.

Lo, A. and MacKinlay, C. (1988). "Stock Prices Do Not Follow Random Walks: Evidence from a Simple Specification Test." *The Review of Financial Studies* 1, 41–66.

(1989). "The Size and Power of the Variance Ratio Test in Finite Samples: A Monte Carlo Investigation." *Journal of Econometrics* 40, 203–238.

Lutkepohl, H. (1993). *Introduction to Multiple Time Series Analysis*. Berlin: Springer-Verlag.

MacDonald, R. (1995). "Long-Run Exchange Rale Modeling: A Survey of the Recent Evidence." *International Monetary Fund Staff Papers* 42 (3), 437–489.

(2007). *Exchange Rate Economics: Theories and Evidence*, 2nd edition. London: Routledge.

MacKinnon, J. (1991). "Critical Values for Cointegration Tests." In R. F. Engle and C. W. J. Granger (eds.), *Long-Run Economic Relationships: Readings in Cointegration*. Oxford: Oxford University Press, pp. 267–276.

MacMillan Committee on Finance and Industry (1931), Cmd 3897, HMSO.

McCloskey, D. N. and Zecher, J. R. (1976). "How the International Gold Standard Worked, 1880–1913." In J. A. Frenkel and H. G. Johnson (eds.), *The Monetary Approach to the Balance of Payments*. Toronto: University of Toronto Press, pp. 357–385.

Meltzer, A. H. (2002). *Why Did Monetary Policy Fail in the Thirties? A History of the Federal Reserve*, Chapter 5, Vol. 1, 1913–1951. Chicago: University of Chicago Press.

Middleton, R. (1996). *Government versus the Market: The Growth of the Public Sector, Economic Management and British Economic Performance*. Cheltenham: Edward Elgar.

(2002). "Struggling with the Impossible: Sterling, the Balance of Payments and British Economic Policy, 1949–72." In A. Arnon and W. L. Young (eds.), *The Open Economy Macromodel: Past, Present and Future*. Boston, MA: Kluwer Academic, pp. 103–154.

Miller, M. and Weller, P. (1991). "Currency Bands, Target Zones and Price Flexibility." *IMF Staff Papers* 38, 184–215.

Mills, T. (1993). *The Econometric Modelling of Financial Time Series*. Cambridge: Cambridge University Press.

Miron, Jeffrey (1996). *The Economics of Seasonal Cycles*. Cambridge, MA: MIT Press.

Mishkin, F. S. (1995). "The Term Structure of Interest Rates and its Role in Monetary Policy for the European Central Bank." *Working Paper 5279, NBER*.

Mitchell, B. R. (1993). *International Historical Statistics, Volume 2*. London: Macmillan.

Mitchell, W. C. (1913). *Business Cycles*. New York: Burt Franklin.

Mizrach, B. (1995). "Target Zone Models with Stochastic Realignments: An Econometric Evaluation." *Journal of International Money and Finance* 14, 641–657.

Moggridge, D. E. (1969). *British Monetary Policy, 1924–1931*. Cambridge: Cambridge University Press.

Morgenstern, O. (1959). *International Financial Transactions and Business Cycles*. Princeton, NJ: Princeton University Press.

Moure, K. (1991). *Managing the Franc Poincaré Economic Understanding and Political Constraint in French Monetary Policy, 1928–1936*, Cambridge: Cambridge University Press.

 (2002). *The Gold Standard Illusion: France, the Bank of France, and the International Gold Standard, 1914–1939*. Oxford: Oxford University Press.

Mussa, M. (1976). "The Exchange Rate, the Balance of Payments and Money and Fiscal Policy under a Regime of Controlled Floating." *Scandinavian Journal of Economics* 2, 229–248.

 (1979). "Empirical Regularities in the Behavior of Exchange Rates and Theories of the Foreign Exchange Market." In *Policies for Employment, Prices and Exchange Rates*, Carnegie-Rochester Conference Series on Public Policy, 12.

National Economic Development Corporation (1964). *The Growth of the Economy*. London: HMSO.

National Institute Economic Review (1964). "The Economic Situation: Annual Review." *National Institute Economic Review* 27, 4–12.

 (1967). "The Effects of Devaluation and the Balance of Payments." *National Institute Economic Review* 42, 4–9.

National Monetary Commission (1910). *Statistics for the United States, 1867–1909*. Government Printing Office, Washington DC, Document No. 570. 61st Congress, Second Session.

Newey, W. and West, K. (1987). "A Simple Positive-Definite Heteroskedasticity and Autocorrelation Consistent Covariance Matrix." *Econometrica* 55, 703–708.

Newton, S. (2009). "The Two Sterling Crises of 1964 and the Decision Not to Devalue." *Economic History Review*.

Ng, S. and Perron, P. (1995). "Unit Root Tests in ARMA Models with Data-Dependent Methods for the Selection of the Truncation Lag." *Journal of the American Statistical Association* 90, 268–281.

Nieuwland, F. G. M. C., Verschoor, W. F. C. and Wolff, C. C. P. (1994). Stochastic Jumps in EMS Exchange Rates. *Journal of International Money and Finance* 13, 699–727.

Nurkse, R. (1944). *International Currency Experience*. Geneva: League of Nations.

Obstfeld, M. (1984). "Balance-of-Payments Crises and Devaluation." *Journal of Money, Credit and Banking* 16, 208–217.

Obstfeld, Maurice (1993). "International Capital Mobility in the 1990s." *NBER Working Paper* No. 4534.

Obstfeld, Maurice and Taylor, Alan (1998). "The Great Depression as a Watershed: International Capital Mobility over the Long-Run." In Michael D. Bordo, Claudia Goldin and Eugene White (eds.), *The Defining Moment: The Great Depression and the American Economy in the Twentieth Century*. Chicago: University of Chicago Press.

Officer, L. H. (1986). "The Efficiency of the Dollar-Sterling Gold Standard, 1890–1908." *Journal of Political Economy* 94, 1038–1073.

(1989). "The Remarkable Efficiency of the Dollar-Sterling Gold Standard, 1890–1906." *Journal of Economic History* 49, 1–41.

(1993). "Gold-Point Arbitrage and Uncovered Interest Arbitrage under the 1925–1931 Dollar-Sterling Gold Standard." *Explorations in Economic History* 30, 98–127.

(1996). *Between the Dollar-Sterling Gold Points: Exchange Rates, Parity and Market Behavior.* Cambridge: Cambridge University Press.

Oppenheimer, P. (1966). "Forward Exchange Intervention: The Official View." *Westminster Bank Review*, February.

Osterwald-Lenum, M. (1993). "Recalculated and Extended Tables of Asymptotic Distribution of Some Important Maximum Likelihood Cointegrating Test Statistics." *Oxford Bulletin of Economics and Statistics* 54, 461–472.

Pantula, S. G. (1989). "Testing for Unit Roots in Time Series Analysis." *Econometric Theory* 5, 256–271.

Patat, J. P. and Lutfalla, M. (1990). *Monetary History of France in the Twentieth Century.* London: Palgrave MacMillan.

Perron, P. (1989). "The Great Crash, the Oil Price Shock, and the Unit Root Hypothesis." *Econometrica* 57 (6), 1361–1401.

Pippenger, John (1984). "Bank of England Operations, 1893–1913." In Michael D. Bordo and Anna J. Schwartz (eds.), *A Retrospective on the Classical Gold Standard, 1821–1931.* Chicago: University of Chicago Press.

Posen, B. R. (1986). *Sources of Military Doctrine: France, Britain and Germany between the Wars.* Cornell Studies in Security Affairs. Ithaca, NY: Cornell University.

Redmond, J. (1984). "The Sterling Overvaluation in 1925: A Multilateral Approach." *Economic History Review*, 2nd ser., 37, 520–532.

Renouvin, P. (1981). *Leon Blum. Chef de Gouvernement, 1936–1937*, 2nd edition. Paris: Presses de Sciences Po.

Ritschl, A. and Wolf, N. (2003), "Endogeneity of Currency Areas and Trade Blocs: Evidence from the Interwar Period." *Mimeo*, Humboldt University, April.

Robertson, D. and Symons, J. (1990). "Output, Inflation, and the ERM." Discussion paper 43. Centre for Economic Policy Research, London.

Rogoff, K. (1995). "The Purchasing Power Parity Puzzle." *Journal of Economic Literature*, 34, 647–668.

Rose, Andrew and Svensson, Lars (1994). "European Credibility before the Fall." *European Economic Review* 38, 1185–1223.

Rose, A. K. and Svensson, L. E. O. (1995). "Expected and Predicted Realignments: The FF/DM Exchange Rate during the EMS." *Scandinavian Journal of Economics* 97, 173–200.

Roy, R. (2000). "The Battle of the Pound: the Political Economy of Anglo-American Relations, 1964–1968." Unpublished PhD thesis, London School of Economics.

Sauvy, A. (1984). *Histoire Economique de la France entre les Deux Guerres.* Paris: Economica.

(1969). "The Economic Crisis of the 1930s in France." *Journal of Contemporary History* 4 (4), 21–35.

Sayers, Richard (1957). *Central Banking after Bagehot.* Oxford: Clarendon Press.

Schenk, C. R. (1994). *Britain and the Sterling Area: From Devaluation to Convertibility in the 1950s*. London: Routledge.

Schenk, C. (2002). "Sterling, International Monetary Reform and Britain's Applications to the EEC in the 1960s." *Contemporary European History* 11, 345–369.

Schuker, S. A. (1976). *The End of French Predominance in Europe*. Chapel Hill: University of North Carolina Press.

Schwartz, A. J. (1987). "A Century of British Market Interest Rates, 1874–1975." In *Money in Historical Perspective*. Chicago: University of Chicago Press.

Shepherd, H. L. (1936). *The Monetary Experience of Belgium, 1914–1936*. Princeton, NJ: Princeton University Press.

Shirer, W. L. (1969). *The Collapse of the Third Republic: An Inquiry into the Fall of France in 1940*. New York: Simon and Schuster.

Siklos, P. and Tarajos, R. (1996). "Fundamentals and Devaluation Expectations in Target Zones: Some New Evidence from the ERM." *Open Economies Review* 25, 35–59.

Simmons, B. (1994). *Who Adjusts?* Princeton, NJ: Princeton University Press.

Simon, M. (1968). "The Morgan-Belmont Syndicate of 1895 and Intervention in the Foreign-Exchange Market." *Business History Review* 42, 385–417.

Spiller, P. T. and Wood, R. O. (1988). "Arbitrage during the Dollar-Sterling Gold Standard, 1899–1908: An Econometric Approach." *Journal of Political Economy* 96, 882–892.

Stewart, M. (1977). *The Jekyll and Hyde Years: Politics and Economic Policy since 1964*. London: J. M. Dent.

Svensson, L. E. O. (1991). "The Simplest Test of Target Zone Credibility." *IMF Staff Papers* 38, 655–665.

(1992). "An Interpretation of Recent Research on Exchange Rate Target Zones." *Journal of Economic Perspectives* 6, 119–144.

(1993). "Assessing Target Zone Credibility: Mean Reversion and Devaluation Expectations in the ERM: 1979–1992." *European Economic Review* 37, 763–802.

(1994). "Why Exchange Rate Bands?" *Journal of Monetary Economics* 33, 157–199.

Temin, P. (1989). *The Lessons from the Great Depression*. Cambridge, MA: MIT Press.

't Hart, M. C., Jonker, J., and Van Zuiten, J. L. (1997). *A Financial History of the Netherlands*. Cambridge: Cambridge University Press.

Thomas, M. (1992). "French Economic Affairs and Rearmament: The First Crucial Months, June–September 1936." *Journal of Contemporary History* 27, 659–670.

Tomlinson, J. (2004). *The Labour Governments 1964–70, Volume 3: Economic Policy*. Manchester: Manchester University Press.

Toniolo, G. (2005). *Central Bank Cooperation at the Bank for International Settlements, 1930–1973*. Cambridge: Cambridge University Press.

Ungerer, R., Hauvonen, J. J., Lopez-Claros, A. and Mayer, T. (1990). "The EMS: Developments and Perspectives." International Monetary Fund Occasional Paper 73. International Monetary Fund, Washington, DC.

Vandenbosch, A. (1927). *The Neutrality of the Netherlands during the World War*. Grand Rapids, MI: W. B. Eerdmans Publishing.

(1959). *Dutch Foreign Policy since 1815: A Study in Small Power Politics*. The Hague: Martinus Nijhoff.

von Hagen, Jurgen and Fratianni, Michelle (1990). "German Dominance in the EMS: Evidence from Interest Rates." *Journal of International Money and Finance* 9, 387–375.

Wandschneider, K. (2008). "The Stability of the Inter-War Gold Exchange Standard Did Politics Matter? *Journal of Economic History* (August), 151–181.

Warmbrunn, W. (1963). *The Dutch under German Occupation, 1940–1945*. Stanford, CT: Stanford University Press.

Weber, Axel (1990). "EMU and Asymmetries and Adjustment Problems in the EMS: Some Empirical Evidence." *CEPR Discussion paper* No. 448, August.

Wheelock, D. (1991). *The Strategy and Consistency of Federal Reserve Monetary Policy, 1924–1933*. Cambridge: Cambridge University Press.

Wright, J. (2000). "Alternative Variance-Ratio Tests Using Ranks and Signs." *Journal of Business and Economics Statistics* 18, 1–9.

Wyplosz, C. (1986). "Capital Controls and Balance of Payments Crises." *Journal of International Money and Finance* 5, 167–179.

Index

Printed in the United States
by Baker & Taylor Publisher Services